# I'd Rather Be Writing

## Marcia Golub

**W**

**WRITER'S
DIGEST
BOOKS**

CINCINNATI, OHIO
WWW.WRITERSDIGEST.COM

Visit our Web site at www.writersdigest.com for information on more resources for writers.

To receive a free weekly E-mail newsletter delivering tips and updates about writing and about Writer's Digest products, send an E-mail with "Subscribe Newsletter" in the body of the message to newsletter-request@writersdigest.com, or register directly at our Web site at www.writersdigest.com.

03  02  01  00  99     5  4  3  2  1

**Library of Congress Cataloging-in-Publication Data**

Golub, Marcia.
   I'd rather be writing / Marcia Golub.
      p.    cm.
   Includes index.
   ISBN 0-89879-900-7 (alk. paper)
    1. Authorship. 2. Journalism—Authorship. 3. Creative writing. I. Title.
PN147.G618   1999
808'.02—dc21                                     99-29229
                                                                CIP

Edited by Jack Heffron
Production edited by Bob Beckstead
Interior designed by Tim Kron
Cover illustration by Mary Ross
Production coordinated by Kristen D. Heller and Rachel Vater

For my mother, who knew how to tell a story
For my father, who learned how to listen
For my husband, who believes in me when I don't
For my son, who teaches me

## ACKNOWLEDGMENTS

Many gifted writers, published and not-yet-published, were generous with their time and energy, responding to the sometimes annoyingly New Age questions I posed to them. In particular I'd like to thank Madison Smartt Bell, Maureen Brady, Sam Decker, Barry Denny, Ellen Dreyer, Jodie Klavans, Tom Mallon, Lori Perkins, Marissa Piesman, Ruth Reichl, Zack Rosen, Peter Rubie, Emily Russell, Evan Russell, Susan Saiter, Martha Schulman, Steve Schwartz, and Lore Segal for sharing their insights, humor, and pain about the writing process. I'd also like to thank Peter Rubie and Jack Heffron for suggesting I write this book, which I can't wait to read the next time I find myself organizing my closets instead of writing. My students at Writer's Voice have taught me much about teaching and writing. Their questions and comments continually show me new ways to read, write, and discuss writing. Thanks also are due my husband, Bob, for being that essential first reader, honest but kind, critical but thoughtful. And I would especially like to thank my son, Zack, for sharing his many thoughts, both on writing and life, with me. When I forget why I write, I only have to see him hard at work on one of his stories or books or lists or theories, tongue curling out of his mouth, eyes distant and dreamy, to have it come back to me.

## ABOUT THE AUTHOR

Marcia Golub has published two novels—*Wishbone* and *Secret Correspondence*—and is the author of award-winning stories, one of which, "The Child Downstairs," received the Open Voice Award and was anthologized in *Narrative Design: A Writer's Guide to Structure*. Her unpublished novel, *Tale of the Forgotten Woman*, was a finalist for the Pen/Nelson Algren Award and was twice nominated for the Editor's Book Award/Pushcart Press. She has written book reviews for *The New York Times* and *The Baltimore Sun*, as well as articles on religion, archaeology, literature, and astronomy. She teaches fiction writing workshops at Writer's Voice in Manhattan. She lives with her husband and son in "upstate" Manhattan, where she tries very hard to write and not use her binoculars to peer at every passing barge on the Hudson River.

# CONTENTS

# INTRODUCTION

When I first started working on this book I thought: Oh no, the jig is up. If I write the truth everyone will know how much time I waste being compulsive about cleaning the gunk off the bottom of the electric toothbrush. I'd written novels and stories; I'd written *about* novels and stories; I'd written about literature and mythology and even punctuation. But I'd never written about writing before, and the prospect of doing so was daunting—like trying to talk about talking, making sense while moving your lips without tripping over your tongue.

No sooner would I sit down to write than I'd find myself going into the kitchen to brew coffee or defrost something for dinner. I'd force myself to get back to my desk and sit there, splitting my ends or examining my eyelids in the mirror. I'd put the mirror away and the phone would ring. With a theatrical sigh of impatience (knowing full well how delighted I really was at the interruption), I'd answer and get into a long conversation about skin cancer with a friend who was trying to put off something she was supposed to be doing. In short, I felt like I needed to *read* this book more than write it.

Then I saw *that* was the point. All writers struggle with issues of time management, organization, and productivity, and we develop techniques for coping with such concerns. But we don't often put those techniques into words, even to ourselves. We pace from room to room, muttering and feeling insane, wasting the few minutes we have to be doing what we *want* to be doing without realizing that *that* is our technique for starting—pacing and muttering. Recalcitrant about varying our schedules the slightest bit to accommodate our family's schedules, we feel guilty about hoarding those precious hours but hoard them nonetheless (*and* feel guilty), never catching on to how we have to do just that—hoard the hours for our writing. Reluctant to start, resistant to finishing—and yet we manage to do it. We have figured out ways that enable us to find the time and use it productively, to kvetch and moan but somehow start and continue and finish our projects. But most of us, if you ask how we do it, are apt to stare dumbly and say: Dunno. Sit, I guess. Start. Keep going. Finish.

There's more to it than that, but writers who are successful at managing their time and energy don't waste much of it verbalizing how they get from wanting to write to actually writing. Still, I realized it would be helpful to other writers—new ones who are trying to find their way and old ones who have forgotten theirs—to learn how to do this.

And so I began, doing what I love and watching myself do it. How did I get myself started? What techniques did I have for getting past the demon of doubt, the seduction of laundry? Just as I was building up a head of steam, revealing the secrets of *my* writing life, my husband suggested I interview other writers to find out how *they* got themselves going. My initial impulse was to pick up the first volume of the *Oxford English Dictionary* and hit him over the head with it. Instead, I contemplated his idea for a few days. As reluctant as I was to ask other writers how they coped with the desire and dread of writing—a reluctance built largely on the fear of the telephone, not wanting to interrupt a writer's train of thought with my impertinent questions, thereby incurring his or her eternal wrath—I became curious. Soon I had a series of questions I wanted to ask: How do you find the time? The self-confidence? Do you use dreams? Do you have rituals? Are there secrets to getting yourself started? To keeping yourself going? To finishing? What about revision? What about responses from other writers? I found it easier to mail my questions out than risk telephoning—hey, I'm a writer, I'm used to rejection in the mail—but when the responses began coming in I found most writers were not reticent about revealing their secrets. They had their writing woes, and they had their ways of coping with them. It seemed as if we were all walking around locked in this prison of solitary activity, feeling like the only weirdos on the block when the truth was we were a community of weirdos (and not-so-weirdos). As Firesign Theater put it, "We're all Bozos on this bus."

The purpose of this book is to help the reader/writer make better use of his or her writing time. The book should prove useful in two ways: First of all, there is solace in knowing you are not alone, that there are published, even famous, writers out there who deal daily with the frittering imps, that the great demon god of writer's block casts its shadow over us all, even those who have never actually shivered with its chill. Second of all, there are ways to combat whatever keeps you from writing—whether what stands in your way is the inability to start, the loss of inspiration in the middle, or a general inability to finish a project. People who want to write but have lives that are overextended between family and career as it is will learn techniques for finding time in the cracks . . . and for using such time to write, not eat pretzels.

The book has a narrative flow and can be read from beginning to end, but each chapter is self-contained and can also be read as the topic pertains to issues in your writing life. Tips and quotations are laced throughout the chapters. My hope is that some of these may inspire you. If you only have an odd half-hour in which to write, you may find it useful to work on a "Try This," one of the many exercises that come at the end of chapters or sections within chapters and are designed to help you over a particular hurdle. There is also a whole chapter devoted to exercises, to get your creativity flowing again.

In fact, perhaps you'd like to do the following "Try This" now: Write a few paragraphs on what you would like to find in a book about writing. Do you want it to have ways to help you find inspiration? (Got it.) Advice on getting past the first sentence? (Got that too.) Help in keeping inspiration alive during the times when you have to put your writing away to work on something more pressing? (See chapter twenty-six.) Stuff on how to write and still be a loving, generous parent? How to write and still have a career? How to use magic and rituals and dreams? (Yup, yup, and yup.) Chapters on craft? (Some.) I tried to put into this book anything I could think of to help you do what you love to do. But in the end, you sit, you stare, you start. So what are you waiting for? It's time to write.

# ONE

# I'D RATHER BE WRITING

**W**riters are a peculiar breed. We scheme and plot and lie in order to carve out a section of day—dirty dishes soak in the sink, laundry accumulates in smelly heaps, we don't answer the telephone, having already told our family and friends we will not be home all morning—we do this for the purpose of writing . . . and then we sit, cracking our knuckles, splitting our ends, eating stale bread and drinking enough coffee to keep an entire freshman class studying the night before finals. In short, we do everything but the thing we want to do most.

Perhaps it is the fate of writers, to always wish to be doing something else. When we are laughing with buddies we are thinking of how to use the scene in a story. We hike through autumn foliage, our noses dripping from the cold, making up odes of awe, anxious lest we forget our impromptu poetry before we get to a place where we can scribble it down. But, except during those rare and precious moments when our writing takes off, and voice and mind and pen are one, facing that blank page makes us feel like prisoners in solitary confinement trying to communicate with crickets. Really, we ask ourselves, isn't there something a bit more productive we could be doing?

The sad truth is that although many people say they would rather be writing, when they sit down at their computers they discover they really would rather be doing laundry. They even tell themselves there's a writerliness to sorting through clothes. Separating whites from darks instructs you in how to separate bons mots from clichés. Pour in the soap, push the buttons, wait till it's time to throw it into the dryer, and a little while later you will see your family laid out before you as you tenderly fold your son's T-shirts and your husband's underpants. You can do all this with a Lawrentian lovingness and attention to detail, making of household drudgery an act of religious devotion. The best part is that when you are all done there isn't time to write, oh drats, and you meant to start the great American novel. Guess it will just have to wait till tomorrow.

Tomorrow you discover you'd rather be making a stew.

Our attitude toward writing—a pursuit we do for love because, believe me, there isn't any money in it—is like my son's approach to homework. He is in third grade and has only been doing homework for one week, so he's still pretty excited about it. The first day he worked conscientiously, writing out a poem the teacher had sent home, carefully forming his letters, his tongue curling in unison with the marks on the page. When he was done he held it up proudly for me to read, and I made a big fuss. The second day he made a picture illustrating the poem, but he needed a perfect circle, which he couldn't make till I found something round for him to trace, and he needed new crayons (which luckily I had thought to buy only a few days before), and he worked conscientiously but got up several times to ask me for supplies and opinions of what the teacher *really* wanted him to do. And he stopped to play the drums a bit. And he practiced sliding from his room to the living room, scoring runs for an invisible crowd of wildly cheering fans. The next day he did a little math, played the drums, ate a yogurt, slid into home, and turned on the TV—at which point I said: Uh uh, no way. This is the sad truth about homework, my lad: It needs to be done, and you need to sit there and do it, and no matter how much that crowd roars for its main man you need to sit and finish your homework before you can go sliding around the dining room or watching TV. What intrigues me in all this is how quickly homework moved from an activity he proudly did to one that brought on major bouts of ants-in-the-pantsitis.

But that is the truth about writing too. It doesn't get done unless you sit down and do it. You can't jump up to throw in the fabric softener (does anyone actually use fabric softener?), then come back to finish a sentence. And you can't spend too much time imagining what you'll wear in Sweden when they hand you the Prize instead of imagining what your character is playing with in his coat pocket.

I can remember a time when sitting, notebook and pen in hand, hidden away from family and friends (especially family), was my favorite occupation—and not just when I was doing something else. My attitude toward writing was like Anna Karenina's to Vronsky. My heart would pound as I raced home so we could have time alone, my writing and I, before my mother filled the house with cooking clatter and smells. When it was raining, especially if there was thunder and lightning, I would write my Poe tales with titles like "The Grave Had My Name." I was in junior high school then and had every intention of being a mad genius and dying young. Hiding in my room, I worked in the dusk in what I thought of as a garret (the apartment was all on one level, the second floor of a two-story, two-family semi-attached brick house in Brooklyn; this didn't stop my imagination, however, from conjuring the ambiance it needed for art).

Now I am a jack-in-the-box at my desk, jumping up at the least thought of something else to do. Garbage to throw out? Can do. Telephone calls to make? I'm your girl. The secret is to learn how to push the lid down, to tell the inner jack that jumping up is fun and all, but right now we have work to take care of. Because the truth is I, like you, *would* rather be writing, and seductive though the siren call of laundry and dirty dishes is, I know it's no more than a voice that says: Come, make clean. Don't play with that dirty stuff in your mind. You can't do it, you have nothing to say, and besides it's rather yucky in there, like the closets, but if you clean the closets everything will be organized, the outgrown and torn and useless thrown away, everyone's closet will be clean and you will be loved.

Don't listen to that voice. Listen to the one that says: There's a locked door at the end of the passage. You've been told not to open it, but do it anyway. Let's see what's hidden in there, we'll just take one little peek. After all, what could one little peek lead to?

# TWO

# URGES, VIEWS, AND ANSWERING MACHINES

In the beginning was the urge, and the urge was with you, but first you had to make a pot of coffee, and then the telephone rang, and then you realized you had to defrost something for dinner, and then you sat down at the computer and discovered the urge was gone.

You wouldn't be a writer if you didn't get the urge to write. It's what happens afterward that counts. Maybe you don't have a pen. (Why don't you have a pen? More about this later.) Maybe you can't get to your notebook. (Why not? More about this too.) Somehow you need to keep the urge going. As with sex, you can keep yourself fired up by thinking about it . . . or you can lose the whole thing by calling your mother. Don't call your mother unless she's dead, and even then be wary. My mother died a year ago and I call her a lot, and whenever I do I cry, and when I cry I don't do my work. Probably there will come a time when I won't cry so easily, but right now I try not to call her when I'm trying to write, unless I'm trying to write about her. And writing about her is too hard, so I've made some notes, I've done a few horrible first drafts of stories, I've gathered material for a novel, and now I'm letting the whole thing cook without me as I work on other projects.

When the urge descends on you it's like a blessing, like a perfect crisp sunny day, like a chocolate brownie with nuts and frosting—just the way you like it and nobody makes it that way anymore. What I'm saying is you can't count on the urge, so when it descends do your utmost not to put it off. The muse is temperamental and easily insulted. When she gets a busy signal, she hangs up and doesn't call back. But the next time you're at your computer she'll get back at you. My muse, ignored, tends to look like Mother Nature in that old margarine commercial in which she's fooled into thinking she's eating butter when it's really Parkay. You don't want to mess with her.

> **TIP:** One word on a slip of paper can serve to help you recall a story idea, but if you don't write that one word down you may not even recall you *had* a story idea.

Now, I know (even if the muse does not) that you can't always stop what you're doing to write. You simply can't push the pause button on your professor's mouth while he's telling you the secret of the universe, which is sure to be on the final. You can't tell your boss that it's very interesting about the new filing system and all but hold it right there, you'll be back in half an hour. You can't tell a baby not to poop, you can't tell a toddler not to cry, you can't tell a kid not to relate the day's triumphs and woes for the next fifteen minutes. What you can do is try to memorize the image, the idea, the feeling—whatever it was that brought on the urge. And as soon as you can, jot it down. You don't have to follow it through right then and there, you only have to make a note. One word might do it—"falcon" will always bring back the moment a peregrine falcon flew over my head in Central Park and landed in a tree in front of me. Your note doesn't need detail. That can come later, as you let it help you retrieve the memory, and the urge, when you're in a more appropriate place for writing.

Speaking of which . . .

It's awfully hard to take yourself seriously as a writer if you're working on a TV tray set up in the bathroom. A writer needs an appropriate place to write. Virginia Woolf wrote about the importance of a room of one's own. Well, nowadays that may be going a bit far, especially if you live in New York City, where you're lucky to have a bathroom of your own when you're using it. But you do need a corner, a niche where you can lay out your papers and notebooks and the little finger puppets you like to play with when you can't think of what to write. A spot of your own. I don't think that's too much to ask. That doesn't mean putting off your dreams of writing till you can afford a studio apartment just for you and your computer, which must sit on an antique mahogany desk, the walls wainscotted and lined with books.

My "office" is set up in the bedroom. The desk is a big piece of wood cantilevered out from the wall, with enough circuitry beneath it to alarm any fire marshal. It has ample space for my computer and printer and telephone, with some left over for papers, disks, notebooks, pens.

The good part of this arrangement is that the bed serves as a secondary workspace, at least till my husband gets home. I pile stuff on it—notes for my novel, notes for this book, bills that have to be paid and letters that have to be written, lists of things to do that day and that week, telephone books. It all gets loaded onto the bed and off my mind. That way I don't have to look at any of it when I'm writing. Because if I look at it I think about it, then I do that instead of what I'm trying to do, which is hear a voice in my head and not the one that goes, "You have to buy milk, you have to call the allergist, Uncle Saul was ninety-five and you didn't send him a card, if the insurance company doesn't pay that doctor soon he'll rebreak your arm."

The bad part of this arrangement is that that kind bed, willing to shoulder my responsibilities for a time, is apt to call to me in the late afternoon, suggesting a little na-na. Think how much more productive you'll be afterward, it whispers in the rustle of sheets. Like a lover it offers to hold me, enfold me, warm my feet. Usually I can resist the seductive ploys of blanket and pillow, especially if I tank up on caffeine. Sometimes, however, I cannot. Chances are at those times I'd hear the invitation even if I had a room of my own. In fact, before my son was born I did have such a room, and so I can attest that mid-afternoon, when the sleepy tempter calls to me, especially if my work isn't going well, I sometimes succumb.

That admitted, I must further confess the shame I feel when caught napping. I can remember being woken from such a nap by my mother on the phone. She kept asking me why I sounded so funny, and I kept trying to sound chipper and lively instead of groggy, my thoughts still cottoned by clouds. The more wide-awake I tried to sound, the guiltier my mother seemed to think I was. All I had to do was say I'd been napping, for Heaven's sake, not shooting heroin. She was my mother after all, the world's biggest advocate of naps, especially for her child, but it felt *shameful*, as if she'd caught me holding an orgy while my husband was busy at the office. I'm sure she went to her grave thinking I got up to funny business in the late afternoons.

## YOU DON'T HAVE TO BE VIEWISH

To have an office in the bedroom, I've found it essential that no one be sleeping in the bed. That means your bedmate needs to work someplace else. I know there are marriages in which husband and wife both work at home. I also know there are marriages where husbands push wives out of windows and wives sprinkle arsenic on their husbands' bowls of pasta. I'm not saying the two are related, but you have to wonder. One couple I know, both of whom work at home, is now in the process of getting a divorce. Another work-at-home couple, with a huge suburban house in which husband *and* wife have private rooms in addition to the bedroom they share, came so close to blows he rented an office in town. Space was not the problem. It was privacy. It was the need writers have to pace and mutter and make coffee and not run into someone else muttering. And certainly not to find themselves muttering about the kids and who's going to pick them up today and what should they have for dinner. This is all to say that money is not the solution, although let's face it—without money my writer friend would not have been able to rent an office in town in addition to the ones at home.

The thing my "office" has is a terrific view. It has four windows that look out on the Hudson River and the George Washington Bridge. Hawks fly by; barges, tugboats, and sailing vessels float up and down. Just now, for instance, I looked up from my work and saw a three-masted wooden schooner going across the river toward New Jersey. It's raining, the wind is fierce, and the sails have tilted the boat to such an extreme that I am contemplating dialing 911 before it capsizes. What is holding me back is that several years ago I did call, during a terrific storm in which a shad fishing boat appeared to be in trouble, and I was treated as a lunatic or crank by every desk clerk and police sergeant I spoke to. By the time the Coast Guard went to investigate, the crew was all drowned . . . or would have been if the boat had seriously been in trouble. Which it turned out it hadn't been. Which is why I am loath to call today. And a good thing too, since in the time it has taken to tell you this the schooner has righted itself, made it across the Hudson, and is now heading north. This is all to say that people see my desk setup, right away they "ooh" and "ah." What a terrific place to write, they say. The truth is it's a terrific place to not write. When I'm writing I'm looking at the page or screen. It's when

I'm not writing that I gaze out the window at the view. I wouldn't trade my view for the back of a glue-manufacturing factory, let's say, but just don't *you* feel bad if that's what your desk faces. It's much less distracting. You'll never find yourself running for the binoculars when you're supposed to be getting characters to a costume party.

**Try This:** Write a description of your fantasy writing place. Where would it be? What would it look like? Smell like? What would it have nearby? Anything goes. If you wish you could write at the beach, imagine an ideal existence in which money and sand were no object. Have fun with this. Next, write a description of your actual writing space. Where do you usually write? What surrounds you there? What do you hear? What do you see? What pleases and displeases you about this space? Compare the two writing places. What are the major differences between the ideal and the actual? Are there any similarities? Can you make the reality a bit more like the fantasy? You may not be able to write at the beach on your computer, for example, but you can put a photograph of the ocean on a wall near your desk. Maybe put some sea glass on your sill.

## SOUNDS OF SILENCE

If you write at home it is best either to be alone at the time you like to work or to have a thick door that no eight-year-old can open. It is also preferable not to have a downstairs neighbor who is hard of hearing and blasts reruns of *I Love Lucy* at odd hours. Some things, however, can't be helped, and as the old woman downstairs never complains about my son practicing the drums, I never hit the floor with a broom, screaming, "Turn down the volume, you hag!" Oh, maybe once or twice, but I'm sure she didn't hear.

I have been known to sometimes resort to environmental tapes. I have only one. One is enough. Side A has the sound of spring rain falling in a forest with little birds. It sounds like a leaky radiator. Side B has the sound of rushing water gurgling over rocks. It also sounds like a leaky radiator. The two sides do not sound the same, although they both sound like leaky radiators. It's amazing the amount of variation you can get on a leaky radiator.

This tape does the trick for me though. If you are the Martha Stewart type I'm sure you can make your own environmental tape. Next winter, when the heat is coming up, just record the sound. Label the tape "Adirondack Brooks and Streams in Spring." Then play it whenever you start to hear Ricky sing "Babaloo."

I find the white noise of rain and rushing water muffles the laugh track on *I Love Lucy* so that I can almost not hear Lucy's high-pitched baby voice. Unless I listen for it. Which is what I do. Why we do this is one of the puzzles of human nature, along with why we think of all the disgusting foods we have eaten the past week when we are about to throw up. I can usually force myself to stop listening for Lucy's voice by turning up my own. Sometimes that means reading aloud. Sometimes I work with my fingers in my ears for a while, till I tune in the frequency of WMHG and the static of WLUCY dies down. When my writing starts flowing again I really don't hear my neighbor's TV anymore.

**Try This:** Set a timer for five minutes. During that time describe any sounds you hear—the hum of your computer, the banging of work-men in the apartment next door, the grumbling of your stomach. My brother told me he could hear the sound of his eyelids blinking when he was trying to write. After your ear has separated the different com-ponents of sound, let them merge again into that surrounding cushion we call "silence." The next time you are distracted by noises, write the noises down. Pretend each is an instrument in an orchestra. Now listen for the overall envelope of sound and try not to hear each individ-ual noise anymore, especially if it has words that compete with your own. Blend the sounds into one background Muzak, a soft, boring nonsound that you can easily tune out.

## THE CALISTHENICS OF SELFISHNESS

There is something in friends that does not love a writer. Or does not love the idea that you are one. For, as soon as you announce you are trying to write, people will take to calling you during your writing time. Sometimes they will even ask, "I'm not disturbing you, am I? You weren't (ha ha) writing?" To which you must learn to reply, "Yes, I am. I'll call you later." Then hang up. Practice this a few times a day. Yes, I am, click. Yes, I am, click. It is necessary for writers to develop a set of hardened muscles that do not flinch at the punches of guilt people jab at them.

You need to get so you can hang up without thinking, especially without thinking how you're hurting your best friend's feelings. You may need to practice this a few times an hour, and even then you may not be able to do it. Frankly, I have been writing at home for twenty years and am still unable to do it. Instead I try to convey displeasure through the use of the glum voice. Unfortunately this more often solicits concern than farewell, which makes it even harder to be rude. Before you know it you're off and running, talking about illnesses, depression, and did you hear what happened to Joe Shmoe's stepfather, but first you have to admit you don't know who Joe Shmoe is, and there you go. And that it is why an answering machine is essential.

Screenwriter Steve Schwartz quotes Hemingway (he thinks it was Hemingway) as saying, "The greatest enemies of writing are visitors and the telephone." Whether it was Hemingway or not, *someone* said it, and it shows the long history of writer antisociability. We don't like to be interrupted when we're writing. In the old days when there were no answering machines, I had only two methods of saving myself from telephone interruptions during my writing time. I could let the telephone ring and not pick up, or I could take the telephone off the hook. Letting the phone ring was not ideal. There was always the mysterious caller who would ring twenty or thirty times at a shot, then call back a few minutes later. Taking the phone off the hook was the preferred technique, because at least there would be no derailing of my train of thought with that ringing nuisance. But afterward there would be a price to pay. A repeated busy signal would drive my father-in-law, for example, crazy. The man prides himself on being a nudge. So, as soon as I would put the phone back on the hook it would ring and it would be him, telling me he had called the phone company to see if my phone was out of order. Since it wasn't, they had listened in to see if I was talking. As I was not they had concluded I had "accidentally" left the phone off the hook. I never had it in me to tell my father-in-law I had purposely taken the phone off the hook, although he knew I had, and I knew he knew that. Instead we would play this little game of *Can You Top This?* which went something like: "The telephone company said it was working fine." "Oh, I must have hung it up wrong." "How could you hang it up wrong, didn't you hear the recording come on?" "That had to have been when I was taking a shower." "Odd you didn't notice . . ." ad nauseum.

None of which you have to worry about. Life is easier now. Computers take away any need for the Wite-Out and Correcto-Type I used to hoard. (I still have some in my desk though—you never know when the comet's going to hit, but I'll be ready with clean copy, having a manual typewriter *and* Correcto-Type while everyone else's computer is on the blink.) Tapes play the sound of leaky radiators in a spring forest, drowning out the sounds of Ethel and Fred. The answering machine doesn't even hum or blink, or in any way draw attention to itself, except when it's needed.

The answering machine, however, is not perfect. It will still happen that when you're in the middle of something good, just when you're caught in a dream and the words are flowing faster than your fingers can catch them, the telephone will ring. The machine will pick up, but in the same way you listen in to hear past the white noise at whatever you are trying to muffle, you will find yourself putting the muse on hold so you can hear your own nasal voice say, "I can't come to the phone right now" and your cousin say, "You there? Pick up, if you are. I know you're there. Pick up, I have something important to tell you."

Now, this is important, so make note of it somewhere on your desk. No matter what she says, no matter how many promises she makes to be brief and funny, that what she has to tell you is important, it is imperative that you not pick up the phone. If you even once admit that you were within reach of the receiver but let the answering machine get it, your reputation will be damaged. From then on everyone will assume you're home, not answering the telephone, even when you really are not.

Fellow writer Evan Russell has his own elegant solution to the problem of telephone interruptions, and it is so simple I am amazed I never thought of it. In fact I'm embarrassed to admit it. All he does is unplug the phone. That's it. I'm not sure why I never did this. I think I believed you can't. That it is illegal somehow—a *1984* surveillance thing. That if you unplug the phone, alarms will go off. Before you know it there's a knock at the door. It's the telephone company, come to plug your phone back in. If you don't answer the door they knock it down with axes, as if you were being held hostage. "Miss, you in there? You all right? Stand back, we're coming in." Like cutting the tags off your mattress or stuffed animal, the ones that say what the stuffing is and in big letters scream, "Do Not Remove." Someone out there will know if you do.

But Evan says the only bad thing about unplugging the phone is that if you forget to plug it in again when you're done you can go around for days thinking you're even less popular than you are.

I have a couple of warnings for you. First of all, the worst interruption in a writer's day is when you're working on a story, it's flowing like an unstoppable wound and then, voilà! the unstoppable is stopped by the clotting factor of the telephone ringing. In a moment of . . . I don't know what—generosity, foolhardiness, fear that you're turning down work you desperately need, maybe just the desire to get the damn thing to stop ringing—whatever it is, you answer, and it's someone trying to sell you a subscription to *Kvetch Quarterly*. I'm going to share a secret with you that has been invaluable in my life. When you say "Hello" and there is a lag of a few seconds, what you do before the voice comes on is *Hang Up*. That pause is your signal that this is a telemarketing call. Don't say hello a second time or you're a goner. I'm not sure why this happens exactly. It's an electronic thing. The switchboards of robots who dial numbers all day are hardwired into a living slave who comes on as soon as a real voice completes the connection. Which is to say, it's much harder to hang up on a person than on a machine, so hang up while you still can. (That said, my husband has just informed me that I hung up on him twice last week and once on his business partner. It's not an infallible system. On the other hand, neither of *them* called back, did they?)

Second, when someone calls and promises to tell you something short, it is usually a means of getting you hooked. It took me a long time to realize this. I wondered for years how it happened that this one particular friend would call, and determined though I was not to get involved in a long telephone conversation with her, I somehow always did. The glum voice didn't deter her. She would say, "I know I'm interrupting you. I just have to tell you something funny." Then she would. It would be funny, it would usually be quick, but it was not why she called. That was her key into my day. She had perfected the skill of seguing from that to what she really wanted to talk about— something personal and deep and sad, something I would never have the heart to cut her off from. Which was how I'd end up on the telephone for an hour, right when I was in the middle of what had promised to be a good story and was now stillborn. You would think the muse would understand something like that and say, "Don't worry. We can finish next time." After all, you're being kind to someone you love. But the muse isn't like that. I told you before, she's quick to take offense and slow to forgive, and the next time you need her she's off eating Cheetos in bed.

**Try This:** Write a story about a recent writing session you had that got interrupted—either by someone else or by the cleaning woman in your soul. There can be a confrontation between characters (or parts of your mind), even if this didn't happen in real life.

• Keep a log of your distractions for at least a week. Then review it, looking for patterns. What do you find most distracts you? Create a plan of action to stop it. Think of—and write down—at least three specific steps you can take to combat this distraction.

# THREE

# MY SECRET LIFE

The question of friends, family, and phones brings up a larger issue, the one of identity. How wise is it to strip off the mask of the mundane and reveal your secret life as a writer? Is it better to keep your hopes and dreams to yourself, not giving others a chance to shoot you down through kindness as much as cruelty?

I've grappled with this issue for years. I can't say I have a solution. It depends on you; it depends on your circle of friends and family. A sense of commitment comes over you once you have announced to the world you are writing. It helps people understand why you don't want to have marathon conversations on the phone anymore, why you can't head the PTA and organize the rummage sale like you did last year. I didn't tell my parents for a long time that I was a writer. As a result my mother would call and question me about my day; it always felt like the Gestapo. "I called and nobody picked up. Where were you?" Where was I? I was walking down the street with a bunch of characters I know, or am trying to know. But I couldn't tell her that, so I lied. "I was in the shower." "You're always in the shower. What do you do a whole day, you don't take a shower till the afternoon?" And on and on. My life must have seemed very mysterious to her till I published my first novel, and that only after I'd been writing full time for ten years. After *Secret Correspondence* came out I still couldn't tell her I was writing when she called. It would seem, how can I put it? uppity—as if I were putting on airs, placing myself above her because I was American born and college educated and she was neither.

This is the downside to telling people you are a writer. Some people may be impressed, but some will be angry. And the angry ones may be the ones you have loved the longest. They may laugh at the idea of you as a writer. They may act insulted, as if the whole notion were a bit of pomposity on your part. They won't take your desire to write seriously; they may even sabotage you. Telephone calls are the least of it. There are the unkind things people say, then claim only to be joking. There are the accusations they make, that you only ask them questions because you're planning to steal their material and put it in that awful book of yours. They make jokes about you and your "important" book to other people, a book so important you can't find time to visit your grandmother in the nursing home or have dinner with your parents anymore.

On the other hand there will also be people who, learning that you are a writer, will tell you their stories willingly. Too willingly. They usually take you aside at a party and say something like, "I'm going to tell you something real good, you should put it in a book. I would if I had the time but I don't, so here, listen. This story's a natural for a best-seller." (Everyone would be a writer if they only had time, if they weren't busy in the *real* world doing *real* things!) Watch out for these kind souls. Most of the time their material has nothing to do with you, with what your writing is about, your dreams, but if you do happen to use *any* of it they will claim you stole it. And if you change anything, they will accuse you of lying.

Some people are lucky. Just as some are born beautiful or wealthy or smart, some are born with supportive parents. Madison Smartt Bell told me, "The general attitude in the South is that being a writer is as good a way to be poor as any. I think I picked that notion up from George Garrett to begin with. But certainly it seems to be a less vexatious career choice in Southern families than in families from other regions of the States. My own parents were of a literary disposition and knew a lot of writers so there was nothing peculiar about my becoming one. Indeed they were quite willing to encourage me along

---

**TIP:** People are more likely to reveal themselves to you if they *don't* know you're a writer. The sorts of secrets, anecdotes, and truths people (relatives) tell you once they know you're a writer are usually defensive and/or self-aggrandizing. Nobody but a writer knows what makes a good story. Everyone thinks he or she does.

those lines." And novelist Tom Mallon revealed that he wrote an awful novel, called *Impeachment*, "in bright green ballpoint" when he was thirteen or fourteen. Since it was written in 1965, he likes to take "credit for a certain prescience." What struck me most about this novel, however, was that his parents read it and were "sweetly respectful and impressed," Tom told me.

Sweetly respectful and impressed. Sweetly respectful and impressed. A more typical response in my neighborhood (especially as I got older) was, "A writer! A writer! A curse on our heads. There's no money in it. You'll be a bum all your life. What makes you think you have something to say anyone would want to read, let alone pay for?"

Novelist Jodie Klavans told me she too found her family discouraging in regard to her ambitions. Everyone kept pushing marriage on her as something constructive to do to get the foolhardy idea of writing out of her mind. Even now, with two published novels, a good marriage and two kids, they still think she's some sort of "literature junky." She says, "It's like they want to know, 'Don't you ever want to go shopping again?'"

My second novel came out when my son, Zack, was in kindergarten, and he was so proud. He would announce to everybody that I was a writer. I'd be buying him a pair of shoes and the salesman would say, "How do you do," and Zack would nudge me. "Tell him about *Wishbone*."

The thing about *Wishbone* was that it was very dark and a bit kinky, not the sort of book I wanted to share with the teachers and parents in his school. Or every stranger we met in a store or in line for the movies. Or on the A-train. Certainly not on the A-train.

Or at my parents' assisted-living home, for that matter. There too the revelation of my secret identity caused me to be eyed differently by people. I was approached by the Activities Coordinator and talked into giving a reading. Before I knew it I was standing before a sea of white nodding heads atop afghan rugs in wheelchairs, telling them about this writer being stalked by a character in her novel. Afterward some of them came up to me, hearing aids whistling, to tell me how much they'd enjoyed what I'd read and to ask if I didn't just adore Danielle Steele. There was something so poignant about all these old women clutching their bodice-rippers. My own book seemed academic in this setting *and* perverted. Just as it had felt perverted when touted by a five-year-old to his kindergarten teacher.

Evan Russell advises me that it is a mistake to tell acquaintances you're a writer, because the next question is always, "Are you published?" and there's just no way to keep your dignity after having your nose pushed around in a pile of *No, not yets.*

But he also told me that, after years of listening to them harp, "When will we get to see something of yours?" he finally showed his novel to his family. His mom handed it back and said she couldn't get past the first thirty pages, it was disgusting. His sister said she couldn't read it because she was breastfeeding and couldn't read anything not in paperback. But the surprise came in his father's reaction. A man never known for offering praise or encouragement, he did both—something unexpectedly moving for Evan. And this is a good reason to announce to the world your intention to write. You may find support in strange places. You may also find that the lack of the same fills you with the drive you need to succeed.

**Try This:** Write a scene in which you tell your parents, your wife, your sister or brother, your friends that you are a writer. Describe the overall response, then describe the response of each individual. What do they say? Do? How does the narrator of the piece (the stand-in for you) react? What does the narrator do after leaving the scene? Think about what this reaction means. If he or she is energized by the response received (remember, the narrator's drive can be fueled by a desire to prove critics wrong as well as right), perhaps you will be too. Maybe it's time to take off the mask. Eventually all serious writers do.

- For those of you who have already revealed your secret identity, write a scene in which a striving artist (writer, musician, tap-dancer, clown) confronts the doubts and worries of his or her family regarding this ambition. Or write a scene in which a first-person narrator has an adult child who reveals his or her desire to write. Express the concerns you might have for someone you love who chooses this rocky path. Let that imagined child answer those concerns.

## YOUR SONG-AND-DANCE ROUTINE

Whether you elect to reveal your secret identity to others or not, it is important that you admit your dream to yourself. This is one of the

> ... I'm always sorry when I hear of your reading anything of mine, and always hope you won't—you seem to me so constitutionally unable to "enjoy" it, and so condemned to look at it from a point of view remotely alien to mine in writing it, and to the conditions out of which, as mine, it has inevitably sprung—so that all the intentions that have been its main reason for being (with *me*) appear never to have reached you at all. ... And yet I can read *you* with rapture.
> —Henry James in a letter to his brother, William James

first things you need to do in order to write. You need to take yourself seriously. That means you can't write on a napkin in a coffee shop once in a while, waiting for your pastry to come, and call yourself a writer. (I suppose you could call yourself a waiter, but that wouldn't be true either.) I won't tell you that all writers have writing schedules they stick to, no matter what. Writers are individuals. As soon as I tell you writers do this or that, I see a thousand naysayers saying "Nay." But I know one writer, me, for whom a daily routine is essential.

Why? Because it's hard to write. I don't mean the actual work is difficult. That may or may not be true. Sometimes it flows; sometimes it doesn't. What I really mean is that it is hard to get yourself to sit down and try. You will come up with a million other things that need to be done first. You will clean your desk, sharpen your pencils, make a few quick phone calls, you will put up the laundry, you will run out to the store for milk, you will make coffee, tea, breakfast, lunch, dinner. Clean the windows. Clip your toenails. You will do anything but write. But if you have a schedule that says: Get up, get family off, exercise, shower, write, then you know what you have to do. There's no thinking about it. There's no decision to make. Should I work on my novel or should I make a salad? The salad can wait. Now is the time to work on your novel. Sit down and do it.

"Make it the first priority of the day (and the week)," Madison Smartt Bell recommends. "The trick is to reserve at least a couple of hours of your best-energy time for writing what you want to write, every day if possible, or five days a week, or four, or whatever you can manage. For me that time has become the first hours of the morning, but it wasn't always that way. I used to work better in the afternoon or at night. When doesn't matter, but reserving the time does. Devote your best hours to your own work and do whatever else you have to do afterward."

If you are a screenwriter, like Steve Schwartz, your schedule may entail more selling time and less writing time, but it is still a writing schedule. "I try to restrict myself to my office for at least four hours every day and hope something comes of it. . . . My work falls into two phases: selling a project so I'll get paid to write, and writing the screenplay. More of my time is spent on selling than on writing. This entails thinking up and fleshing out movie ideas."

During the next three hours (or whatever amount of time you set aside for your writing) you write—and think about your writing. You don't answer the phone unless it's an emergency. You don't plan your son's birthday party or fill the goody bags. And when people ask you if you are free, you look at your appointment calendar and shake your head sadly. You are busy every morning till one, or every afternoon till four, or every evening after work till ten. You don't have to tell anyone that you are busy writing, because people will assume your own work is less important than the work you do for someone else. Don't explain. Just say, "No, sorry, I'm busy." That's what I mean by taking yourself seriously as a writer.

That doesn't mean that everything you write during that time is gold. Mostly it's crap. But there is something to be gained from writing crap. For one thing, it keeps the fingers in practice for when the gold comes along. And it helps you hear a voice, to feel the rhythms, the buildup and the punch-line effect of a good delivery. Writing every day is like a musician doing scales. It keeps you limber. And, perhaps most importantly, it holds fear at bay. Because the longer you go without writing, the harder it is to actually do.

You may have a thousand ideas in your head, you may hear characters conversing, you may see the action before your eyes and know that what you have is great . . . if you would just write it down. What you are building for yourself is one gigantic writer's block, embuing this project with a halo so that nothing less than perfect will be allowed to escape from your brain to the page. But if you write every day you get used to terrible phrasings and clichés and malapropisms. That doesn't mean you let anyone else see them, but they're not so terrible for you to see. You can fix them the next day. You can discard them. And you can also find stuff hidden in your writing that you never intended and are blown away by. But this happens only if you allow yourself to write down the imperfect—what you never meant to say.

Bear in mind that being a writer means *being* a writer. It's not just when you have a pen in hand that you are a writer, although you're not a writer at all if you never write. But the state of being a writer means you are a writer all the time. It means catching a snatch of dialogue and memorizing it until you can find a place to jot it down. It means describing scenery to yourself, and gestures, and evocative occurrences. It means staying alive to the miracles around you, the tragedies and comedies of the marvelous and the mundane.

**Try This:** While you are doing something that is a necessary part of your day—grading papers, marketing, taking a bus or shower—mentally "write" what you are doing, seeing, hearing. Describe the kid twirling around the passenger pole on the train. What is he wearing? How does his body move? What does his face look like? Examine a package of chicken breasts not only with an eye to buying it or not but to describing it. What *is* that color? How does the wetness of the package feel? ("Yucky" is not a good enough description.)

## GHOULISH GOULASH

You need to train yourself to be a writer even when you're not at your desk. Writers are never bored—or shouldn't be. There's always something to observe, to think about, to make mental notes on. Sometimes this aspect of being a writer can be troubling. John Gardner wrote about stopping to help someone who'd been in a terrible automobile accident, all the time making observations about his surroundings, his own emotions, the responses of other people, in case he ever had to write a scene in which a terrible accident occurred. When my mother was dying, and then six weeks later when my father was dying, I found myself standing off and observing the scenes I was part of. Writers *are* ghouls, vampires of experience, their own as much as anyone else's. That doesn't mean they don't feel, or that there is a coldness in the way they make note of the horrors, and wonders, of life. I wept, I consoled, I held my mother's hand and I kissed my father's cheek. I also saw her gnarled fingers and felt his rough bristles. His confusion about the canes, about the catheter, the way my father sucked at the spongy thing we used to give him water—my revulsion at this, and my revulsion at myself for feeling revulsion. Part of me took things in and said, "Remember this. Don't let it slip away. Remember." There *is* something ghoulish about this attitude. There is also something quite remarkable about it. For, in remembering my parents I keep them alive. In writing about them I bring them back for a little while.

> James Joyce wrote *Ulysses* "to preserve the speech of my father and his friends."

You probably know this if you're reading this book. You've been writing in your head a long time, keeping your stories alive, keeping the voices you know so well still speaking. Now I'm going to tell you about an essential tool and an essential technique for getting yourself to write on paper. The tool and the technique are so essential in fact that each gets its own chapter.

# FOUR

# THE LITTLE NOTEBOOK

I t's little, it's unpretentious, it slips easily into a back pocket or purse and can be pulled out without fanfare. It's the little notebook, and without it some of our best ideas would get lost. After all, it is much more difficult to jot down an idea for a story that pops into your head when you have to ask someone to borrow a pen and some paper. It is also more difficult to retrieve that idea when you know it's some-place in your bookbag, but first you have to empty the whole satchel out on the bed and go through every dirty tissue and crumpled To Do list, searching for it.

Anne Fadiman writes, in her book *Ex Libris: Confessions of a Common Reader*, "One day, when Sir Walter Scott was out hunting, a sentence he had been trying to compose all morning suddenly leapt into his head. Before it could fade, he shot a crow, plucked a feather, sharpened the tip, dipped it in crow's blood, and captured the sentence." Whether you go for this or not you'll agree it is much easier to get into the habit of carrying a pen and pad with you.

I have four pockets in my jeans—one is for my wallet, one is for my keys, the third contains my card case, but that fourth pocket, the back hip pocket, holds an unostentatious notepad and a pen. All day long I neurotically touch my pockets to be sure that all four are filled. When I have to wear a dress I feel like a transvestite, especially negoti-ating the pocketbook thing. I never know what to do with my bag when I get to where I'm going. In restaurants I dangle it off my knee. At parties I hide it behind a chair and then can't find it. When I walk down the street I clutch it like a soldier with important documents for the general.

You may be comfortable carrying a pocketbook or a backpack. On the plus side, this won't make your pants tight and restrict your wardrobe. On the minus side, this means you have to carry a pocketbook or a backpack.

Pocketbooks aside, the point is that the notebook should always be with you. When you are in line at the drugstore and when you pick your kid up from school. Aunt Tessa's funeral. Cousin Betty's wedding. The only time my notebook isn't with me is when I go for a run. None of my pocket items go running with me—just a key and a quarter wrapped in a piece of paper with my name and address and my husband's office phone number, in case my body is ever found.

Now, perhaps you have a notebook, a big black notebook that says JOURNAL on the front in gold letters and plays "Hail to the Chief" whenever you open it, shouting to every passerby, "I am a writer's notebook, and here is a writer . . . writing." Should you use a notebook like that in your daily life? That depends. Do you like the blaring of trumpets announcing your presence when you come into a room?

Personally I like my little notebook to be, well, little. Not heavy, not bulky, and I don't like pictures of puppies on it. I want it to draw as little attention as possible when I take it out to note something. I don't want people to notice. Or if they do, I prefer they think I'm making a shopping list rather than planning a major opus. I tend to jot observations like a detective following a suspect. I duck into telephone booths (oh, all right, so they're half-cubicles now—no place for Superman to change, but they grant me a bit of privacy). I hunch over myself on a park bench like the nerdy girl in sixth grade who didn't want anyone to cheat off her test. I probably draw more attention to my activity by the secretive way in which I do it than if I took a more casual approach. Boris and Natasha in cloak-and-dagger attire look less conspicuous. You can probably do it better. But take my advice— a small notebook fits into your back pocket and doesn't set off any car alarms when you take it out.

In general, you may find it useful to have several notebooks. Notebooks are one of my fetishes. Pens are another. I drool when I see a stationery store. I can't walk by one without poking my head in, or at least ogling the window. One of the more difficult things about my son's infancy was how it kept me out of stationery stores. Our northern Manhattan neighborhood—what we call Upstate New York City—is blessed with woods, flowers, a grand river, and wildlife, but it sorely lacks such amenities as stationery stores, booksellers, and trendy coffee bars. Negotiating the subway with a baby in a carriage was not a task I took lightly. To go to the pediatrician I'd do it. To buy a new pen . . . maybe not. One night my husband and I got a babysitter and went downtown to one of my favorite paper haunts, where I loaded up on notebooks, pens, artpads, envelopes, reams of paper, and other writing supplies like they were canned goods and I was stocking my fallout shelter.

"But what do you write in your little notebook?" you ask. You write whatever interests you. Story ideas, character names, overheard dialogue, a scene, an image, a thought. An extended riff on what passes through your mind while waiting for the school bus. The point is that if an idea or an observation comes your way you're ready for it.

Writing something down often works as a magnet for other thoughts. It's almost as if the muse, or whoever is in charge of passing out ideas, gets off on your appreciation so much she just keeps throwing the stuff at you . . . as long as you keep bending to scoop it up. You show your gratitude by writing it down, and she shows her generosity by continuing to bestow it. It gets to the point where you want to say, "Enough already. If you don't let me walk a few blocks without stopping to write I'm never going to get home." Don't do that. I told you the muse takes umbrage easily—nothing insults her faster than being ignored or turned away. So write down all the ideas she gives you, even the junk that's only half good. And be grateful. For a time will come when you are at your desk, trolling for ideas in an empty head. Then you can reach for that little notebook and voilà! an abundance of things to work on awaits you.

When I was writing my first (unpublished) novel, *Tale of the Forgotten Woman*—a book that took seven years to write before I'd even show it to my husband—I'd go for a walk in the park and have to stop every few feet to jot something down. I was in the grip of a full-blown case of inspiration. I had no idea how rare this infection was, nor how I would long in subsequent novels to come down with it again. All I knew was I was self-conscious about this style of walking, sure I looked pretentious or insane, a woman talking to herself and scribbling notes. Which in fact I was. But who did I think was watching? If someone noticed my odd way of taking a walk—stopping every few feet to plop on a bench and scribble—that person could only have been another writer. And he or she would understand. Possibly hate me, but surely understand.

> **TIP:** Carrying a small notebook and a pen can function as your secret identity card. No one has to know what is in your back pocket, but you know it is there—because you are a writer, always . . . even when you're on shopping for underwear at K-Mart.

Bear in mind these manic states, if they come at all, don't come often. Depression—the downside of the non-Lithium swing—visits frequently and stays long, like in-laws from out of town. So encourage the ups, even if you seem like a raving lunatic a while. I had an analyst once who thought my ups and downs indicated a manic-depressive personality. She advocated drugs to keep things on an even keel. I didn't listen to her, and I am glad to this day. Even keel means floating in still water, waiting to die of starvation and thirst. Now, I know some people really *can't* function because of the mood swings, and that's a different case. But doctors often overprescribe drugs—they're more afraid of your moods than you are. So, if you're prone to ups and downs, and these ups and downs are manageable, manage them. Encourage the ups, discourage the downs, and full speed ahead. For me, the highs are worth the lows. That first novel I told you about had a story in it called "Tale of the Thinking Cap," about a girl who is given a cap that makes her burn with ideas. Everyone warns her to take it off, she'll be consumed by it, but she says that *that* is exactly what she wants.

You know what? I still do.

**Try This:** Buy a small notebook you are comfortable carrying everywhere, and carry it everywhere. Use it to jot down those passing ideas, even the ones that aren't so good. Refer to it during your writing time for a phrase to help you get started or for a jolt to reawaken an earlier plan. Make the notebook as essential a part of your leaving-the-house accoutrements as the door key. And don't forget your pen.

- If the habit of note-taking is a hard one for you to start, make a game of it. Each week come up with something to be on the lookout for—a treasure hunt for detail. One week you may jot down any unusual thing you come across having to do with blue. You can extend the word across the boundaries of pun so that you can list a blue garbage bag tied up like a present, the way the wind blew, the *blooo* sound it made, blue feelings. The following week you may go scavenger-hunting for love—divine, romantic, Platonic, familial, sexual. Another assignment you may give yourself is to search for laughter—things that make you laugh, instances of other people laughing, laughing sounds. Or one week you might use your notebook to copy down dialogue. Eavesdrop on people at work, on the bus, at the next table.

Once you have established the habit of note-taking you won't need to search for specific things, although it's not a bad thing to do now and then to hone your writing vision and sharpen your senses. Specific details always make for stronger writing than airy generalizations. As you get used to noticing and noting such details, you will find a treasure trove to use in your writing—both in your notebook and in your writing mind.

## GOLDIBOOK AND THE THREE PADS

Doris Lessing undoubtedly mined my psyche when she wrote *The Golden Notebook,* although I was only nine when the novel came out and didn't have much psyche to speak of. (I seem to remember a five-year diary with one or two entries filled in, along the lines of "Tony smiled at me today. Joy.") I am now a woman of many notebooks. My system is arcane and not necessarily practical. It's an individual thing: It may not work for you. The essential notebook is the small public one. You may also want a big notebook for writing big notes at home. I like unlined paper so I buy sketchpads of various sizes for my various needs. I have a big book for writing out ideas and first drafts and for thinking on the page. I have a middle-size book for taking on trips, because there's room for the roomier thoughts I always think I'm

> I have lost too much time by losing, or rather by not having acquired, the note-taking habit. . . . I ought to endeavor to keep, to a certain extent, a record of passing impressions, of all that comes, that goes, that I see, and feel, and observe. To catch and keep something of life . . .
>
> —Henry James

going to have time to think, forgetting that with a child there isn't any time for thinking. *Especially* on vacation. And I always have my little notebook in my back pocket. I also keep a dream notebook. And a notebook in which I write things about my son. And a cheap, cheap, indescribably cheap notebook for my freewriting. Which brings us to the next chapter.

FIVE

# FREEWRITING

More than twenty years ago Gail Godwin published an essay in *The New York Times* called "The Watcher at the Gates," and I have been carrying it around with me ever since. In it she says that there are two parts to the writing mind—the artist and the watcher—and that it is essential to shut the watcher up while the artist is working. Later you need the watcher to come in and help tidy things, straightening thoughts, syntax, and stuff, but during the initial stages of creation you must be free from the self-doubt an overactive watcher can instill.

She quotes Freud quoting Schiller: "In isolation, an idea may be quite insignificant, and venturesome in the extreme, but it may acquire importance from an idea which follows it. . . . In the case of a creative mind, it seems to me, the intellect has withdrawn its watchers from the gates, and the ideas rush in pell-mell, and only then does it review and inspect the multitude."

How do you get past your watcher? The best technique I know of is called "freewriting."

Freewriting, as many of you perhaps know, is essentially what the name implies—free writing. It is writing about anything, trying to get past your censor, trying to get away from the Miss Grundy who only wants to ball you up with questions of spelling and punctuation, not to mention mentioning unmentionables.

It is useful, if you are having trouble working on your magnum opus, to freewrite a bit. It is also useful to do it if you want to write but don't know what to write about. Many writers start their day this way, having a set amount of time for doing it. Ten minutes, half an hour. It is a period of time when you put pen to paper, or fingers to keyboard, and you write without looking back. There is no such thing as a dictionary. Anything that comes into your mind comes on the page. You can use dirty words and have dirty thoughts. You can even write about how you hate your family, those slimeballs who don't understand you can't go home for the holidays because you don't want to see them . . . ever. You can lie. You can admit to shameful thoughts about your best friend's husband. You can make up fantasies that might get you committed to an institution for the morally insane if anyone knew them—the one about the Doberman pinscher, for instance. You don't have to worry though, because no one will know about them, unless you choose to show your freewriting around. Now, why in the world would you do that? Freewriting is for you. For Your Eyes Only. It's a spy mission to your unconscious.

> The unconscious creates; the ego edits.
>
> —Stanley Kunitz

The one rule about freewriting is that you can't erase or cross out. You shouldn't even read back while you're doing it. And you have to go for the appointed amount of time. If the telephone rings, pretend you are in the shower.

Freewriting enables you to be productive in two ways. It can be a laboratory of ideas. Crazy associations and memories may come out while you're doing it that might not have occurred to you if you were not. Freewriting, in this case, may give you material in the same way that psychoanalysis might, only it's much *much* cheaper.

The other way freewriting helps you make better use of your time is by oiling the machine: It gets you going. You're not so afraid of starting if you've already started. The connection between fingers and brain has been made, and the charge between the two hasn't blacked out the entire northeast sector, not even when you wrote about your brother's weird personal habits. Freewriting lubricates the finger joints; it gets you into the writing mode. It clears the cobwebs from your brain and helps focus your vision. And it gives those nasty voices that keep telling you what's wrong with you a chance to be heard. You can then shut them up and hear your own voice again. Ten minutes of freewriting about nothing is a better use of your time than an hour spent staring at a blank screen. Freewriting may feel like a waste of precious minutes, but if it helps you get past the paper dragon it's a waste of nothing more than some scrap.

In the past, it was common for many writers to keep diaries or work on their correspondence as a means of loosening up before the day's real work of writing began. Virginia Woolf, of course, is the most famous of this lot. Diaries and letters were how Edwardians freewrote. It was as free as they got, which wasn't as free as I'm telling you to get. I'm just trying to prove that doing warmup writing as a means of getting limber has a long pedigree.

Some people freewrite in their heads. One of my former students, Evan Russell, for instance. That is, when he's not actually writing he has these extended conversations with himself. "It's actually just like writing," he says, "only you can go so much faster, which is wonderful, but then there's no record of it, which sucks. What is it that I babble about in these imagined conversations? Pretty much everything under the sun."

I also have these long conversations with myself, but of late they're more annoying than interesting. I'm usually defending myself to parents, friends, sometimes ladies and gentlemen of the jury. I rehearse unpleasant scenes I will have to enact in the not too distant future—demanding the doctor give me a referral to have this thing on my face looked at before its roots dig into my brain. Sometimes I make lists of things I need to do, then I recite them over and over. I've found one way to get such annoyances off my chest is to get them on paper. They tend not to go around and around if I write them down. I can stop myself and say, "Hey, I wrote that already. Let's think about something else."

Freewriting is nothing if not free. It is what you make of it, with few rules. Steve Schwartz, for example, just types facts about himself when he's having trouble starting. "My name, where I live, etc. Anything. After a paragraph or two of drivel, somehow I'm loosened up enough to actually write." You will find that for you, as for Steve, "The act of writing makes easier the act of writing."

So, aside from the essentials—no correcting spelling, punctuation, grammar; no pausing or searching for the felicitous phrase; no holding back from disgusting, painful, stupid, boring thoughts—anything goes. There are, however, a couple of ways to do it.

Let's look at the keyboard/pen controversy first. I like to write on paper with a pen, but I have a terrible handwriting. Sometimes I do my freewriting on paper, knowing that I will never be able to read back what I've written but that's okay. I just want to get something written. I want the tactile sensation of ink scribbling across the page in curliques of meaning only I can decipher. Other times I freewrite on the computer. I have a file in the computer set aside for this. I make a new file each year, and I keep adding to it so that come December I have a long scroll of unhappy thoughts. A Christmas card from my most neurotic self. The stuff I write on the computer is readable, but I'm not sure I want to read it . . . or have anyone else to. I also find it impossible not to correct typos when I work at the computer, which makes me tidy up a bit. It's important not to tidy when you freewrite.

The two other things I don't like about freewriting at the computer are my back and the shimmy. My back hurts when I work at a keyboard. Sometimes I sit in a regular chair; sometimes I sit on a kneeling chair. It doesn't matter. There is only so much time I can spend writing at a keyboard, and since it's more important to write my stories and novels in a legible way, I tend not to freewrite at the computer for extended periods of time. But it does get me to turn the computer on, and sometimes that is enough of a plus to do away with oh-my-aching-back considerations.

The shimmy is something my monitor has begun doing of late. It probably means I need a new monitor. But every new piece of equipment I get sets me back not just financially but emotionally. I hate to admit this but my computer has a name. I know it's just a machine but, like Norman Bates' stuffed mother in her rocking chair, my first computer still sits in my closet. It doesn't work; there's no logical reason to save it. It's just it feels like a person or a pet. Maybe there should be a cemetery for old hardware. More likely there shouldn't, since I seem to be the only one with this problem. I also still have my old manual typewriter on the floor under my desk—a Royal upright that looks like something Lois Lane wrote her articles about Superman on.

Emotional and financial considerations aside, setting up a new piece of equipment, even one as simple as a monitor, somehow manages to kill at least a day of work. So for the time being my words shimmy and my back aches, and my computer and I manage to hobble along like ancient sisters, leaning on each other's frail arms.

Other variables about freewriting concern time and theme. It is sometimes useful to write for a set amount of time. Much more than half an hour I wouldn't go. The line between sanity and schizophrenia starts to blur after forty-five minutes, and you may find yourself walking the streets, mumbling to yourself, when you thought you were freewriting in privacy. Frankly, at a certain point you have to stop freewriting and start hitting the expensive stuff.

Thematic freewriting means choosing something you want to explore ahead of time, then freewriting about that. Maybe it's your sister's divorce. Maybe it's the people you've dated who turned out to be losers. Maybe there's a character in your novel you want to get to know. The material you end up with is not necessarily stuff you want to use. But it can be helpful to know your character hates broccoli, has sexual fantasies about a woman who sells bagels, and used to think she was adopted because her parents kept telling her to stop behaving like a wild Indian. Ibsen was asked how he came up with the name Nora for his heroine in *A Doll's House*, and he said that she was really Eleanora but her family had called her Nora since she was a little girl. This doesn't appear in the play. It's just something he discovered about the character in the process of getting to know her.

Whatever approach to freewriting you use, the essential thing about it is (I repeat) that you don't look back. Like Orpheus, you hear the voice behind you and let it guide you. If you turn, the Eurydice of words will disappear into the underworld again. Especially if you tell her she's looking a bit piqued and the shroud has absolutely got to go, it's positively déclassé.

**Try This:** Buy a cheap notebook or make a freewriting file in your computer. The notebook should be so cheap you don't feel bad about wasting paper. Some people like to freewrite in pencil, to further add to the aura of temporality that should surround the event. If you use a computer, don't bother printing out. Make a commitment of five minutes (or more) a day of freewriting for one week. At the end of the week think about the exercise: Did freewriting help you get started doing other writing? Did it raise your self-esteem, so that you *felt* more productive and therefore could be? Did ideas come to you via free association that may not have otherwise? Remember this technique when you are having trouble starting.

## AND FOR YOU VISUAL TYPES . . .

Another way to free the creative side of your mind and get past your censor is similar to freewriting but is more visual. It is called "clustering," a process popularized in Gabriele Rico's *Writing the Natural Way*, one many of you may already know about and use. It's the sort of thing you do naturally when you're trying to think something through. You write a word or short phrase in the center, the thing you are trying to think about—a character's name, a mood, a place, a short idea. Then you free-associate other words around it, drawing circles around the words and lines from the center to the new associations. You might also draw arrows from one association to another. The key here is not to think too carefully about what you're doing, just to keep throwing ideas out. After a few minutes of doing this you end up with something like a cobweb. If the urge to write overtakes you at this point, you start. If not, you continue clustering until it does, or until you can't cluster anymore. Don't read the cluster through thoroughly: Just glance at it before starting, then put it away. You don't need to use every association. But it's a technique that promises to help you get in touch with elements of your writing that have been eluding you. It takes the strain off what you're doing and bypasses your watcher by getting him or her to think you're just doodling.

**Try This:** Find a word that evokes a subject you'd like to write about. Cluster associations around it. "Childhood" might bring up "Fears," for example, which might sub-cluster into "nightmares," "bugs," "closet," "dark," "hedges I had to pass to get home from Debbie's house," etc. Another major cluster group within "Childhood" might be "Pleasures," which could sub-cluster into "digging," "candy," "fantasies." And some of these may sub-cluster again—"digging" could bring to mind something found in the backyard; "candy" could evoke memories of the candy store across the street; and "fantasies" will probably end up as the central cluster on a new page. Use unlined paper for this technique so you won't feel hampered from moving diagonally, vertically, or any old way as associations occur to you.

After you cluster awhile, make sure you write something. It should be rough and free. Later, you may wish to polish it or you may choose to leave it as is, taking some of the associations it has helped you find to a work already in progress.

**TIP:** Freewriting is a great thing to do while waiting for someone in an espresso bar. You can hide your self-consciousness behind a facade of working. It makes you feel like you're not alone. And who knows, you may even find something back there, on the other side of the wall, as you mine your anger, resentment, self-doubt, and delight in the smell of good coffee.

SIX

# SCHEDULES

Schedules are a good thing. In fact, schedules are a great thing. People complain about their busy schedules, how they can't possibly fit one more thing into their lives, their schedules are making them crazy. What they don't know is their schedules are keeping them sane.

It is important to have a schedule if you are a writer. A day can too easily be spent clipping your toenails and drinking tea if you work at home—what one of my students, Martha Schulman, calls working as "an underemployed writer"—or running from one urgent matter to the next if you have an outside job. Or kids.

Depending on which of the above categories you fit in, there are two reasons you need a schedule—too much time and not enough. If you have too much time on your hands you tend to waste it. Having all that time begins to feel "less like a privilege," Martha told me, "and more like a burden." It not only gives you hours to fill, which can make you profligate, casting hours about like rose petals, throwing time on projects such as putting new shelving paper in your kitchen and straightening the utensils drawer. It also removes your confidence that, as she put it, "I'd write something great *if* only I had the time." A humbling crisis for an already indecisive lot. When there's no pressure to get something done you lollygag rather than make a commitment to your work—should I write now or go for a run? How about I just sit here eating bonbons, thinking about it awhile?

I am an indecisive person, always the last to order in a restaurant. My husband knew what he was getting into—on our first date, I needed lip balm and ended up buying two because I couldn't make up my mind. A person like me needs a schedule. It is 8:15. I sit down at the desk and begin. I begin by making lists—the things I have to do that day, the telephone calls to make, the things I need to buy. I allow myself five minutes to get this all out. Then it is time to turn on the computer or take out the manuscript.

If you work in a busy office and maybe have kids too, you need a schedule so you don't forget to write. My friend Sam Decker says that he doesn't get anything done without a schedule, he's juggling so many balls. When you have a busy life, writing may seem a luxury you can't afford. It's the first thing that gets cut from your day. Cut it often enough and you are not a writer anymore.

Someone juggling all them balls will necessarily have a different writing schedule than someone clipping toenails. For the latter—the wide expanse of day opening before her, nothing but a bed on the horizon—it is important that she know the time. It is time to write. It doesn't matter what. It matters that it is *now*. But for the juggler the important thing is that he or she makes a commitment of writing time, and *when* it gets done doesn't matter as much as that it does.

For both kinds of writers the amount of time matters less than the commitment. How long you write depends on other things—what's going on in your life, your finances, your attitude, your back. If you work a nine-to-five job it's unrealistic to plan to write three hours a day, seven days a week. You'll burn out. The same is true if you have children. Even people with nothing to do but write make a mistake, pushing themselves till writing is no longer a pleasure but a life sentence of hard labor. It's as though we all believe we're really into bondage and discipline, only to find, the whip coming down, we're thinking how to escape. No wonder we rebel and end up doing nothing.

It seems to me too often we lose sight of why we write in the first place. If you are writing for the money or the glory you're reading the wrong book, because I don't know anything about money or glory, except that they are more often missing from a writer's life than part of it. I write for love. "Writing is like Prostitution," Molière wrote. "First you do it for the love of it, then you do it for a few friends, and finally you do it for money." About the last, hmm. . . . Whether it will come your way or mine, or even what exactly would be so bad about that, I can't say. I'm not inclined to literary liposuction or breast implants on my cover, but getting paid for my writing doesn't cheapen it. It just isn't why I do it. As long as I keep sight of why I do, I don't mind being able to afford a skim capuccino now and then. But I write for love. I believe this is why you write too. Perhaps we're fools, but we would want to continue writing even if we never got paid, depressing though that would be.

So why is it we hate doing this thing we love?

Because we are afraid.

We forget sometimes that we *are* doing it for love. Chances are no one is beating down your door to read the next thing you write. No one cares, probably, if you write another word, not even your mother (least of all your mother). You are doing it for the fun of it. To amuse yourself. Because there is no better feeling. Because you are good at it, or used to be before it became a grind.

My son at eight says that if he were a professional writer he would "write all day because I only get to work on my story at school for fifteen minutes." For him the love is still alive. Peter Rubie, my agent who is also a novelist, told me that when he was a kid they'd give him paper and pencil as a means of shutting him up for a few hours. (I've tried this with Zack, but it doesn't work. He talks a big storm about writing all day, but when I give him a notebook and pen he'd still rather tell me what he plans to write than do it.) Another novelist friend of mine, Jodie Klavans, said she writes so she'll have something she'd want to read.

This is really why we do it—to amuse ourselves. To tell a story to the Kid . . . and to anyone else who will listen. Because we were once little and bored and no one was interested in what we had to say, except ourselves. So we told ourselves stories. And we told ourselves poems. And we made up long, involved dramas of escape, treasure, and ghosts. And after a while we got hooked.

Somewhere along the line, though, it became drudgery. But if gold was made into dross, there must be a way to make dross back into gold.

I have a friend who told me that the writing life is a curse—this after waxing poetic about how writing calms her and how she has no trouble starting and how easily success came to her. It was as surprising to hear, after all this buildup, as it would be if she'd been showing me pictures of her little darlings and then dropped how she'd murdered her eldest daughter just that morning.

The truth is we're conflicted about writing. It is the love we love to leave. We need to find the fun in it again. Part of that, believe it or not, is having a schedule. I know this sounds like I'm promising you great desserts that will help you lose weight, only to admit that my brownies are made from tofu. But really, if you find a schedule you can live with, you can start putting the fun back in your writing.

The first thing is that you don't have to write eight hours a day to be a writer. It's okay to write in short blocks. If all you can manage is twenty minutes a day, half an hour, that's fine. But you need to make a commitment to that. Promise yourself you will write for that amount of time, and that is all you need to do, then feel good about it. You can write more. If the spirit is with you and your boss isn't about to fire you, keep going. But if you struggle for half an hour and have accomplished exactly zilch, well, that's it. You have lived up to your commitment. Now go do what you want. It's recess. Take a run. Eat lunch. Nap. Browse in a bookstore. Do whatever you want. The only thing you are not allowed to do is feel guilty.

Chances are you will want to go on past that half hour, but if you don't, you don't have to. That is the key. Writers often feel locked in a prison of self. They think everyone else is out there having fun, and here I am, trying to make these wooden puppets come to life. That is why you give yourself thirty minutes to do it, then you can leave. If you want. But if you'd rather be writing. . . .

The other thing, and this is particularly helpful for people with already busy schedules, is that the amount of time you spend writing can be cumulative. It's okay to write for ten minutes three times a day. And it doesn't have to be grand either. Freewriting counts. What is important is that you get into the habit of writing, you live up to your commitment to yourself, you get limber and stop feeling guilty about all the writing you are not doing.

In the end, this is why it is crucial to have a schedule—so you do not waste time feeling guilty. I am assuming, as I said before, that you

I have forced myself to begin writing when I've been utterly exhausted, when I've felt my soul as thin as a playing card, when nothing has seemed worth enduring for another five minutes . . . and somehow the activity of writing changes everything.

—Joyce Carol Oates

write because it is what you love to do. Having a schedule gets you started doing that activity you love. It's how I feel about exercise. I know I will feel great when I get myself running, and I will continue to feel great all day afterward, but if I think about it too much beforehand I find reasons to postpone doing it—it's cloudy, the park will be empty and unsafe; it's late, the park will be empty and unsafe; I don't have enough time; I need to buy milk; and so on, ad nauseum. But with a schedule you know what you need to do; you can stop thinking about it. There are no decisions to be made. Whether it is the ten minutes that come to hand in an otherwise ridiculously hectic day or the fact that it is 8:15 and there's really no pressure to do anything— you turn on the computer or take out your notebook. And you begin.

Ah, begin. But how do you begin, you say. And that brings us to our next chapter.

**Try This:** Make a writing schedule for yourself, nothing so unrealistic you are setting yourself up for failure. What is the minimum amount of time you can write each day and get something accomplished? Start small. You can always go longer than that minimum. But you must stick to this schedule for at least a week. Keep a log of how it goes: How much time did you intend to spend writing? How much time did you succeed in squirreling away for this purpose? How did you deal with interruptions? Did you find yourself wasting time in the beginning, then getting involved in something only to have to stop because of other obligations? Alternatively, did you start full speed ahead, then run out of steam? When the week is up, read the log. Can you pinpoint particular problems you have in making a schedule and sticking to it? Remember: Writing is not just writing. The time you spend thinking, reading, re-searching, and/or daydreaming is also "writing," as long as it pertains to a writing project. It's madness to imagine a writer who says she writes four hours a day is actually scrawling sentences across the page nonstop for that amount of time. For one thing, she has to pee.

**TIP:** Plan your day around your writing schedule, not your writing schedule around your day. Then you won't ever find yourself without time to write.

# SEVEN

# BEGINNING

There is beginning, and there are beginnings, and there are chapters in this book about both. After all, beginning is one of the three most difficult parts of writing (the other two being continuing and ending). Maybe beginning is the *most* difficult aspect of writing, inertia being what it is. Basically, two things make beginning difficult—ideas, and the lack of them. So let's look at these two problems separately for a moment.

## WRITING WITHOUT IDEAS

It is in your soul to write, you know you are full of wonderful thoughts and perceptions and characters, but the moment you find yourself alone you can only think of shopping lists. So here's what you do. Write out the shopping list (or the list of people you have to call, or the list of things that must be taken care of this week). Write it down and get it out of your mind. Promise your guilty conscience that you will buy the food and make the calls and do the laundry and write the report. You will do it all later—if your guilty conscience will leave you alone for a while. It's really up to you, Conscience. If you want me to call Aunt Esther and find out how Uncle Lou's prostate operation went you'd just better go sit in a corner somewhere and let me work, because I'm not doing a thing till I get some writing done.

So now your good-niece/nephew demon is at bay, but you find yourself like the narrator in a book I read as a kid. You've sharpened the pencils; you've gotten the notebook. You sit down and a wail issues from your mouth: "I don't have anything to write about!" You do. You have lots to write about, you've just forgotten it all in this moment of stagefright, facing the audience of yourself (we all know what harsh critics we can be). Don't give up. There are things you can do.

First of all, you can take out that little notebook and see what ideas you have jotted in it to develop at a future date. This is your future date, so mine that pad for something to ring your creativity bell.

But it may happen that your little notebook is empty just when you finally have time to write. And your freewriting hasn't opened up any associations you want to explore further. So, do you just throw your hands up and eat cookies? Maybe, if that's what you really want to be doing, but then why aren't you reading a book called *I'd Rather Be Eating Cookies*?

Here's what they did last year in my son's second-grade class: They kept story envelopes. In these envelopes they put slips of paper with things they had jotted down that they wanted to write about. My son's envelope was full of ideas like Hitting a Grand Salami, Longest Baseball Game Ever Played, I Make the Game-Winning Play. Your ideas may be slightly different. How about that weird old woman who lived down the block when you were growing up? What about that dream in which you were making love to a mountain? Put that in the envelope. Don't forget Momma's gefilte fish ordeal, the time the cops came because they thought she was chopping someone up. How about Pat's argument with the fruit man about her eyebrows? The smell of the old basement after it rained? Your paranoid fantasy about the guy with the binoculars?

And while we're on the subject, let's talk about paranoia for a moment. I think paranoia is great. Especially for writers. We all agree it is easier to begin writing if you have an idea, but we don't know where ideas come from. Well, my own ideas come from a deep-seated paranoia. It works like this:

I start out having a pleasant little fantasy about being a great writer, getting my novel published, my picture is on the jacket. I have a little smile on my face, I'm humming to myself. The next thing you know I'm thinking about someone looking at that picture. Someone distinctly not nice. Three years later there's a novel called *Wishbone*, about a writer who starts to receive threatening letters and phone calls from a character in her novel. Now my neighbors don't want to send their kids over for playdates at my house anymore. My next novel will probably be about *that*.

Another good place to look for ideas is in reminiscence. I once took a writing workshop in something called Reminiscence Therapy. It was for social workers learning how to conduct such a workshop with people who might otherwise have trouble talking about anything deeper than the weather. I found it wonderful to learn I had this storehouse of story ideas inside me, that the misery of childhood had a purpose—to give me something to write about.

And hey, it's not all misery either. There's joy in reminiscence too, although you want to make sure you don't let the gold of nostalgia coat everything in its sickly yellow haze. But if you're having trouble coming up with ideas to write about, think about the ice cream man you used to chase down the block with the quarter in your hand, shouting, "Mr. Ice Cream Man, Mr. Ice Cream Man!" Remember the knife sharpener in his horse-drawn wagon and the sound of the dangling pieces of scrap metal he would rattle to let people know he was coming down the street. What about the red patent leather shoes your mother made you save for a special occasion, so you outgrew them before you got to wear them?

And how about old photographs when you were a kid? Maybe your family kept them all neat in albums with captions below. My mother had a drawer. It was in a china closet in the living room. All our pictures were thrown in, a hodge-podge of times and places. Every so often we'd go into that dusky room, my mother and I, and open the drawer. She'd pull out a bunch. "Here's Aunt Shirley when Alvin was a baby," she'd say. "Look, it's Little Molly with her sister. They had a fight and haven't spoken for thirty years." Some of the photos were really old, from Europe. Some were from last week. The grab-bag style of our selection made a *I Ching* of memory whose wisdom I would try to discern. What did Tanta Chava and her infant, murdered by the Nazis, have to do with last summer at Niagara Falls with Rose and Dave? Writing can be like that too. You call up these vignettes and images. You don't know what they have to do with each other, but you sense they belong. Or at least you trust in your unconscious for a while. In the end you find these disparate images really do go together, that your unconscious mind was working all along at a design you couldn't begin to see.

Our old memories are mysterious. A lot of what gives them their narrative drive is trying to figure them out. They are so powerful, so distilled, these memories. It's like drinking vodka straight, through a straw. After all, a lot happened to you growing up, but most of it is gone. These are the few glimpses that remain. Why these? Of ten years of three months of summer days, why does the time the bees banished you from the backyard stay with you, or the smell of concrete on the sidewalk as you gazed into the garden but were afraid to enter? You remember your uncle's ink-stained fingers, but not your grandmother's rice pudding, even though everybody says what a wonderful woman she was and you love rice pudding. What does the cleaning woman showing you two waterbugs in the bottom of the garbage can mean? And when you screamed she laughed and laughed. When my aunt was dying she was on painkillers, having wonderful dreams of running through a forest, giggling, stopping to pick mushrooms. I don't remember her ever talking about the forest in Poland before this. I didn't even know they had lived near a forest. But here was her last memory—a time in her girlhood when she was running free, laughing in the woods, stooping to pick mushrooms for her mother.

So you take those early memories and explore them, and what you don't remember you make up as you go. Nobody ever said you can't lie. That is what fiction, in any case, is—a pack of lies. But it's different from the usual I-didn't-take-the-last-cookie variety of lie. Fiction is telling lies to find the truth. One of the problems in the Reminiscence Therapy workshop was that some people got caught up in trying to catch the ephemeral exactly as it was. If something didn't work as narrative—it was too long or boring or confusing—they would say, "But that's what happened." You must remember that writing is an art: It is not taking dictation from personal history. You search the storehouse of memory for those weird or wonderful moments, but then you shape them. You edit. You elaborate. You *lie*. This is as true for writing memoir as for writing fiction. You can't remember the exact words the druggist said to you when it was raining, so you make them up or you leave them out. Or maybe he said something to you another time, but it fits better if you write that he said it this day, the day your baby sister was born.

If you allow yourself to search memory for the numinous moments, you will find a story. The wide field of childhood is too vast, however. Try to cut it down. Be specific. Where did you live as a kid—what was the house like? Your room? The kitchen? The basement? Each room

> Genius is childhood recalled at will.
>
> —Charles Baudelaire

might be a story. How did you get to school? It's not enough to say the school bus picked you up. Think about the bus. Did it have a certain smell? Who sat next to you? What was he doing? What were *you* doing? If you walked to school, think about the particulars of that walk. What did you pass? Did anything happen the day your friend didn't join you and you had to go alone? Remember the big house that everyone said was haunted? Did you ever go inside? Did you ever *hear* of anyone going inside?

There are other gems in the distant past. I'll throw out a few, but I'm sure you can come up with your own. How about the oddballs in the neighborhood? I remember Rosemary, an old woman who lived across the street when I was growing up. She had no teeth and terrible breath, and every day she called to me, "Girly, girly, come here. I got to tell you something." Sometimes I would pretend not to hear her, but most of the time I went to listen to her sad stories about her husband who beat her, then abandoned her, leaving her with an infant that died. I stood at the gate, crying, listening to her stories, smelling her breath, wanting to get away, to play stoopball with my friends, but not wanting to hurt her feelings or leave her alone with her sadness. One day she wasn't there. The next day she wasn't there again. Then there was the smell and the police came.

Was there an old woman in your neighborhood everyone said was a witch? Or an old man who gave you pops and looked like Jiminy Cricket? Is there a holiday gathering that stands out in your mind? If not, how about making up one, a composite perhaps of a dozen Thanksgivings or Chanukah parties? Put your grandfather in it, even though he was dead by the time Aunt Rose threw the turkey at your mother. And what did your mother wear on such occasions—did she have a special dress or apron? Did she smoke cigarettes with pastel papers to match her outfit? Did your aunt bring her Jell-O Surprise everyone hated but ate anyway, no one having the heart to tell her Jell-O was bad enough but the fruit surprise made you all want to puke? Who were your friends in the old neighborhood? What happened to them in real life and in your imagination? Did you have a magic object—a doll, a feather, a tooth? Describe it and how you used it. Perhaps there was a place of power for you, somewhere you'd go when you were feeling sad or scared. I used to like to hide under the desk and have my mother look for me. Only she never looked. Still, I liked to hide there and pretend she *was* looking for me.

Did you have a favorite game? I don't mean Scrabble or Candy Land. What about the game of Lava you and your brother made up, where you'd hide under the blanket and he'd be the lava, trying to creep under and touch you? What about rituals you had—what were they for? I was very neurotic for a while about not stepping on any cracks.

There's a lot of material to be mined from your past. You don't have to understand it to write about it. In fact, it is better if you don't. And especially if you don't explain it to us. Just tell us the stories. Describe what existed then. Don't chew it up and digest it, then regurgitate it on paper and expect us to eat it. We're not baby birds. We like to do our own chewing. Just give us the bugs.

**Try This:** Write about an old or weird person in your childhood. Write about this person from your perspective now, looking back. Then write from the point of view of the child you were, how you saw that person then.

• Where did you hide when you were a kid? When did you hide there? Why? Use action to give us this story, not exposition. You have permission to lie. If you don't remember something, make it up. If something might have been blue or purple, make it purple. Next time you write about it, make it blue.

• Who was your best childhood friend? What did you like to do? What happened to him or her?

• It's Thanksgiving. The family has gathered around. Who is there? What do they say and do? Bring one holiday, any holiday, to life. Stick to a specific time—the time you were twelve and your parents were getting divorced but hadn't told you yet. Don't suddenly bring in the time you were in college and were drunk. Save that for another story.

• Take a mental walk through the neighborhood you grew up in. *What* do you pass on your way to your friend's house? *Who* do you pass? Make it spring. Make it daytime. Another time write about a summer night. Be specific. If you don't remember a neighbor's name, make one up. If you call him Pop and later remember his name was Pappy, you can change it—or you can leave it as Pop.

• Write about getting to or from school. Is there a teacher or schoolchild who stands out in your memory? Write about that person.

• Write about storekeepers in your neighborhood when you were little.

• Write about a really early dream that has stayed with you. Give us the kid who dreamed that dream. Write it in first person. Later, write it in third person.

• Describe the house or apartment where you grew up. Give us specific events that happened in the various rooms. Each room might be a different story. Don't forget the basement or attic.

• When you were young a monster lived in your house. Where? What did it look like or do? How did you appease it? How did people around you react to your fear? What was happening in your life at the time that fueled the monster's wrath?

• Write about forbidden places on your block. Did you ever go where you were expressly told not to? What happened? What might have happened if you weren't such an obedient child?

• Explore on paper a haunted house in your neighborhood, either where you live now or where you lived as a kid. Go in. What do you see? Hear? Feel? What happens to you?

## READ ALL ABOUT IT

Another place to find ideas is in your reading. If you want to write, you have to read. It always surprises me when people in my writing workshops say they don't read much. I'm embarrassed for them, as if they had no clothes on and didn't realize it. Do you know of musicians who don't listen to music, artists who don't look at pictures? I don't think there's any other art in which the practitioners think they can do it without studying what's been done.

Often such writers will rationalize their non-reading habits by saying they are working on something and don't want to be influenced. The things people come up with to worry about! I'm not suggesting that it's okay to plagiarize. I take it on faith that you are a basically decent, honest person. There *are* cases where writers, sometimes celebrated ones, unintentionally plagiarize something they've read, but that won't happen to you. It's rare, like getting hit by lightning, and I think you need a photographic memory for it to happen anyway. You don't have one, do you?

What *will* happen to you is that most of what you read will be forgotten the moment you finish the book or story. But some of it will be taken in deep. It will get mixed with everything else you've read and taken in, as well as what you feel, your memories, hopes, dreams, ideas. There, in the unconscious, the whole thing will mix and churn and cook. And when your book or story comes out it will be you, it won't be Ann Beattie. It will be as individual as your fingerprint, and not even identical twins share the same fingerprint. In the same way that you are made up of genes from your mother and your father but you aren't either of them, reading will supply you with a series of narrative genotypes that will combine and mutate into something unique.

Reading gives you a feel for the shape of writing. It teaches by example the kinds of effects you can get by breaking the paragraph this way, by changing the point of view or not, by setting something off with a line break. There may be something you need that you will find in a story entirely different from the story you will write. You haven't even started thinking about that story yet, but when you do you will know how to develop it because of a story you read a long time ago and don't even remember.

Reading helps you develop an ear for rhythm too. Good sentences need to vary in length and complexity and structure. This is true for paragraphs as well. When you read you take in the music of writing.

Then, when you come to write, you have a record collection of drum-beats in your head, as well as orchestration techniques and harmonies. It's all there, imprinted on your brain. It becomes the shape of your mind, the way you dream.

If you don't read you don't have ready access to any of that. You still have stories because you have imagination. And you may have a sense of plot line derived from movies and sitcoms. But you lack a sense of written narrative, which is entirely different from stories told in pictures on the screen.

The point is, wherever your ideas come from you need to save them someplace where you can find them. If you use a story envelope, put in it anything that moves you, anything that gives you the urge. Then when you have the time and the inclination to write but think you don't have any ideas, pull one out from your story envelope and begin.

**Try This:** Give yourself five minutes to come up with at least ten topics you'd like to write about. Put each one on a separate slip of paper and place it in a story envelope. Keep adding to this envelope as ideas occur to you or by periodically forcing yourself to think of them, using a five-minute deadline to do so. Once you have a collection of ideas going you will never have the excuse that you want to write but don't know what to write about. Just pick one out and begin.

Ah, but there's the rub. You still have to begin, even though now you have an idea. And so this brings you to the second problem with beginning to write.

## WRITING WITH IDEAS

It's important for you to know that beginnings are hard for everybody. You thought having an idea would be the solution, but then you find your ideas are like those little waterwings toddlers wear, and here you are jumping off a high cliff into this pool of water that looks like an eight-ounce glass, but then again maybe it only looks like a glass of water but it really has no bottom—it's so deep you'll never surface after jumping in.

Now listen to me: You *will* come up again. All writers come up. All writers have trouble with beginnings. No matter how many novels or stories you've written that initial leap is terrifying. Writers who tell you otherwise are lying—if not to you then to themselves. Maybe they turn the switch on their unconscious so that they start writing before they have time to feel the fear, but it's the fear, after all, that made them switch off consciousness to begin with.

My son, a miniature wise man at the age of eight, said to me, "I had some writer's block yesterday, but I got over it." How, I wanted to know, leaning forward like one of those eavesdroppers in the Merrill-Lynch commercial. "Well," he said, "I was having trouble starting. I mean, I knew what I wanted to write but I didn't know how to begin. So I just started and pretty soon it was okay."

That is the secret, in a nutshell. When you have an idea and can't get started on it, you . . . start. Sorry this advice is not more profound. I believe it was William James who called an event of this kind a "catastrophe." He didn't mean it in any negative sense but more as a sudden switch. You're going along on one track and all of a sudden you find yourself on the switch track. It's how you get out of bed on a cold morning. The bed is so cozy; the quilt is your mother and your lover. You don't want to get up, no way, no how. The next thing you know your feet are on the cold wooden floor, you're standing, you find yourself in the bathroom and you're not even sure who you are, let alone how you got there, but there you are, brushing your teeth. It's the zag on the zig.

Some people tell themselves they can't write without a perfect beginning. They're looking for that opening sentence, that great scene, the bit that's going to bring the whole together. And so they can't start. But they can't get that beginning without actually beginning. No amount of kvetching and moaning and pushing is going to get it out of them. The only chance one has of finding that beginning is by beginning. This sounds like a koan, some kind of irritating wisdom along the lines of the sound of one hand clapping. I don't mean to annoy you. There's no other way to say it. You start by starting. You give up your perfectionism. What has perfectionism done for you lately? It's kept you frozen in dread of that first step. Instead of giving into that feeling you say: okay, this isn't how I want it to go, but it's a start. Then you tap out an inane sentence or two or two hundred.

It will almost assuredly be rough going at first, but you are not going to get over it by sitting there pulling your hair out. You are going to get over it by writing a terrible first sentence, a terrible first paragraph, a terrible first page. Eventually it will start to flow. You don't have to know how to get from A to B to C. You don't have to know anything. Just turn on (the computer), tune in (to the voice in your head), and start. By the time you get to the end you will know or at least have a better idea of how to begin. Then you, like Michael Finnigan, can begin again.

First drafts are essentially freewriting on a theme. If you think of them that way, maybe you can keep from freezing up. You're not writing in blood. No first draft is meant to be read. Many times writers start with an idea, not knowing where that idea will take them. Sometimes they know where they want to end up but not how to get there. So maybe all you have is a name: The little girl on the boardwalk is called Pinky. And you have this image of seagull being tossed by a storm. You don't know anything else—not how the two connect or if they even do. Okay, you won't find out by sitting there. You have to start, then maybe you will learn more. You don't have to know everything. So long as you're willing to discard much of what you write, you can start anywhere. You may need to write five pages before you get to the actual beginning of your story, but you will never find it without writing those five pages. So get started already.

Later on we'll talk about revising. For now, suffice it to say that you will have to revise, no matter how elegant your prose is, no matter how easily it flows out of you in a natural state. Just remember, revising is mostly discarding, and it's a lot harder to discard those sentences you labored over than the clichés that burst full-grown from your brain like Minerva from Zeus. Give yourself permission to write dreck. Nothing good gets written without dreck. Dreck is fertilizer: Without it there'd be no crops.

Virginia Woolf put it more elegantly. She called this sort of thing the "diamond in the dustheap." Dreck, dust—we're talking dirt. We're talking the stuff you throw out. Don't be so afraid of it. I won't tell your mother you're playing with dirt when she thinks you're working.

When I say you freewrite your first draft I don't mean you give

---

The best thing is to write anything, anything at all that comes into your head, until gradually there is a calm and creative day.

—Stephen Spender

yourself a set amount of time to write. Although it's fine to freewrite a first draft for a set period of time, I mean something more along the lines of taking your idea and playing with it. Maybe control the material a bit more than if you were actually freewriting, but just a bit. You don't want to get caught up with questions of punctuation, spelling, propriety. You might try to be less autobiographical than otherwise, unless you are writing an autobiography. Using a third-person narrative voice helps a lot of writers to remove themselves from personal material. If you tell us what Harry said and did the day of the big snowstorm, instead of what you did, you may feel freer about making up the accident with the snowplow instead of telling us how you *almost* got hit and *probably* would have died.

**Try This:** Take an idea from your story envelope or one you've been planning to write for a while. Give yourself half an hour to write it. (You can take longer, of course, but making your unconscious believe you only have half an hour can often prod it into starting.) For half an hour you will freewrite on the idea you have chosen. You will not go back to change or correct anything. You will not stop to look up a word. You will not pause to think about what *should* come next. There are no *shoulds* now. Trust your unconscious to dream it. See what it comes up with. When you are done (the half hour is up or you have gotten to the end of the piece), put it away. It's not time to revise yet.

> **TIP:** If you have trouble beginning try freewriting for the first five minutes or so of your writing time. Moan, kvetch, write about the problem you are having beginning, write about what you want to write about. Eventually you will find a way to begin, just to get you away from that annoying, querulous voice.

EIGHT

# BEGINNINGS

In terms of what makes a good beginning, you may find it helpful to get out a collection of short stories and look at some first paragraphs. A good beginning draws the reader in right away, even if he or she doesn't quite know what's going on. Something surprising or a non sequitur may spark a reader's curiosity enough to continue reading. Starting in medias res (that is, in the middle of the action) often tantalizes the reader. You need to be able then to fill the reader in on what happened before in a way that is not overly confusing. This means being adroit in the use of flashbacks, and the movement in and out of them.

Mostly a good beginning needs to be clean. To have a style and a rhythm that is interesting. I like things to be spare, at least at first. Old-fashioned writers—and I'm talking Tolstoy, Dickens, the greats, you understand, but those with the sensibilities of a different time— tended to set the scene in their beginnings, to do involved paragraphs of what in filmmaking is called the "long shot." Afterward they would zoom in on the characters we're really expected to care about. Writers don't do that so much anymore. As a matter of fact, if you do this you will most assuredly be advised to cut all that introductory stuff and start on page fifteen. That's no reason not to have written all the introductory stuff in the first place. It was probably necessary to get you in the mood, to bring you to that point where the story really begins.

Call me Ishmael.

—Herman Melville

And some of it may come up later. But the tendency in contemporary fiction is to start without the slow buildup. To start as if the reader already knows the characters and the events leading to this point, and here we are, up to our necks in a situation. A lot of the stuff that used to come in the beginning will follow, once the reader is caught enough to withstand the impact of time travel—flashing back here and there. This is probably a fad, but it is the fad of our time. And starting in the middle of things does have this going for it: Your reader gets involved right away, if only in trying to figure out what the heck is going on.

You of course can do whatever you want, and if you want to be a turn-of-the-millennium Tolstoy, then in the words of Joseph Campbell, "Follow your bliss." But it's hard enough to get anything published without developing a nineteenth-century style, unless you're writing historical novels.

Let's face it. It's unlikely you are trying to write *War and Peace* unless you are my son. He is writing a book called *The Chronicles of the Candy Wars*, and his original intention was that it be seven hundred pages long. I suggested that that was too long, so he cut it down to four hundred, and when I said that was probably still too long for a third-grade writing project, he said, "Look at *War and Peace*. That's over a thousand pages." He likes to look at how long the books are on my bookshelves, and *War and Peace* impressed him by its mass. "And just see how small the letters are too," he said, as if the one-thousand-one-hundred-thirty-eight page length weren't enough. He kept asking me what it was about, and I kept saying, "War. And peace." So now I'm reading it, after years of meaning to but never finding the time. And you know what? That *is* what it's about.

According to Brenda Ueland in her book *If You Want to Write*, Tolstoy said you should never write something that can't be understood by an affectionate seven-year-old boy. Happening to have just such an affectionate boy, although he's eight, I can attest that either Tolstoy or Ueland is mistaken. There is much in *War and Peace* Zack could never understand. There is much in *War and Peace* I do not understand, especially why everybody has to have so many names and different military and aristocratic titles.

But Zack's feeling is that if Tolstoy can do it, so can he. This is a great feeling to have, but don't let it be yours unless you're in third grade or you're some sort of mad genius who's been traveling in time.

By the way, Zack is planning a sequel to his book when he finishes the four hundred pages he now has planned. It's the story of the Candy Wars, from the vegetables' perspective.

**Try This:** Get a book by a writer you admire and write the first lines of each story, chapter, or essay in it. How do these lines draw you in? Do they intrigue or mystify? Do they clearly set up a situation you want to know more about? Pick a first line of an unread piece of writing (story, chapter, essay) and write your own piece from that starting point. Make sure you note where you got the first line from. If, at a later point, you decide to try publishing the piece, you may need to change the first line or attribute it to another writer in some way.

TIP: How you actually begin matters less than *that* you actually begin. You may need to cut the first three pages of a story to get to the real beginning anyway. But if you can't begin till you have a starting sentence, drum one up before you sit down. Do a repetitive movement—pacing is my favorite— till a way to begin comes to you. If you have an hour and a half to write, it is more productive to pace for ten minutes than to sit staring at a computer screen and your watch for the full ninety minutes.

# NINE

# IN A DARK WOOD

**Y**ou thought beginnings were hard. Well, just wait. For, if all goes okay with the beginning, a time comes when, like Dante, we find ourselves in a dark wood and don't know how to proceed. This is the dread middle, where we lose sight of our original inspiration. Things never planned happen to our characters, and what we have been planning all along just won't jell. How are we ever going to get to that super ending, which was the initial germ for the book, if the action won't move in that direction?

First of all, take a deep breath. Next, tell yourself that most writers go through something like this in the middle of a work. As Peter DeVries wrote: "Every novel should have a beginning, a muddle, and an end." The same holds true for nonfiction, where you knew what you wanted to say when you started, and you knew where you wanted to end up, but you don't know what you're doing right now. I wish I had some magic words I could teach you, that I could tell you what "real" writers do at this point and it was something easy, like eating forty hard-boiled eggs without anything to drink. But the truth is you just have to force yourself to continue.

As with the beginning, you are going to have to do some bad writing. You might as well get it over with. Events in your writing may not pan out as you've planned them. If you try to make them happen according to your abstract scheme, they will get back at you. They will turn ludicrous, like that wedding that was supposed to bring everyone together and it turned out they were all wearing clown noses because of the day they'd spent at the circus school. They will turn tragic, the way someone left the meat out of the refrigerator too long and that wonderful dinner party turned into the ending of *Hamlet*, with all the characters falling into their plates. Or else those carefully planned-for events will just drop dead at your feet. Nothing leads to stilted action and dialogue faster than forcing your characters into places they don't want to go.

You have to trust your imagination. *You* may have determined that your character takes a left turn, but *she* has decided to go right. Okay, so go with her. See what happens. You can get rid of any developments you don't like later. Then you have ammunition; you can say to your character: Look, we tried it your way. It sucked. So do me a favor, just take that left turn and see if my idea works any better. Remember, some of the best ideas are the ones you didn't plan. This is why outlines, useful as they may be for a long work, need to be written in pencil, with big margins and double-spacing. You simply can't plan for every contingency in writing. Sometimes you have to let your characters take the lead.

When I get to this point, I say: "Fine, take the lead," and my characters shrug and look at each other like the three mystery guests on *To Tell the Truth*. No one wants to stand up. Sometimes they'll have long telephone conversations with each other and talk about the weather, but no one wants to *do* anything. If this happens to you, you may need to prod your characters into action. Okay, they want to make telephone calls. Fine. Let one of them call you. Or you call one of them. Then you can ask some questions. Personal questions you would never ask a real person. Information and revelation you acquire in this way won't necessarily make it into your writing. Don't worry about that, because understanding your characters has to help you get them moving eventually. Sometimes it's just that you need a handle on a character's psyche before you can get him to go swimming in November.

Asking questions of characters is like talking to children. If you say to your kid, "How was your day?" he or she will answer, "Fine." And there you are, knowing no more than you did when you started out. You need to learn to ask the right questions. Try asking your kid, "What was the funniest thing that happened today?" You may learn all about how Pete balanced a plate on his head during lunch, then slipped in some spilled ketchup. You'll get a much more interesting answer.

As I said before, you can ask things of your characters you would never ask in real life. Pry. Be insulting. Make assumptions. "Parents fighting again?" "Where'd you hide Jessica's doll?" "Still love your wife?" "Tell me about your first sexual experience." It may turn out that events have happened in a character's life that never make it onto the page, at least not this page. But if you ask the right questions you may find out something interesting, and if it's interesting enough it may turn into a subplot in your novel. Or another story about this character in a different setting. At the very least it may give you a way to have that character speak, gesture, or move that makes him come alive.

The same is partly true for nonfiction. You don't have the power to lie when you're talking about real people's real lives. But so much of what we know about people is limited. You can ask questions of the ghosts of once-living people. "Gram, why did you dress Uncle Joe as a girl for that photograph?" You won't get the one and only definitive answer, but you may be able to translate yourself into that time, into your grandmother's head, and hear possible explanations.

The most important thing to remember about the middle of any work is that you have to keep going. Your hatred of the material you are producing is resistance to finishing the project at hand. You cannot know how to proceed unless you do it. Usually it turns out that what you produce is not as bad as you thought when you were writing it. But in the event it turns out to be just that bad, so what? So you've wasted some time. Maybe you got a key sentence out of it. Maybe a twist you weren't expecting. Or maybe you didn't get anything: Even then you got something—you now know that was the wrong turn, so you can go back and turn the other way. Nobody said writing was going to be like sledding down a big hill, all fun with shouts of glee. There are rough spots, dry patches where the dirt pokes through. In fact, sometimes it seems like there are mostly rough spots, with just a few exciting dips and thrills. But those thrills, aren't they worth the price of the ride?

**Try This:** If you are stuck in the middle of a long work, it can be useful to outline what you already have, leave a big blank, then outline the ending you foresee. On a separate piece of paper write all the possible ways you can get from A to C, then pick the one that appeals to you the most and write it.

- Or you can skip the middle and write the ending, then go back to the middle. You don't have to write it in order, although that is usually how it is done. If something is exciting to you, but you feel you have to wade through this swampy middle to get there, it is probably a better idea to write the exciting part while it is still exciting. Postponing the writing of it may make you lose the thrill, and then you've got a middle *and* an end that seem a vast wasteland.

- If you have a half-finished manuscript hidden in a bottom drawer, take it out and read it back from the beginning. Let the momentum push you into new territory. Force yourself to keep going, even if you feel like you're running a marathon wearing cement sneakers. Remind yourself that it is a first draft. Or tell yourself that it is just a writing exercise. After a certain amount of rough going you should find you've gotten to the top of the hill. It should be easier to keep going. The important thing here is: Don't look back. Keep moving forward. Now is not the time to stop to revise. Try to get to the end before you start making changes.

- Begin a new piece in the middle, based on what you have so far. Use the same characters in the situation in which you broke off, but start on a fresh page. Trick yourself into feeling like you're beginning something new. Of course, you don't have to reiterate information you know has already come up in the earlier writing. You don't have to introduce your characters, for instance, or explain their relationships, if this has been made clear in the first part of the piece. But try to put a fresh spin on the writing. Take those characters and start again, in the middle—give us the wedding implied by Judy and Kip's engagement in the first part of your story; Uncle Lumpy is already drunk and making passes at Judy's grandmother. Later you can knit the beginning of the piece to what follows, or you may choose to keep the division between parts by using a line break. Sometimes a clean sheet of paper can grant you a new outlook and enable you to continue a project from a slightly different angle.

**TIP:** If you force yourself past the middle, your writing will start to move again. If you put something away, waiting for inspiration, it is more likely to stay put away. Write the middle quickly and carelessly—just to get things moving again. Nothing is written in stone. Think of the middle as a shaky rope bridge, something you must pass to get to the other side. Later you can go back and make a bridge of cable and steel, but for now all you've got is that skinny rope, and the sooner you get across it the better you'll feel.

## FRESH IDEA OR OLD PATTERN?

If you have a lot of half-finished work, you may need to take stock of your writing before starting any new projects. One thing you can do is outline each of these partially done stories, novels, or articles, and compare the stopping points. Do you tend to get stuck when the conflict between characters becomes most extreme? When something unpleasant has to happen to a character you like or identify with? When you need to do more research or interviews to back up your assertions? Outlining may help you see a pattern to your resistance. Sometimes just knowing such a pattern exists can help you overcome it. "I am going to force myself past this," you may say. "I tend to give up whenever I try to write about work, but I'm not going to give up this time."

Sometimes writers abandon projects they may have worked long and hard on because they are seduced by the siren call of a new idea. Anything new can seem fresher, more exciting than something you've been struggling with for a while. That's why it's good to finish at least the first draft of a project before going on to the next one. You can keep notes on your new idea while you finish the old one. But if you let yourself be tempted away by every new thought, you won't finish anything. Remember, the excitement of a new idea is momentary. Once you start working on it, it too will demand slogging through the dull parts. You have to write past that, till it becomes exciting again. All work has to be worked at. Only an unhatched idea seems perfect as is.

**Try This:** Organize all your half-finished work into two piles—writing you can see yourself finishing *someday*, and writing you can't ever imagine resuming. Take the latter pile and bury it. I'd even suggest throwing it out, but throwing any of *my* writing out makes me come down with malaria, so how could I advise you to do it? But if you have an attic, that's a good place for it. The point is put it somewhere you don't often go, so it doesn't stare you in the face, going *nyah nyah* when you're trying to write. Now organize the other stuff, putting the project closest to your heart on top. Make a commitment to finishing that first project before starting anything else. Think of it as a marriage vow. You will not allow yourself to be tempted by any new idea that bats an eye at you. You may need to use brute force to get yourself to be faithful this way, but you know that sticking to one project till the end will prove more meaningful than starting up with the occasional floozy. The middle you muddle through does not have to be perfect. It can be crap. In fact, I *demand* it be, just so long as you write it all the way through. You are going to finish a rough draft of that story, novel, article, or memoir in entirety before putting it away, or you are going to put this beloved project on the other pile, with all the stuff you have buried in the backyard. This is your moment of truth. *Someday* is today. Write the damn thing or admit you never will. No matter how dull or awkward or stilted or forced the writing feels, it is better to write through till the end than to stop, waiting for renewed inspiration. You know what Edison said: Genius is one percent inspiration and ninety-nine percent perspiration. Get sweating.

There is no great talent without great willpower. These twin forces are needed to build the huge monument of an individual glory. Superior men keep their brains in a productive state, just like the knights of old kept their weapons in perfect condition. They conquer laziness, they deny themselves all debilitating pleasures. . . . Willpower can and should be a just cause for pride, much more than talent. Whereas talent develops from the cultivation of a gift, willpower is a victory constantly won again over instincts, over inclinations that must be disciplined and repressed, over whims and all kinds of obstacles, over difficulties heroically surmounted.

—Honoré de Balzac

# TEN

# DEATH AND OTHER ENDINGS

A nd so we come to the third of the horrible triplets: The ending. Ending a writing project can be as hard as beginning one and as tedious as plodding through the middle of it, plus there may be an accompanying separation anxiety. Especially when it's a longer work, one that may have been with you for years, the desire to finish the damn thing is often offset by the terror of what comes afterward.

As a result, some writers make themselves crazy looking for a grand finale. Something with fireworks, the way they end Tchaikovsky's *1812 Overture* in Central Park. Writers will pull out all the stops. There's a shootout. There's a tragic love embrace in which the main character dies in the arms of a woman who only now realizes his worth. There are hints of eternity, the meaning of life, and all this goes along with a sense that the weather is weeping too, and the scenery is a veritable chorus of backup emotions. And that's for the lighthearted comedies.

Then there are the writers who just end it, practically in midsentence, scarcely bothering to finish a thou. . . .

How you choose to conclude your work is as individual as anything else about your writing, but there should be a sense of completion, of resolution, implied if not spelled out. Other than that, there really are no hard-and-fast rules. Some works end with a bang; some do not.

There *is* something to be said for the undramatic conclusion, a kind

---

A good rule for writers: Do not explain overmuch.

—W. Somerset Maugham

of winding down in the windup. It is contemporary, for one thing. Modern literary tastes tend to run from the melodramatic, sometimes running so far that they head toward the insignificant. But it is possible to achieve a balance between the two—a way to conclude with meaning but not fanfare. Such a low-key ending can grant a greater sense of verisimilitude to a work. Life is like that, the reader may feel. Stories don't conclude; they stop. Ideally, the reader is left with the feeling that life continues for the characters, just as life continues for his friends after he leaves the party. If you've given the reader a strong sense of character, of the life that character has on the page and seems to continue to have after he or she shuts the book, then such an inconclusive conclusion is successful. The grand finale, in modern terms, is apt to seem ridiculous.

Writers sometimes feel the need to tie up all the loose strings when they get to the end of a work. While it's generally a good idea not to leave too much laundry flapping in the breeze, you don't want to create something as tidy and fusty as a maiden aunt. It's best to leave some things up to the reader. What he or she figures out will grant a greater sense of satisfaction than can be gained by having meanings handed over. After all, we all like to pat ourselves on the back, telling ourselves how wise, how perceptive, how positively brilliant we are.

But this is one of the hardest things to do—to leave some things up to the reader. We all have this inclination to explain our meaning. We have to fight this urge throughout our writing, but as we get to the end it becomes a demonic possession, the desire to tell, to make sure no one walks away without *getting it*.

Now, I agree that it's important for *you* to know what your story means. You must understand why that hobo entered the conversation for a paragraph, then wandered off and was never seen again. You didn't necessarily know when you were writing it. You can't say you planned for him to be there. But his presence works, and by the time you have finished a piece of writing you should have a sense of why it does. Nonetheless, you need not be like the Ancient Mariner, stopping all wedding guests to tell them not only what happened but what you've learned from those events.

In the same way, you didn't know what you'd find when you interviewed women at a homeless shelter, but you were drawn to their plight and you wanted to know their stories. Sometimes nonfiction assumes the shape of fiction, things working out more poignantly, more unexpectedly, than we could ever intend them.

## TO THE FINISH LINE

Perhaps the real question for us as writers is not so much what works—a personal thing, after all—but how we can get around our reluctance to finish something.

You and I both know why we're reluctant to end it all. Amateur psychologists can tell just by the way I shape that sentence. After all, who knows what exists afterward, where we go when we're finished. While you're writing a long piece, especially if it's something you've been writing a long time, a project you've been obsessing with, you know what you have to work with every day. You've named the characters, set the setting, you have put certain events and consequences into action, have given the characters desires and have kept them from achieving them too easily. You have yourself a tidy little universe in which you are God. And it is for exactly those reasons you'd like to end that world and start over again. It's the way God felt before the Flood. You can do it so much better next time. Right now your characters are making you sick. They're turning insipid and whiny. The setting is about as interesting as the tour of the Wonder Bread factory you went on in third grade. (Actually we did this as a class trip and it was great. The best part was the smell. Then they gave us these miniature loaves of Wonder Bread to take home that were the size of hotdog rolls.) My point is that you develop a love/hate relationship with your writing as you near the end. As much as you'd like to finish that novel and move on to something else, the thought of finishing it and not having anything else to move on to makes you procrastinate and *potchka*, as my mother would say. Play around, fixing what doesn't need fixing.

So, thank you, Dr. Freud. Now we know our problem with endings may have something to do with our fear of death. So what? So how does that help us?

It probably doesn't. Just as one day we are going to die, no matter how afraid we are of this, and no matter how much we're kind of looking forward to it because there's no laundry in heaven, one day we have to finish our writing project and move on to the next one.

But how? I can feel you gritting your teeth, longing to shake it out of me, as if I had the secret. All I can say is you write till you've said it all, then you stop. You have nothing more to say about these characters. You could create other scenes, other conversations, but they would reiterate what has come before. Oh, but they are such good scenes, you say. Can't I just add another chapter to my two-thousand-page novel?

The answer is no. Those other scenes, you can jot them down in one of your multitude of notebooks. Stop thinking about your ideas as stuff for this old work you are finishing. Can the new scene appear in another book with different characters? Can the new material be the subject of another article instead of augmentation of this one? Try to keep notes for the next work, so that when you finish the current one you're not left with a big fat nothing to write about staring you in the face. You don't have to know what the next story is about. Just take notes. The scene you dreamt up, the image or the phrase— eventually it will all come together and be a new work, and this will be some of the new stuff in it. The stories about your father's side of the family didn't fit in this book about your mother and grandmother, but maybe they're chapters of a book on its own. Start a new notebook to jot down the ideas that come to you.

Annie Dillard writes that you should "spend it all," when it comes to writing, "play it, lose it. . . . Do not hoard what seems good for a later place in the book, or for another book." I agree that, during the writing, when a scene, image, or expression you were saving for later wants to be written *now*, it should be written now. It will never be as good in a place you try to squeeze it than in this place it cries to be. But when we are involved in a long project, especially if it is a first novel, we want to put everything into it. Every witticism, every funny event or meaningful revelation—this is great, we think, got to put it in. It's as if we think we are never going to write anything again. But really, these thoughts you get as you near the end of a long work, sometimes they are your treasure trove for the next work. It's like putting away the baby clothes when your kid starts school. That's what you have to do now. Start putting aside notes for the next work, even though you don't know what it is. Have faith in your creative spirit. It will come. Especially if you start thinking about it. That's like putting a light in the window, guiding the new work home. You can use these new ideas that are coming to you in an entirely different way. You're not stuck with those same old characters, as you were in your last book. There is life after death, at least in fiction.

**Try This:** Read half a story by a writer you admire and finish it in your own way before reading to see how the author did it.

- Read the last page of a story and write your own version of what came before it.

- When you read a feature article, stop halfway through and think how you would continue it. You don't have to write it, but you can contemplate how you would proceed: Would you have more quotes from the environmental activist? Would you talk to people who live in the community? Would you end with a summary of your own views, a vignette of the congresswoman planting a tree or two kids using branches to mock-swordfight?

- Take a piece of writing you are having trouble ending and make a list of as many possible ways to end it as you can think of. Choose the one that most appeals to you and write it.

> **TIP:** If you don't know how to end a piece of writing, go back to the beginning. You will sometimes find a clue there—an image, an event, a phrase or rhythm—that can help you find a way to make the piece come full circle.

# ELEVEN

# DEADLINES AND LIFELINES

**A**nd now is the time to sing the praises of deadlines.

My husband wants to know why I make arbitrary deadlines and drive myself crazy trying to meet them. Since I work for myself, he doesn't see why I am not a nicer boss. Take a vacation, he says. Sleep late. Take the day off. Except for the freelance work I do for hire, my deadlines *are* self-imposed. Therefore I can change them. Be more lax in assigning them.

First of all, my deadlines are not as arbitrary as he thinks. They usually involve finishing something before my son's vacation schedule interferes with my writing time. Or before I have to turn to an assignment I'm doing for someone else and won't have the concentration to work on my fiction. Or before my teaching responsibilities eat away at my writing time. I don't just put on a blindfold and stab at the calendar like some kid at a birthday party playing Pin the Tail on the Donkey.

But he is right that since I am assigning the deadline, I can change it at will. In the back of my mind I know this. I just try to forget it. I try to take my deadlines as seriously as I would if someone else were making them for me. I have learned that deadlines enable me to be more driven in my work, and therefore more productive, than I might be without them.

Nothing is worse for a writer (at least for this writer) than great gobs of free time. Those of you who work full time at high-pressure jobs and have to squeeze your writing in during your coffee break may not think so. For you it must be like hearing someone in Tahiti complaining about the weather. Nonetheless, it is true that it is harder to be self-disciplined than to be disciplined by a policeman.

Take Wednesdays, for example. Wednesday my son has school till 5:30. It's a long, exhausting day for him, poor kid, but it gives me a taste of the free world, having an entire day in which to work, just like a normal person with a normal job in a normal office. I should accomplish a lot on Wednesdays, wouldn't you think? And in the beginning I did. Of course this was before I got used to having such a nice long day, before I really believed that I could go till 5:15, that no one would come along and take this away from me. After a while I noticed something. For one thing, it took me longer and longer to get to my desk on Wednesdays. And once I was there, I tended to clean it rather than write. I would make phone calls, lengthy ones to my sister in which we'd talk about everyone in the family *and* the meaning of life and death. I'd call back all the people I'd been snappy to on the phone when they had interrupted me on Monday and Tuesday. I'd call my mother-in-law. When my parents were still alive, I'd call them. I'd take care of correspondence, usually bills, then call the insurance company and argue over medical expenses. I'd plan my son's next birthday party, spend an hour or so searching for Beanie Babies. Arrange a few playdates. Or sometimes I would just sit and split my hair till I looked like something newly risen from the dead. Then maybe I'd wash my hair, because no one can go around looking like that for too long. After all, I had eons before I had to pick up Zack. My husband was right. I could be a kinder boss to myself. I could relax my schedule. If I didn't start writing till, what was it now? Eleven? Well, I could work in the afternoon. And since it was already nearly lunchtime, maybe it didn't make sense to start now. I was getting hungry. No sense in working at something, then having to stop in the middle to eat. I could always write after lunch. It was Wednesday. A whole day in which to work. Anything goes on Wednesday.

Anything does go on Wednesday, especially the hours. It's like the fable about the Tortoise and the Hare, but I can't quite figure out why, so you do it. All I can tell you is that suddenly on Wednesday it gets to be 4:30 and I realize I haven't gotten anything for us to eat for dinner. Hell, I haven't even gotten dressed yet. Before you know it I'm rushing out the door to get my son, picking up a barbequed chicken on the way home. When I try to figure out where the day went, I can't think of anything productive I accomplished. Except it's great to have my desk clean, all ready for me to get going early on Thursday.

Now, don't get me wrong. I would never willingly give up Wednesdays. Maybe it's my Sabbath, the day I cease from my labors. It's just not my most productive day. Not like Fridays.

Friday is my early day. It's the day I have to pick my son up at 1:00 from his school, which is inconveniently placed about six miles downtown. Since I don't drive I need to take the subway. The ride takes half an hour, but you never know how the trains will be running, so I leave the house at 12:00. Which means my day effectively ends around 11:00 on Fridays, because I need time to shower and eat something. Fridays I race around, muttering to myself, sipping coffee like a bee nectar. I am so energetic—or maybe I'm hyper from all the caffeine. I have so much to do, so little time. I don't know how I am going to accomplish everything. I waste not a minute. Zip zip, beds are made, dishes done, coffee dripping, computer humming. Telephone rings, I don't give it a glance. No time to split my hair. Hell, there's no time to comb it. For now all I have are a couple of hours to write, and boy do I get things done on Fridays.

If I could make my Fridays into Wednesdays, long lazy days in which I don't have to turn back into Mommy till 5:30, I would. Listen, if I could live on chocolate I would do that too. What I'm saying is all that free time is not necessarily good for you. And there's something to be said for stress.

## USING DEADLINES

So make a deadline for yourself. Look at your calendar and say, "St. Patrick's Day falls on Tuesday this year. I absolutely must have this story done by then or I won't have time to go to the parade and get drunk." Then drive yourself crazy. Drive your family crazy. Work yourself up into a state. "I have to finish this. I'm running out of time. I only have thirty days."

You and I know this is a game you are playing. But it's a serious game. If you miss that deadline, okay, so you miss it. You can finish your story after the parade. Still, it's important that you invent that deadline and believe in it. And convince others to believe in it. Tell them how you have this deadline to meet so they better stay out of your way. And no, you can't chair that committee because you have a deadline. And you can't take your great-aunt to the doctor next Tuesday because of that deadline. Because, you know what—you *do* have a deadline, the one we all have, whose date we don't learn till we meet it. And if you want to write, you really do need to finish your work before *that* deadline.

And you will have a better time on St. Patrick's Day if you meet the other deadline.

I'm telling you what works for me. But you may have the sort of fragile psychic constitution that falls apart at any sign of pressure. A deadline? The thought makes you shriek and go running in hysterical circles. You can't possibly handle such a thing. Fine, then don't. You'll have to find a kinder way to beat your reluctance to finish a project into submission. Maybe you can promise yourself treats. The carrot instead of the stick approach. Finish the story, you tell yourself, then you can take a week off and just go to movies. Or maybe your fragile psyche likes Häagen-Dazs and you're skinny enough to indulge. But only after you finish that story. Or you can do a Lent sort of thing—no chocolate till after you complete your novel. After all, you're so close.

One last thing about deadlines. There are some people who laugh in the face of them, or cry is actually more like it. For such people arbitrary deadlines will not work. Real ones don't either.

I have friends, accomplished writers, experts in their fields. One has been publishing art history papers for years to the acclaim of critics here and in Europe, but he is unable to finish his doctoral dissertation. As a result he doesn't have his Ph.D. and so can't teach at the university level. He'd get a teaching job in a minute if he had his degree. I mean, he's an authority, a published, respected historian. And he's done all the work for his dissertation, independent research, much of which has produced the aforementioned touted articles. Most of his dissertation is written: I think all he has to do is type the footnotes or something stupid like that, but he can't do it. He just cannot do it. And now he is so beyond his deadline that it's like he was in a race and went in the opposite direction from everyone else, heading for the finish line by going around the world.

Another friend is a respected music journalist. He writes jazz criticism easily, and he knows so much it's unbearable going to a concert with him. He has a great ear and can analyze riffs famous musicians are playing that I can't even hear. The worst thing that happened to him was that he got a book contract some years ago, and he has been close to finishing the biography of a famous jazz musician ever since. But he can't do it. He quit his full-time job in order to give himself the hours he needed to accomplish his goal. *That* was two years ago. He told me about a dream he had in which he was carrying this musician and his piano up the stairs but couldn't get to the top. Sisyphus of the ivories. Or maybe it's like that Little Lulu cartoon in which she gets hit in the head with a baseball when she's supposed to be practicing her music and is chased up and down piano keys by musical notes. Could it be any clearer? The deadline passed a number of years ago. I think his editor may have since died.

For these people—published writers, mind you—finishing a writing project of some magnitude means facing the music, so to speak. They know there are people ready and willing to tear their work apart as soon as they hand it in. It's probably not insignificant that both these writers are themselves critics—they know what they're up against. Reviewers and professors await, guns at the ready. More likely my friends' books would be lauded. That doesn't matter. They are still immobilized by the fear of failure. It's a very public humiliation they fear, a humbling by their peers. Certain failure by choice is preferred to possible failure by others.

And you thought it was bad, writing and not knowing if you'd ever get your work published.

**Try This:** Look at the calendar and find a deadline for the project you are working on—the vacation your family is planning to take three months from now, for example. You want to have the first draft of your book finished by then. That doesn't give you much time. You better hustle. (If you find you've given yourself an unreasonable deadline, you can change it at any point. You can't possibly finish the first draft by then? Well, how about the first draft of the first section?)

**TIP:** Once you have a deadline in mind, your unconscious will often apportion the amount of time you have so that you find yourself getting to the end just when you're supposed to. It can seem miraculous, but the mind has a better sense of these things than we give it credit for. But if yours doesn't (or you think it doesn't), look at the amount of time you have till your deadline and figure out how much you need to accomplish each day in order to meet it. That way you won't be left with a hundred pages to go the night before something is due, having rested content too easily with a daily quota of five till that point.

# TWELVE

# WRITING THROUGH

There's a hexagram in the *I Ching* called "Biting Through," which seems to be about persistence, seeing something through to the end. I'm not an adept at consulting the *I Ching*, although I have been known to throw sticks or coins (and sometimes up) trying to figure out where to send a story. While it's always given me good advice, generally it's not anything practical but more along the lines of the original clichés my husband's grandmother would come up with: "You never see the hunch on your own back" and "Building, building, building, everywhere is building."

But "Biting Through" is excellent advice for the writer struggling with a novel or story. It means persist, keep working at it: Eventually you will get all the way through. It doesn't mean "Send it to *The New Yorker*." I take "Biting Through," in fact, to mean "Writing Through," that the work in question is not quite finished.

Writing has a certain organic shape, which it gets when the writer follows the dream till the end, not going back and revising until then. It's important to do a first draft, knowing in the back of your mind that any part is subject to change. But if you don't get to the end, you don't know what you have. That makes it impossible to know what to discard and what to keep. Also, there is an audience of negative critics in every writer's mind. Like Romans watching the lion and the Christian, they are more likely to give the thumbs-down sign than not. These negative critics are your mother, your father, your siblings, your children, every other family member, every person in your field whether you know them or not, every friend and enemy—a vast collection of melon-headed naysayers who take umbrage easily but are insensitive to the effect their insults have on you. If you let them they will kill any idea you manage to have. First they try to kill the idea before it's born. But if you do manage to get around them and give it birth, they sneak to the cradle and try to kill it while it's rocking. You know the expression, "Throw the baby out with the bathwater"? That's what the naysayers want to do, and then they will tell you how they've saved you from a life of worry and woe. Stick with them and you'll never be a writer.

I try to write a story in one sitting. When I say "story" I am not talking about something fleshed out and alive. I am talking about a skeleton with a few shreds of skin, maybe one eyeball. The sort of thing that scares me when I'm alone. I hate to think anyone might find it and believe this is what I do all day. Especially before I published anything, I lived in fear that my husband would look at my first drafts and arrange for a pickup from Bellevue. It was worse than that really, because I thought maybe I *was* deluded. After all, being insane meant I wouldn't know it. And surely, never having gotten anything published seemed a clear indicator that the "real world" didn't think what I was saying made a whole lot of sense.

With all this negativity free-floating around my brain, it was much easier to put my work aside than to continue. I went back to the beginning of my first novel ten times. I would get as far as the third chapter and decide I needed to change the first paragraph. It looked as if I was never going to get past chapter three. Each time I had a very good reason for going back, but it could have waited. I could have made a note to myself. What I really needed was to plug through to the end. And finally a writer friend of mine, someone who *had* published and was therefore legit, told me, "You're just making ex-cuses. There are always reasons to go back and fix up what you have. But at some point you actually have to sit down and write the damn thing." So that's what I did.

Now, as I told you, I write or try to write the first draft of a story in one sitting. But you can't write a novel in one sitting unless you have a mighty comfortable chair. So with novels I try to do a chapter in one session. In both cases I try not to go back till I get to the end. Sometimes with a novel or a long work of nonfiction (this book, for example), I read the chapter I wrote the day before, as a means of regaining entry into my material. A lot of times I get so caught up in making changes in that chapter that I don't move on. When this happens I stop myself. I then allow myself to read the last paragraph of the last chapter. It's not enough for me to get into the revision mode, but it can help me make the transition to what comes next.

## OTHER METHODS

Not everyone agrees with this approach. I don't always agree with myself. Madison Smartt Bell, who used to work "twelve hours at a stretch to finish a story in one sitting," sees the reason for having done this as fear of losing his "conception of how to make the whole thing work out." He no longer works to finish a draft this way because he has more confidence that the story will be there when he gets back to it, although he still works quickly—"a story in two or three days typically, a novel chapter in four or five."

Some writers, Hemingway being the most famous, believe it is important to stop yourself midway through a sentence so you have a place to pick up the next day. Hemingway called it "leaving water in the well." I would sooner leave my pet chihuahua in the well. I'm sure it has as much chance of surviving as my inspiration after a night of treading water. But hey, it worked for Hemingway. (On the other hand, he did end up killing himself.) So maybe your creativity needs a dousing at the end of the day. You have nothing to lose by trying this approach. See if it helps you to continue working on a long project, to hold on to your inspiration during the stretches of time that you simply cannot get to write.

When I'm beginning to work on a novel, I try to dream it through first. I tell myself the story over and over before actually starting to write it. I daydream it. I take it for walks. I go from the beginning and write it in my head till the end. As with all dreams, there are vague parts. I'm not sure how I got from a woman in her nightgown to the couple standing on the George Washington Bridge. And I'm not sure how my narrator meets the guy who introduces her to a new way of singing, or what that has to do with the baby. In other words, it's diffuse and cloudy in parts, but I tell myself the dream over and over—and as I do, more of it comes clear. When I start to actually write I have a vague outline in my mind, which I have also jotted down. The outline is ink on water. It's that wavy; it's that subject to change. But I have dreamed it through. I do not start from an image and see what unfolds.

Other writers do precisely that. I read somewhere that Joan Didion started with the image of a woman in an airport and ended up with *A Book of Common Prayer*. Whenever I tell my students that they should try to dream a novel through before writing it, that they should have a broad outline in mind, I always get someone who disagrees violently with me. He (for some reason it's always a "he") proceeds to tell us all about the involved crime novel he wrote, how he could never have done it if he'd tried using an outline. I usually don't pull rank on my students. I'm extremely nice and self-effacing, but I ask you: This novel he wrote, is it published? Now you and I know there are many good novels that don't get published. The fact that his is unpublished is no sign that it is lacking in merit. But you know what? It is. And you know why? Because he didn't have a clue of what he was writing about beforehand, and he didn't have the discipline to go back later and take out all the stuff that didn't belong and put in all the stuff that did. Okay, so now you know I'm not really as nice and self-effacing as I seem in front of the classroom. Behind this kind smile lurks one of those dread naysayers. I've taken off my mask and revealed my mean inner face. But you need to realize you can't believe every know-it-all who comes along and tells you to just write, you'll discover what you're writing about as you write it.

The process of writing *is* different for everyone. And it will be different for you each time you start something new. You have to reinvent the method each time. Some people, like the guy I mentioned above, really do just take off and see where they end up. But then that writer needs the discipline to go back and cut, add, switch things around. Essentially what such a writer is doing, whether he realizes it or not, is he is writing an outline—albeit a fleshed-out one. No novel comes out like Minute Rice, perfect first time, every time.

## TO OUTLINE OR NOT TO OUTLINE

I did ask a number of writer friends about outlines though—actually what I asked was whether they used them or did they believe *outline* was to *creativity* as *cirrhosis* was to *liver*. I found some people outlined and some didn't, but even writers who didn't had a sense of destination before they began.

Marissa Piesman quoted her agent: "Writing without an outline is like flying without a map." Evan Russell said he didn't formally outline but knew where he was going. "It's like driving. When I was learning to drive I was told never to look at what was right in front of me, but to keep my eyes on the farthest point down the road. The driving takes care of itself that way."

The driving metaphor was also used by Steve Schwartz. He doesn't outline because "writing is an act of discovery," but he won't start writing till he knows how his piece ends. "It's like I'm going to drive," he told me. "I know I'm going to start in New York and finish in Chicago. I have an idea I might stop in Pittsburgh and Cleveland. But that's not certain. I may change my route while I'm driving. I don't know who I'll meet en route. I don't know what will happen between us. I just know I'll wind up in Chicago."

Madison Smartt Bell finds it essential to know the ending of a long work before he starts. "That way I have a clear target. The journey toward it is undetermined, but the destination is known. This method saves a lot of rewriting, though some writers are tempermentally unsuited to do it that way."

> I write to find out what I'm writing, and once I get the sense of that the hard work begins. It's like driving a car at night when you can't see beyond the headlights but somehow you get through the night.
> —E.L. Doctorow

Tom Mallon told me that, though he might change his mind in the course of writing, he had to have the novel's plot and ending laid out when he started. Unlike a number of writers I spoke to, he outlines "in minute detail, scene by scene, almost line by line. By the time I have the outline as I want it, the writing almost amounts to rewriting."

Madison, on the other hand, finds detailed outlines too stifling. "I like to have a device for shaping the work that's somewhat independent of content," he told me. "With a modular work like *The Year of Silence* I relied on a sort of drawing that balanced all the units together in a patternistic way. With a more linear novel I will sketch outlines for each larger section as I get into them, but in a flexible, non-binding way. If the thing is too completely synopsized in advance you'll get bored writing it and express this boredom to the reader. . . ."

My own worked-over outlines look like ransom notes from anal-compulsive kidnappers. "Leave here and move A to B—or leave where is and move second half after line break. Run in to opening." If I don't follow my own instructions soon after writing them, I'm lost. I might as well have written, "Take ten steps from the shadow of the great oak tree at noon and dig where the boulder meets the root. *X* marks the spot."

According to Sam Decker, outlining is a gift. "Without outlines my writing would be babbling." That being so, why do so many people shudder and break into a sweat at the mention of the word? Jodie Klavans told me outlining would take the joy out of writing. "The fun is in peeling back the layers and watching the story write itself. It's there all along, only I'm not completely aware of it." Ellen Dreyer also told me that outlines seemed at first "unfair fetters to my creativity," although she has since come to see them as useful tools.

The problem, I think, is bad press. Nothing brings back the dusty, overheated, stifling atmosphere of the fifth-grade classroom faster than the word *outline*. We tend to see them as these dry, formal things we were forced to make, with Roman numerals, capital and small letters all following an arcane, meaningless system. A pox on your head if you didn't follow exactly the form laid out by Mrs. Rubinsky. And what about those topic sentences? And what about all your thought disregarded, degraded by a grade based on form, not content? Nobody ever seemed to care what you were writing about in fifth grade, as long as you broke your paragraphs according to plan. And the plan was so ancient, so removed from your actual writing, it might have been worked out by Napoleon.

But an outline doesn't have to be this formal, dead thing. It can simply be a list of things you want to include in the book, put in the order they seem to go, for the time being. No one is going to ask to see your outline when you hand in your novel, or give you a *D*-minus because your novel doesn't follow it. (This is not entirely true. Agents like to see outlines. *My* agent likes to see outlines. But not the outline I worked from. He'd have to have experience in cryptography to break my code. The kind of outline agents and sometimes editors want to see are ones you write *after* you've written the book. Cliff Notes on your own fiction.) The outline is simply an aid for you, the writer. "Something to bounce off of," as Sam Decker put it.

The thing about outlines is that you can change them at will. You don't have to make a whole new neat outline afterward. Just add and subtract scenes, move things around, use arrows to indicate where stuff should go. Post-its are also fine. "No one says you have to stick to the outline if you get a better idea," my agent and fellow writer Peter Rubie told me. Which is why, after all, my outlines have those inserts and minuscule writing that runs horizontal to the page's vertical.

Steve Schwartz's experience as a screenwriter has taught him to regard outlines "as selling documents." He told me, "The way the movie business works, I'm often required to write an outline. Once I start writing, I try to forget it. . . . If I deliver something good, no one will care about the outline either." But he admits they *are* helpful when it comes to plotting. His latest approach to outlines is to "think of them in jazz terms. Take a solid melody (plot outline), then feel free to improvise (character, dialogue, situations) on that melody."

## SHUFFLING THE DECK

Some people outline on index cards, with one thought or scene or image per card. Then they shuffle the cards around and try to come up with an order that makes sense. I first read about this approach in Kenneth Atchity's *A Writer's Time*. I have never tried it, but there are two things about it I like.

First of all, the outline you come up with, such as it is, is very flexible. If, during the writing, you discover that the scene with the baby flows naturally from the scene in the hospital, you just take that card and move it up from the back of the pile. And there you have it! New outline.

What I also like is how Sam Decker uses Atchity's method. Sam is a teacher, the father of three, a very involved parent as well as writer, and he doesn't have a lot of time to fool around, tempting the muse. So in the spare moments he can find to write, he just pulls a card from his pile. On it is a scene he needs to do. And he starts. He can write the scenes out of order. He can write them in small chunks of time. Later he will have to string them together, he will have to provide a sense of time, the passage of seasons, the movement and development of characters, but at least for the time being he is accomplishing something.

Whether you make a formal outline or not, most writers agree that having a sense of destination when you start out is beneficial. John

Irving, in *The New York Times*, said, "I begin with an idea of an after-math or something close to an epilogue. I don't start writing a book not knowing where it's going." In fact, he writes the last line of a book first. He may change his mind about the beginning during the writing process, but that's how he starts.

This is where the dreaming-through process comes in. I take an idea from the seed to the plant in my imagination. If what I end up with seems lovely and alive, able to stand on its own and even nourish others, then it's worth all the digging around in dirt and lugging water back and forth I will have to do. Knowing what I will end up with gives me the stamina to start.

## THE UNFOLDING APPROACH

Novels and stories make different demands on writers. For example, I dream a novel through before I begin writing it, but I do not usually dream a story through. A story unfolds. It is short enough to do that, with the proviso that it will change during subsequent drafts.

Most often a story starts from an idea, and I do not know what it will turn into till it does. The characters may be wooden at first and develop personality during the writing. Sometimes I start from a sentence. Sometimes an image. I write it down and see where it goes. But sometimes I know where it's going, and it's the beginning I have to fake.

But there *have* been stories I have dreamed through before writing. Or actually, not the story itself but the fragments that made up the story. Each fragment was self-contained, a prose poem that could never stand on its own but could form a block, what Madison Smartt Bell in his book on writing, *Narrative Design*, calls a module. In the end, in conjunction with other modules, these build a story in the same way tiles make a mosaic design. I still had to erect a story frame to hold them, and that frame was discovered in the writing. I'm thinking in particular about my story "The Child Downstairs," which is about a tired marriage, an aborted love affair, an unhappy child, and a miscarriage. Until the point where I actually started writing it, I didn't realize the fragments would all go together, that it was one story, not two or three separate ones.

Whether you dream on paper or in your mind, you need to accept that the first draft you write will be dreck. Mine certainly is, but it gives me something to work with later. It is my raw material, and very raw it is. I would never serve it to you that way. It is all I can do to stomach it myself. But I have learned not to take these first drafts and toss them straight into the garbage can. For what happens next is the process of cooking. That's when things get pretty hot around the ol' computer console.

**Try This:** If you have a book idea in mind, spend ten minutes of your writing time dreaming it through. Afterward, jot down any ideas that come to you. Do this for a week, then look at your notes, trying to find an order. Use this dreaming-through technique, in a modified form, to work on individual chapters too. Dream the chapter through for a short amount of time before sitting down to write. But don't jot notes. Just follow the path your unconscious has laid out.

> **TIP:** The mind knows more than you think it does. It has a sense of shape, of pacing, of narrative. You don't have to plan everything in advance. Give it free rein and see where it goes. If, however, it goes nowhere—your writing is too discursive, you go off on too many tangents and end up with a woolly mess—try reading an entire story, chapter, or article at night before going to sleep. Train your mind to sense the shape of good writing. Don't force it; don't teach or point out or scold. Just read and enjoy. The creative mind learns best by osmosis.

# THIRTEEN

# COOKING

I don't cook. Oh, I can bake a potato or broil a steak, but anything fancy annoys me. I follow recipes like someone practicing witchcraft, carefully stirring in my eye of newt, terrified to do anything not in the book. Except when I decide a cup of sugar is entirely too much sugar, half a cup will do, and yogurt is a healthier alternative to mayonnaise, and I don't have vanilla so I'll just leave it out. Which explains why no one cherishes a dinner invitation from me.

But there is one sort of cooking I excel at. That is the kind that uses a computer, not an oven. I've found that after a piece of writing takes its shape, it needs to be put aside a while. No amount of struggling and straining will be as effective in helping you improve a piece of writing as a simple break from it. With this in mind I keep two story files in my computer—Cooking and Cooked. In the Cooking file are the first drafts, the second drafts, the third drafts. It may take years before a story gets transferred to the Cooked file, which means it's ready to send out. And sometimes it is sent out, only to be returned to Cooking. But, however long it takes, the process is easier to do if I allow myself to forget what I've written before trying to revise it.

The reason the process can take so long, however, is that each draft of a story needs to simmer before revision. After I write a story, I put it away and try to forget about it. I give it a few weeks, often more. But I don't stare at the computer during this time, going, "Come on, come on, come on." Like the proverbial watched pot, I know it won't boil if I don't leave it alone. So I try to use the time productively, to work on other things. Other first drafts get written during this time, then put to a slow boil. Or I take something else out of the Cooking file to taste, trying to determine what it needs. I may get involved with writing chapters for my novel or for a nonfiction writing project. I'm always working on various projects at once, so the time it takes for a piece to cook never goes to waste. There's always something new to write, something old to revise, or even something cooked to send out. Generally the time goes by quickly.

Too quickly.

At a certain point, instead of being eager to see what that first draft is like, I become filled with dread at the prospect of reading it. I know it is going to be worse than worthless—it is going to be embarrassing. It is only when I can't find anything better to do that I finally call up that first draft.

> First drafts are learning what your novel or story is about. Revision is working with that knowledge to enlarge or enhance an idea, or reform it.
> —Bernard Malamud

Sometimes what I find *is* embarrassing, but here's the catch: It's never worthless. No matter how bad a piece of writing is, there always turns out to be some good stuff in it. Oh, it may be just an image, just a phrase or an interesting transition. It almost certainly will be surrounded by clichés and excessive wordiness, by sentences that hang off it like dead twigs, going nowhere. But they're easy to see and easy to cut. And it's easy, too, to elaborate on the part where the writing is strong. I can hear where the language is clunky; I can sense where it needs filling out. The unexplained developments and the witticisms that turn out not to be funny—they are as evident as a lack of salt or an overabundance of pepper to a chef. I can taste a deliciousness too, the promise of something that is just right. The phrases I came up with that *I* thought overwrought turn out to work after all. And there are things I never meant, but there they are, as if a kitchen sprite spiced my stew after I went to sleep. Echoes, psychological truths, rhythms, images, puns—maybe I never meant them, but they're good. I can add to them and make them stronger. I can foreshadow events, now that I know what is going to happen. I can set things up better earlier or, get rid of the introduction that doesn't belong.

And so I make changes—some of which I love, others that I am sure have destroyed whatever tickled my tastebuds in the first place.

Then I get to put the story back in the Cooking file and forget about it. Again.

Forgetting is good. It means you can surprise yourself. You can regain your objectivity and read your writing as if someone else had written it.

Steve Schwartz told me he actively works to forget what he's written. "I rarely remember my lines," he said. "This can be a little embarrassing when every actor, director, and producer on a project knows them, but the writer can't remember!"

You too may need to work at forgetting what you meant here when you call the brother a marble-eyed satyr. Oh sure, you could spoil it by forcing your memory back to the day of composition, but don't do that. *Refuse* to do that. Recite nursery rhymes to avoid letting your memory remember. For then, when it turns out that your narrator surprises the brother in the basement with his girlfriend, you will be able to feel the narrative gasp that means it worked. Or you will hear the little voice that says, "Blech, this is so obvious." But if you let your memory remember, you spoil any opportunity for fresh tasting, like someone who takes a spoonful of chocolate sauce after cleansing her palate with lemon sorbet.

## OVERCOOKING

One word of warning though: Sometimes you *can* forget for too long. I have some first drafts in my Cooking file that I haven't looked at for ten years. I am a different person now. My concerns, my maturity, my influences are entirely different. And I'm talking about a first draft, which is by nature an embarrassing prospect to look at, full of mistakes.

A few weeks ago, however, I did call up some old stories. I didn't have anything else to work on. I didn't want to force myself on my novel—I hadn't figured out the subplot enough to move forward on it; the main plot was too flimsy without it. I had stories I was working on, but they hadn't been simmering long enough to revise. So I called up a story from my distant past, one I had never worked on after writing it.

The good news is that it wasn't so embarrassing that I had to assume the fetal position in a dark closet after reading it. In fact, it was kind of interesting, in a relic sort of way. Like finding a time capsule. It put me in touch with the person I had been then, when I wrote it.

There were some turns of phrase that filled me with the kind of pride I have for my son's accomplishments. They were nothing I'd send to the Booker Prize people, but they showed promise. They enabled me to see that I had talent back then; I was not deluded. It was a worthwhile first draft, although it wasn't anything I could work on now. Too much had happened in the past ten years for me to go back to it.

Giddy with newfound wealth, I started calling up more ancient first drafts. The next one I looked at also had some nice things and some embarrassing things. But its overwhelming irrelevance to my current situation made it something I could never work on. Then I got to the ending—and that ending blew me away. Somehow the story came to life. I went back to the beginning and started revising. I tried to get rid of the glaring cutesiness. I tried to salvage the story for the ending. Whether I have succeeded in doing so, I can't tell you. It's back in my Cooking file, simmering, only this time I'll watch the pot a bit better. Another ten years would surely turn the thing to mush.

Most of the time this won't happen to you. There are enough occasions when you want to be writing but don't have a fresh idea for you to go back and revise a first draft. Just remember not to let an initial repugnance get in the way. It takes a long time for an uncooked story to cook, but it doesn't take ten years.

**TIP:** If you use a computer, BACK UP! Cooking as well as Cooked. Those rough drafts are as valuable as the ones you've been laboring over. They contain your ingredients.

**Try This:** Make a Cooking file, either in your computer or in a folder. Do a first draft of a story about cooking. Cooking with your mother or grandmother. The cooking class you took in junior high. Teaching your kid to cook. Find something about cooking that resonates for you, and tell that story. It can be autobiographical or fictionalized. It can be a poem. The important thing is to write the whole thing. You'll know when you get to the end. Don't read back. Put it in the Cooking file. Make a date with yourself for two weeks from now to take it out to read and revise. Try not to even think about it till then.

• Although I find the two files (they're really subdirectories in which are contained files, which are the individual stories—if you want to get technical), Cooking and Cooked, adequate for my purposes, you may want to make a third division—Half-Baked. In it you could put stories you are revising, which are not yet ready to send out, distinguishing them from the purely first-draft material in Cooking.

# FOURTEEN

# RE-VISION

So now you have some things cooking. They've been cooking for at least a couple of weeks, and it is time to taste one of them to see what it needs. That is to say, it is time to revise.

My son is under the impression that revision means you fix the spelling and the punctuation, then you copy the whole thing over in your best handwriting. He says if he were a writer he would write all day and never go back to make changes or write over in his best handwriting. You may feel the same way. This attitude doesn't work in third grade, and it won't work for you.

Revision is usually a bit more complicated than spelling, punctuation, and handwriting. You may even need to change things. What things? you ask. Well, spelling and punctuation are as good a place to start as any. But you may also need to move, shape, add, or subtract. You often have to take Faulkner's advice—"kill your precious darlings," those metaphors and phrases you've labored over, sometimes writing the whole story in order to give them a place to exist. Taking these out can be like tearing a baby from its mother, or me from my Häagen Dazs. Nonetheless, if they impede the movement of your writing, they must be removed. What I do when I have to cut something I really like but that doesn't fit in my story is I put it in a file called "Scraps." The idea is that my self-rejected writing is not banished to the vacuum of cyberspace with a touch of the Delete button. It continues to exist, right there in my computer, to be called up whenever I have need for it. Do I ever have need for it? No. But it's a comfort to know it's there. Just in case.

Revising is like cooking with one of my mother's recipes. None of this half a teaspoon here, add a cup of that. No, instead you sprinkle and taste. You keep tasting and adding, reading over and over—and over. Unlike cooking, though, you get to take out. In fact, sometimes it seems all I do is take out. It's a wonder anything is left on the page when I'm done.

That first read-through is valuable. It is as close to objectivity as you will come, ideally having put the first draft away long enough to have forgotten what is in it exactly. Take advantage of that. You will never again be as detached from your work as you are now. Read carefully, and make changes as you go. Paradoxically you must also read lightly, with an eye to the big picture, not getting too caught up in the minutiae of grammar and word order. What I'm telling you is to walk and fly, to do what is impossible. How do you do this? You react to what is on the page, but you don't let it trap you in its undergrowth. You float overhead, even as you bend to weed.

Have faith in your ability to do this. If you are a writer, you have a writer's ear. That means you will hear the clunkers. The grammatically disadvantaged turns of phrase. The metaphors that don't work, but might if you changed the sentence structure a bit. The metaphors that wouldn't work if all their children were out on the street and starving. That's how you go through it.

When you've read the whole thing, you should get a sense of what you were writing—the shape and the focus (even if you didn't know what the focus was when you began). The part where you write about your sister is interesting, but it's not long enough. You need to give more detail about sharing a room, the kinds of games you played at night, how she would get you into trouble by making silly faces. You might add some of this stuff now, as it occurs to you—in the margins, between the lines, on the back of the page, or on a separate page. Or you might make a note to yourself—"add more about bedroom setup"—to remind you, the next time you go through the manuscript, what you wanted to add.

The part where you write about your father, on the other hand, goes on too long. It is not a piece about your father or your relationship to your father, or your father's relationship to his brother. That's good stuff, but it doesn't belong here. So take it out. As I said before, you can relegate this to a scrap file, where it may serve as a story starter for you on another occasion. But some things you will just want to take out and make them disappear. Presto, digito! The magic of Delete.

When you are done with this first read-through, you might put it back into the Cooking file, allowing at least another week to go by before taking it out again. But if you wrote notes to yourself about what you want to add but haven't written yet, you might want to do that fleshing out before putting it away to cook. Ideally, you should take it as far as you can each time you work on it, before putting it back to simmer. Revision is done by feel even when the problems are complex. You can just tell the action is too simple and you need a subplot; the foreshadowing is heavyhanded; the sequence of events needs reordering. You are your own best reader. What you lack in objectivity you make up for in attention. So you change things, you add things and, when you can no longer can tell the words from the letters, you put it away until you forget it again. The second and subsequent times you do this you will not be able to forget as completely as you did the first time. Still, you must get to the point where you don't have the sentences memorized and are reciting them as you read, creating an internal chorus that can make even bad poetry resonate.

## PRESSURE COOKING

This process of revising and putting away, revising and putting away can go on for years, so don't get discouraged if you keep finding things to change every time you go back to a manuscript. S.J. Perelman was asked how many times it was necessary to revise a story, and he said, "Thirty-seven. I once tried doing thirty-three, but something was lacking."

But even for writing with a pressing deadline, it is useful to work on it and put it away, then work on it again. The deadline works as a pressure cooker, making the whole thing happen faster. You put the piece away for a few days, not for a few weeks. During the stewing time you work on another part of the project—a later chapter or the bibliography, or maybe the cover letters. The time the piece is cooking is never spent filing your nails and humming, "Happiness Runs in a Circular Motion." There is always something else to work on. But the deadline, if you have one, functions as a tight lid on a concoction. The whole thing cooks faster *because it has to*. A couple of days, even one day, away from a piece of writing *can* work as well as a couple of weeks. The pressure builds but there is no explosion, and when you take the lid off you'll find your ideas softened, flavored by other ideas, your words ready for tasting.

Some people, myself included, find retyping a useful aid to revision. There are things you won't catch till you're typing in changes on a second or third draft. Madison Smartt Bell has an arduous technique of handwriting the first draft, typing it with changes, reading over the typewritten pages and making additional handwritten changes, then typing it all over again. "When I start work the following day I begin by making polished notes on the typescript from the previous day (starting this way helps me get back in the current of whatever I'm working on before I begin writing all the new stuff by hand again). At the end of the story or chapter I'll read the whole thing through and perhaps make a few more changes for the finished draft."

**Try This:** When you have worked on a piece to the point where you think it's good, read it aloud. This will enable you to hear the echoes, weird rhythms, klutzy phrasings, and lapses in tense you might not otherwise be aware of. Try reading into a tape recorder. Later you can *listen* to the piece being read. (I wouldn't read it aloud and listen to it all on the same day. There's only so much a writer can take.) These are tricks you can use to help you regain objectivity and detachment from your own writing, so you can do the hard work of revision.

In my writing workshop we start our discussion by having someone other than the writer read the story we are going to critique. This gives the writer the opportunity to hear his or her words in someone else's mouth, which can be excruciating, but it is one of the ways to regain a modicum of detachment from work that has been put away for cooking too many times for that to be effective.

Bear in mind that revision is part of writing—an essential part. It is what distinguishes writing from conversation (that and the fact that it is on paper). It is necessary to revise unless you, like Muriel Spark, are taking dictation from God, and even then you may need to go back and clear a few things up. Perhaps you are under the illusion

**TIP:** When revising for the second or third time, you should have a good idea of what you are trying to get across, although this may differ from your original intention. Ask yourself if you have succeeded in bringing out something meaningful. If not, what can you do about it? The meaning of a piece of writing doesn't have to be didactic. In fiction and poetry, in fact, it needs to be evoked more than baldly stated. But writing should add up to something, even if you can't succinctly say what that is.

that professional writers do not revise, or alternatively that they love doing so. Listen to me: No one loves revising. Although, wait a minute. Let me revise that—come to think of it, *I* love revising. I adore playing with punctuation, taking adjectives out, moving a word from here to there and back again, changing sentences around and breaking paragraphs in different ways—what Martha Schulman calls "arranging commas." I'm happy as a clam to delete clichés and tinker. I love to tinker. What I don't love is to make any real changes. A bad day is hearing from my agent that the book I've worked on for three years is really a short story and should be cut by three hundred pages. *Plus* the main character needs more development.

Which brings me to my next suggestion. It is very good to have somebody else read your writing. The question is who. Friend, family? Writer, plumber? It's really a matter of chance in some ways. Who is there in your life you would want to share your work with, whose intelligence you trust, whose sensitivity? Memoirist and food critic Ruth Reichl shows her work—"after I get it to a place where I'm not too embarrassed"—to her husband. "He's a good reader who believes that the best criticism is a gift." Novelist Susan Saiter finds her twenty-six-year-old daughter an excellent critic, but her husband, a writer, is too scathing for her to consult.

> I work over my manuscript many times until I feel there is nothing more that I can change to improve it.
>
> —Saul Bellow

We all have the secret hope that the loved ones we show our work to will come back and say it is perfect. When they don't do that we are crushed. When they do, we don't believe them or value their comments anyway since "What do they know?" as Martha Schulman put it.

This is a real problem, finding sympathetic, encouraging readers whose criticism is nourishing but doesn't taste like pabulum. Emily Russell told me that she tends to discard people as untrustworthy readers as soon as she gets to know them as friends. "After that, they become suspect of too much sympathy and not enough . . . detachment." There is one family member, however, she trusts to give her the tough love she needs. "My sister can be relied on to maintain a cold and dispassionate eye."

Madison Smartt Bell is lucky enough to have that relationship with his editors, whom he trusts quite a bit. "They are both very smart readers who I feel will understand what I meant." Most writers prefer to get responses to their work *before* sending it to an editor. Even writers who never used to show their work to anyone before submission prefer sharing it once they find that essential reader whose sensibilities are like their own. Novelist Tom Mallon, for example, met writer Andrea Barrett at the Bread Loaf Writers' Conference one year. Because of similiar interests, they got into the habit of showing their work to each other and find this arrangement mutually beneficial.

Ideally your early reader needs to be someone whose taste you admire. Who is on your wavelength. Who knows how to encourage as well as criticize. Who knows how to make suggestions without making you feel like a flea on the behind of Literature. The reader you would be if you could split into another person. That reader is probably a figment of your imagination, a Platonic ideal never to be met in the flesh, so you must settle for someone honest who doesn't appear to have a sadistic streak. Remember, there's nothing wrong with sympathy, especially from your first reader. We get knocked down enough by strangers. While you may not want to share your work with your mother, who says, "That's nice, dear," about everything you write, you also don't want to give it to someone who snickers through his nose while reading your stuff, then says, "I don't *think* so." If the person you share your work with leaves you feeling more discouraged than hopeful, get rid of Clyde Snide. It's more important to find someone who says nice things you don't believe than one who makes jokes at your expense. You can't afford that kind of expense.

Bear in mind, too, that it's easy, in revising, to get caught up in the details. Sometimes you need to stand off and look at the whole picture. It's like plucking your eyebrows. If you put your nose to the mirror to examine each hair, by the time you stand back you may find yourself *without* eyebrows. In writing also you need to sense if the arch is arched enough, too arched, and if it is properly placed.

**TIP:** If you think, in revising, that the overall design may be the problem, make an outline, after the fact. Looking at the skeleton can help you see what you might otherwise miss—that the story is standing on one leg and lacks support; that it's missing a middle, and the torso could use a few ribs.

# FIFTEEN

# WORKSHOPS

The best way to get responses to your work that are honest, intelligent, and sympathetic is to become involved in a writing workshop. Doing a revision is all about having a *re-vision*, seeing again what you have and what you don't have, not what you thought you had or meant to have. There's no better way to see freshly than through someone else's eyes. People in a workshop are not your friends, although they may become them. They are fellow writers, and they know they will get as good as they give—that is, it is in everyone's best interest to respond generously to one another's work, by reading carefully, thinking comments through before making them, devoting time to examining the writing.

A good writing workshop can provide not only guidance but the support you need to make unpleasant decisions. An additional benefit, pointed out to me by Martha Schulman, is it imposes deadlines on you, which can be very useful in getting you off your butt (or actually on it, at your desk).

Workshops can be informal—living-room gatherings of fellow writers who have found each other. You may be in one now. The informal workshop happens when a group of writers decide to form a peer review. No one is the leader. No one starts the discussion or keeps it going. As a result, such discussions can often disintegrate into bland nice-nice or jagged barbs. Participants have to work hard to prevent this.

Such groups may meet in a neutral place—a park or a coffee shop—or in someone's home. Sometimes the workshop is set up to meet on an appointed schedule, every other Monday for instance, and if you can't make it you miss that session. More often, especially with a small group, the next workshop meeting is arranged at the end of each session, at a time convenient for all participants. This can be as problematic as planning a dinner party for musicians, doctors, and teachers—people with wildly varying schedules.

If you are not in such a group, you are probably wondering how such groups form. Usually there's a writing connection involved. Mystery novelist Marissa Piesman, for example, was in a group that formed out of Sisters-in-Crime, a mystery-writers' organization. Novelist Lore Segal's group is composed of "a colleague and two graduate students who have turned into writers," people she knows from Columbia University, where she taught for many years. They don't submit "unfinished" work to one another, she told me. "I share work I *think* is finished, knowing that this is merely the first attempt to think it finished."

The easiest way to meet fellow writers is to take a teacher-run workshop. Many YMCAs offer writing workshops, which are run under the auspices of Writer's Voice, a national writers' organization. The workshop I lead, for example, is offered by Writer's Voice operating out of the West Side YMCA in Manhattan. Workshops also come out of continuing-education classes taught at nearby colleges or high schools. Published writers and/or editors sometimes lead workshops in their homes. Other workshops are run by independent writing schools, whose brochures are often strategically placed in bookstores or corner kiosks.

There are different levels of workshop: those for beginners, who get in just by signing up and paying the fee; those for people at a more intermediate level, who usually submit a sample of their writing before being accepted; and those for not-yet-published-but-would-be-if-the-world-were-fair-(which-it's-not) writers. In addition, workshops are often devoted to a particular writing form or genre—personal essay, for example, or poetry; science fiction or mystery.

Beginning workshops are geared to helping the new writer find a voice and—since the desire to write often precedes the sense of what to write about—helping the writer find material. New writers tend to stiffen up when faced with the prospect of actually writing. They sometimes resort to archaic words and stilted constructions, using "thine" and "'Tis" and "O Honey-Lippéd Muse" under the misguided conception that *authors* wear cloaks and spend fortnights sharing the good fellowship of country cousins.

Such workshops should also instill in the writer the courage to explore personal material, as some of our best contemporary writers do. I don't mean intimate so much as day-to-day, *lived* experience. Nicholson Baker, for example, spent many pages in *Room Temperature* writing about peanut butter jars, and many more pages exploring the endless varieties of nasal mucus. In dealing with such odd specifics of daily life he reaches a generality of truth, something he could never have expressed so well if he'd stuck to "writerly" topics like "The Fate of Modern Man a Fortnight Hence."

Most important of all, the workshop provides the solace of camaraderie to new writers. This is especially important for writers just starting out, people who may feel weird or deluded, embarrassed to be trying to do something no one around them fully understands. Being with other new writers, everyone in it together, helping one another do what we *know* to be worthwhile, can provide the support necessary to accomplish what we might not have the courage to do on our own.

More advanced workshops give writers who have been revising in solitude an opportunity to learn what *others* think they're writing about. Such writers work very hard, not just on their own stuff but on their critiques. Chekhov said that the practice of medicine was his wife but that writing was his mistress, and the same is true for many of the people in my writing workshop. They are married to their work—sometimes it was a love match, sometimes a marriage of convenience—but writing is what they do from ardor. They sneak it in at odd hours—early in the morning, late at night, or at lunchtime, cheating on their regular jobs to finish a story or jot down a poem. Such writers tend to read a lot and are almost as excited at the prospect of discussing other people's work as they are to have their own work discussed. Because there is a sense that they are all in it together, they are considerate of one another's feelings. They all want honest criticism, but quickly learn that honest doesn't mean harsh. Along with pointing up flaws in one another's work, they offer praise, suggestions, encouragement. Sometimes the criticism is so thought-provoking I wish I could submit my work to them—like the lifeguard who'd like to join the splashing fun but whose job it is to keep everyone from drowning.

Workshops give the writer an opportunity to *hear* what he or she is writing about. You may think you know, but you're in for a surprise. After you listen to intelligent readers discuss what they got out of your work, you're not so sure. In some cases such readers will point out things you didn't intend. If it turns out you like these accidental themes, you can accentuate them in your next revision. On the other hand, sometimes your readers will say things that show that they didn't understand what they were reading. That, too, is helpful. Now you know the piece has the potential for being misunderstood. If enough people misunderstood it you need to address that issue. If only one did, you have to judge your judge. Is this a careful reader or a lazy one? Is he sane? If he objects to the gratuitous violence in your story, for instance, and there is *none,* you can pretty much disregard his comments. Especially if he later brings in a story about a serial murderer who freezes his victims' fingers and eats them as ice-pops on hot summer nights.

Once you have taken a formal writing workshop you will have met fellow writers, some of whom may wish to keep the workshop going. Martha Schulman is in such a writing group now, which formed out of classes she took at Writer's Voice (including my own), although "We've all added a few people we've met in other classes since," she told me.

Not all informal writing groups meet physically to discuss each other's work. Some operate through the mail. What's nice about this sort of arrangement is that you don't need to schedule meetings. You just send stuff when it is ready. After you get your work back, you can take your time reading over the comments. Such comments are not abstract. They're right there on the page. Things are circled. There are arrows and check marks.

The downside is the lack of a spectrum of comments. You are not privy to a dialogue in which your readers agree or disagree with one another about flaws and strengths in your writing. You are not hearing the sorts of things that are only discovered in discussion. But Steve Schwartz has been in such a group for about ten years, one of four fellow filmwriters/directors who circulate material back and forth, and he's found the arrangement works for him. Because they've been at it for so long, "Most of the mean-spirited, competitive, egotistic, destructive kinds of comments are not made—although every so often one sneaks in," he told me. In addition to commenting on the significance of the work at hand, his peer group makes "assessments as to whether something's ready to be seen, almost ready, or has a lot of work left." He explained that, as screenwriters, "We all exist in the marketplace and know that the world is much less kind than we. Better we be supportively critical as friends than allow one of us to go prematurely into the buzzsaw of that marketplace. Friends don't let friends drive second-rate material."

**Try This:** Make an effort to form or join a writing workshop. One place to look is in local libraries, which sometimes run reading and/ or writing groups. If the one in your vicinity does not, speak to the librarian about starting one. Offer to coordinate it—that way you're guaranteed a slot.

• Bookstores also often run workshops. Writer's Digest Books sponsors a nationwide library and bookstore writers' group program, for instance. Again, if your local bookstore does not offer such an opportunity, speak to the manager about starting one.

• Look at the classified advertisements in writing publications. *Poets & Writers* runs ads placed by writers looking for other writers. Or you might consider placing such an ad yourself.

• There are organizations to consider joining. People with particular interests—whether history, mystery, or needlecraft—often write and may wish to share their work with others who have that interest. Put out some feelers. You'll be surprised how many secret writers are out there.

• Workshops are also offered on the Internet, although I have had no firsthand experience with these and am inclined to shy away from faceless critics. We get enough of that when we send stuff out. But you may feel different. You may live in a small town where you are hard-pressed to find literary-minded people to share work with. You may be far from a college campus, YMCA, or other location that offers writing workshops. If so, the Internet workshop may be just the thing for you.

Some Internet workshops are affiliated with college programs, in which case you generally have to pay for them. But there are also workshops that are more like gatherings of writers, everyone looking to give and get considerate criticism. These are worth checking out. They operate through mailing lists posted on the Internet. Two mailing list addresses recommended to me are: http://www.liszt.com and http://www.listtool.com. Once you call up these lists you can pick a site that interests you— poetry writing workshop, for example, or romance, nonfiction, or young adult. You must subscribe to these lists (which, unlike magazines, cost nothing) in order to read the comments people have been making, as well as to submit your own work for review.

• Consider going to a writers' conference or a writers' colony, both of which offer opportunities to meet other writers. Conferences are offered all over the country. They are often given in the summer and usually last around two weeks. They can be expensive, but no more than a nice vacation. And there's nothing more exhilarating than surrounding yourself with fellow writers, often in a beautiful setting, going to lectures and readings, taking workshops. You also have a chance to meet editors, agents, and well-known writers at such events.

Writers' colonies are less social events than conferences. They emphasize solitude during working hours and are geared to the requirements of writers in need of blocks of uninterrupted time to finish projects. But, they too, offer an opportunity for writers to meet one another—at dinner and in the evenings. Novelist Maureen Brady finds them crucial to her work. Being at a writers' colony enables her to "open up a story further because there's enough time ahead to actualize the ideas." In addition, there is "the feeling of being taken care of, that *someone* cares that I *write*, and that have the right conditions for it. Good for the soul, this!"

"I was puzzled and would marvel at how something that would take three months in New York would take ten days in Yaddo," Lore Segal told me, regarding the famous writers' colony. "Then I realized this is why the aristocracy and the men get things done. It wasn't that I was working more hours, but that after I finished working I could lie fallow. I didn't have to shop or cook or even go to the theater or out for drinks. The work went on, underground." It was also stimulating, she said, to know that in the very next studio someone else was writing too.

Ellen Dreyer, an as-yet-unpublished novelist, concurs that the atmosphere of a writers' colony is inspiring. She found it to be a little "like camp for writers and artists," although one in which she managed to do a lot of good work. On the days when her work wasn't going well, however, she spent her time thinking about the "black, industrial-strength lunchboxes" her food would be delivered to her studio in, whether she'd be getting "a deviled egg, a tuna sandwich, or swiss cheese, and what kind of cookie."

## LISTENING BEHIND THE WORDS

What can drive you crazy about a workshop, whether formal or informal, is that some readers will rhapsodize over what causes others to hold their noses. This is where the proverbial grain of salt comes in handy. You need to take people's comments with it. Don't assume everyone else is right, especially if they don't like your work. Don't try to reconcile conflicting views either. Listen to old Auntie Polonius here. If you try to please everybody, you will end up with a hodge-podge of gobblydegook. As Bill Cosby said, "I don't know the key to success, but the key to failure is trying to please everybody."

In a workshop *you* are the filtering intelligence. You take in the comments. You make notes to yourself. The comments that strike you as wise you mark with an asterisk or underline or check. The other comments you write down, but then don't feel bad if you can't read your handwriting later. When people offer suggestions, listen—not to the suggestions but to the meaning *behind* the suggestions.

I have a story, for example, about a young girl who is instructed by her parents to lie about her age so they won't have to pay for daycamp in the bungalow colony they're in. The lie sets her up for sexual situations she is not ready for. It also makes her feel like a spy in the group of teenage girls she's trying to fit in with. When her mother blurts out the girl's real age as twelve, not fourteen, it transforms her into a total outcast—not just for the summer but, implicitly, for the rest of her life.

If someone tells me, as recently happened, he doesn't see the significance of the mother's action and thinks I should cut it, then I know I haven't succeeded in presenting that action as the betrayal I mean it to be. I have no intention of taking the mother's action out—that is the suggestion. I know that the mother's betrayal is the crux of the story. But I also know that if enough people don't see it that way, my intention be damned—the story doesn't work. Perhaps I sweetened the mother too much in an earlier revision when people complained she seemed too sour. This, after all, is what drives writers mad: Everything you change changes everything, not just the thing you wanted changed.

"You have to be a little insane to write," Maureen Brady told me, "to grapple with the complexities of a world that starts out under water and only draft by draft surfaces enough so you can see it. And when you make a change on page 1 it affects page 350, and you can't bear to go through it again. But," she went on, "there's no other work that is so transformative."

What I'm trying to tell you is you need to listen deeply to people's comments—more deeply than they themselves mean them. Listen *behind* the comments. Don't listen to their *advice* but to their perceptions, what they got, what they didn't get. And then listen to yourself. What did *you* mean your writing to be about? What kept *that* from coming across?

Some people cannot listen to their readers, even when they've gone out of their way to find them. In a recent interview John Irving said that "the idea that what inspires you is untouchable either by your own revising or by an editor's thoughtful suggestions is a kind of hubris." It's good to keep that in mind when you find yourself playing the genius to an audience of stunned friends.

> The feeling that the work is magnificent, and the feeling that it is abominable, are both mosquitoes to be repelled, ignored, or killed, but not indulged.
> —Annie Dillard

Evan Russell admits he had such a problem at first. "I had this attitude that said: I know what I meant to say, dammit, and if you're not on my wavelength you can go to hell." But he has since learned that in discussing a book, trying to explain why something is in there or to justify a character's behavior, "You often stumble upon gold" and discover what you should have written in the first place.

Martha Schulman has found that polishing her prose before giving it to readers is what makes her resistant to listening to criticism. "If the surface gets too buffed and glossy it's hard to get back into it and start troweling, messing everything up." Nonetheless, you need to give it your best shot, each draft, each time. And each time you need to try to gain some objectivity, seeing it through someone else's eyes.

There's no doubt that trying to detach yourself from yourself can drive you nuts. "What is objectivity anyway—a mood more than anything else," Sam Decker told me. That may be so, but objectivity is still the fox we chase, knowing as we do that editors out there don't love us and won't try to see past the flaws of our work. In the end it is up to us to determine what is good and what needs to be changed. We take in what our family, friends, and writing group say, but ultimately the decisions are ours.

Be as objective about your writing as you can be. Listen to what your readers have to say. But don't lose sight of this fact: There is no one out there, no godlike Objective Judge whose acceptance or rejection of our material deems it valuable or worthless. Truly. Objectively. For, truly, objectively, it is ourselves we need to please.

**TIP:** You can learn a great deal from other people's mistakes. If you are in a workshop, don't dismiss the stories that fail as unworthy of your attention. Put energy into your analysis of them. Figure out what makes the failures fail and how they could be salvaged. You will benefit from this in two ways: It will help you develop your critical facility, which will make you a better critic of your own writing. You will also get the reputation of generosity, and others will extend the same courtesy to your work.

# WRITECRAFT

For the next few chapters we are going to shift our focus from getting yourself to write to dealing with specific concerns of craft. In this chapter, for example, we will look at a variety of topics. It's a compendium of advice writers have given other writers. The following chapter will explore various points of views you can use in your writing—the strengths and weaknesses and dangers of each. A short chapter on hooking the reader comes next, followed by a chapter of exercises and story starters, to help you write when you have the time but are drawing a blank.

> **TIP:** Questions of craft belong in the back of your mind when you are writing. They move to the forefront only when you are revising.

## RULES MEANT TO BE BROKEN
Although I do not believe you can teach writing, there *are* some flexible rules, Bendits rather than Legos, for writing vividly. But as soon as someone tells me a rule I look for ways to break it. You may feel the same way. So, in this chapter I'll tell you what writers have found helpful through the years, and you can try to prove me wrong.

### Clichés
The biggest cliché about writing is that clichés are bad. This is true, but not because of something innate in the cliché itself. In fact, the best metaphors are clichés. That is what makes them clichés. They are so perfect that everyone uses them until they no longer work. When something is red as a rose no one sees it as anything but red.

The rose part is just extra words. But if something is red as a squalling infant's face, that may make the reader pause. Then, if the baby image is apt—that is, it fits in well with the story's content, either in its themes or action—the reader may smile. On the other hand, if the baby image is merely decorative, the reader probably will be annoyed. The baby image in a story about a mother may be just right, but in a story about logging in the Northwest it will be less so. You *never* want to use clichés in your writing unless the cliché is the point—that is, if you have a character who talks in clichés, it is okay to use them.

Remember, substituting an inappropriate, albeit fresh, metaphor for a cliché is almost as bad as using the cliché itself. There's nothing wrong with something being red. Not red as a tulip, not red as a pimple you just popped, just plain old red.

> Every cliché once had its moment of truth. At the moment of conception it was a new and wonderful thing.
>
> —Wright Morris

**Try This:** When you revise, circle all figures of speech—metaphors, similes, images. Make a list of them. Are any of these too familiar to surprise or delight your reader? Can you say the same thing in a fresher way, perhaps using images that are appropriate to your story? If your main character is a carpenter, for example, you have a carpentry vocabulary available to you that is both appropriate and fresh. Alternatively, can you remove any clichés altogether, expressing what you are trying to say simply, without figures of speech?

## Details

Writing grounded in particulars is stronger than that which is full of fuzzy generalities, no matter how grand. Give the reader something to hold on to, and that reader will remember it long after tomes on justice have turned soupy in the mind.

The secret in using details is not to overload the reader with the insignificant but to choose the right ones. A young, black-haired widow and her tiny blond infant with blue eyes who is wrapped in a pink blanket, snowflakes falling on her knit black shawl and trembling bare hand with two broken fingernails do not move us, except to laughter. The details are superfluous, the situation a cliché. A kid with a bag of cans he's collecting for the deposit money bragging to a schoolmate that he's doing it to help the environment might better convey the shame of poverty.

**Try This:** Write about a character or person who evokes an emotion in you. Give us details about the character—appearance, smell, habits—that convey the emotional charge and uniqueness of the character. Go further with the idea. Give us the setting in such a way that the few details make the place vivid and the character who is in that setting alive. The trick in this exercise is to come up with as few details as possible to create the effect, not to weigh the reader down with extraneous facts that add up to nothing.

> Descriptions of nature should be very short and always be apropos. . . . You have to choose small details in describing nature, grouping them in such a way that if you close your eyes after reading it you can picture the whole thing.
>
> —Anton Chekhov

## Dialogue

"I love dialogue," she said. "It's so airy."

"Yes, but, but, like whatchamacallit, I don't know, sometimes it gets so—"

"Disjointed?"

"No, not exactly. It's more like, um, uh, it goes on and on and it doesn't seem to have a point or it has a point but it takes too long to get to. And then, like, uh, uh, I don't know, it just—"

"But that's how people talk, isn't it? That makes it real, doesn't it?"

"Yeah, well, I guess. I suppose so. But I don't know. I—"

You don't want to write dialogue the way people talk: You want to write dialogue that *feels* the way people talk. Just as you don't want to show everything, even though in real life that is how the story goes, in dialogue you want to say a lot in as few words as possible and still have it feel real.

Here are a few things to keep in mind about the way people speak that can be translated into narrative:

- People do not speak in full sentences. They interrupt each other. They pause. They dribble into ellipsis points.

- People do not say what's on their minds. They skirt the issue. They say one thing and mean another. They lie. They stop themselves. They get distracted. Sometimes they get distracted in very telling ways, revealing more of what they're thinking by fiddling with their wedding rings than by the words they are using. Gesture and pause are very important aspects of dialogue. This kind of nonverbal communication can have even greater weight than spoken words.

- People generally do not lecture one another, filling each other in on the whole story and providing background information that is so useful for the reader to know. Some bits of information can come out in dialogue, but these should slip out. If they are planted they will feel planted—and the reader won't like you anymore.

- "Said" is a perfectly acceptable way to say someone said something. They do not have to reply, whisper, answer, question, query, growl, yell, or respond. Sometimes you do not have to specify he or she said it at all, if it's apparent who is speaking from the way the dialogue is going back and forth.

And here is something to keep in mind about the way people speak that cannot be translated into narrative:

- They speak badly.

People *um* and *whatchamallit* and *like* and repeat themselves, but if you do it on the page you will annoy your reader. If it is important to have a character speak like this, the trick is to do it occasionally. To place an *um* here and there that stands for ten *ums* in real life.

People have accents in real life, and they use words incorrectly, but you had better be sure of your accent on the page if you don't want to offend your readers. Again, you don't want to write every word as it is spoken by someone with a Latvian accent. You get the accent across by inflexion, by sentence structure that feels Latvian, by the occasional (very occasional) misuse of a word. If you try to write in dialect you will accomplish two things early on: You will insult people who think you are making fun of anyone who has an accent, and you will annoy your reader, who will have to concentrate very hard on the dialogue (which should be the airy, easy part of reading, the breathing section). It is not that you *can't* write in dialect, but youse betta gotta good 'scuse faw doin' it, aw yaw riting's gonna bees bad az dis.

**Try This:** Set up a tape recorder at the table before a meal. Later, transcribe the dialogue verbatim. Make a copy and go through it, taking out unnecessary repetitions and meaningless blather. Add some gestures (you can invent them or rely on your memory). Let both versions of the conversation cook a few days, then go back over them—reading the second one first. Did you lose anything from the first version? If so, reinsert it into the revised dialogue. Are there more things you can take out of the second version and still be left with the *feeling* of that discussion?

## Imagery

Apt, vivid imagery makes strong writing stronger, but the images need to be appropriate. A beautiful girl whose skin is "pink as a pig's rump" seems less than beautiful to us, unless we understand the compliment to be the height of praise, coming as it does from a hog farmer. "The man looked at her with Dracula eyes" may convey a sexual tension, a danger that is part of the man's attraction. But if you're trying to present a character who is nurturing and gentle, giving him Dracula eyes is probably not the best way to go about it.

Too much imagery is not enough—it is too much. It causes the reader to lose patience. Like being lost in someone else's dream, the whole thing can be hard to follow. It may even make the reader feel schizophrenic . . . or certain that you are.

A mistake otherwise talented writers often make is to mix metaphors. It's like the writer's brain gets overloaded with poetic ideas, and he changes horses in midstream, ending up with an olla podrida of disparate parts in a five-and-ten of notions, sundries, and half-formed thoughts. If you catch my drift.

Metaphors can also get overextended. In reaching for an idea, the writer stretches a similarity beyond the breaking point. Then it either snaps and falls apart or else gets tangled up in knots. The hairdressing of bad writing needs the shampoo of revision and the conditioner of editing before a ribbon of felicitous phrase can tie it all together, but please don't write like this or I'll shave your head. (I think I've illustrated my point baldly enough.)

**Try This:** Describe an object you are very familiar with, not allowing yourself to use any metaphors or similes. Next, write about the object using as many figures of speech as you can come up with—even to the point of the ridiculous. Now think about the object and pick a central image to use in describing it, perhaps one of the many you used in the first description. A week or so later read the three different descriptions. Which do you find most effective?

### In Medias Res

A lot of times writers start at the beginning, and they may go on for quite a while before they get to the good stuff. You don't have to do this. You can start in the middle, right when the big event is happening. Then you can give us background, interweaving it into the exciting part through the use of flashbacks and summary. The thing is that by starting in the middle you hook the reader. The reader will probably stay with you through your protagonist's childhood and subsequent bad marriage in order to find out what happens to her, standing there on the windowsill talking to pigeons. It can be tricky to move around in time this way, but it pays off in creating more dynamic writing.

**Try This:** Take the action of a well-known fairy tale—Goldilocks and the Three Bears, Little Red Riding Hood, Jack and the Beanstalk—and start writing the story from the moment before the climax. Goldilocks is sleeping in the littlest bed, for instance, and the three bears are looking at her. Make it tense. Fill us in by giving us earlier scenes, but keep coming back to that tense moment. The scenes that occurred earlier chronologically will eventually catch up to the present you started in. Now take the action from there, when Goldilocks awakes to find three bears watching her.

## Likeable Characters

If readers like your characters they will care about them. If they care about them they will want to continue reading about them. If they continue reading about them you will be published. Regularly. For money. You will be successful, the world will throw gardenias at your feet.

The key here is *likeable*. Likeable doesn't mean good. It doesn't mean morally upstanding. Likeable characters aren't necessarily goody-two-shoes. In fact, goody-two-shoes are probably the least likeable characters around. Funny is probably a good way to make a character likeable. Everyone likes funny people. Everyone likes to laugh. Especially if your funny, likeable character isn't a wiseass but humble, maybe a bit of a dork, so that the humor is blended with sympathy because we're all bits of a dork—different bits, same dork.

Now, not everyone can create likeable characters. I can't. I try, but readers seem to come away from my stories shaking their heads and moaning, "What a creep." I don't know why this is. It's not that I don't try. I do. I never intend my readers to think, "God, what detestable characters!" But that is what seems to happen. You, on the other hand, are no doubt very likeable, I daresay lovable. And you can take that charm, wit, and intelligence, and invest your characters with those traits. If you do this you will find publishing a friendlier business than I've found it. It's all a matter of attitude.

## Show, Don't Tell

This is the oldest rule in the book, and a very long, very boring book it would be if you followed it to the letter. You can't show everything. Writing is an art, and that has to do with artifice and artificial. It is not life. In life we observe actions, hear dialogue, each day is a chapter, our life is a book—the problem is no one but God would want to read it. It's long and dull, and the part where you goo-goo at the ducks with your kid goes on for years.

Narrative writing is an artful compilation of showing and telling. You want to show key scenes, dramatic points, and parts where character is revealed through dialogue and gesture. One scene of a family together bickering and irritating each other by leaving the cap off the soda bottle or taking the last slice of bread without offering to share is probably enough. Two such scenes would be overkill. Even if something comes out the next time the family gets together, you don't have to *show* that. Maybe you can *tell* us that Bip squirted ketchup in his sister's eye and she had to be rushed to the hospital. Then you might show us the scene in the emergency room.

Sometimes you can show *and* tell. You start out telling, then you throw in a smattering of dialogue so the reader gets the feel for the scene without having the whole thing laid out. Conversely you can give us part of a scene, then summarize the conclusion. These half-scenes give the writer a lot of mileage. A sentence of dialogue can bring a page of exposition to life, and a summarizing paragraph can cap off a scene that might otherwise meander for another few pages.

In a writing workshop you are almost certain to get responses that say, in effect: I want *more*. I want you to show me the whole scene, not tell me any of it. This is one of the failings of writing workshops. Everyone knows the same bunch of rules and they spout them to one another like old ladies talking clichés over their knitting. You have to judge the weight of your writing to determine if it is too heavy with exposition or too light with scene. In the end what helps you most in developing this sense of judgment is reading. By reading a lot of narratives you learn, through osmosis, how to handle showing and telling. Then when it comes to writing your own narratives you know how to do it. You're carrying your own bag of tricks.

**Try This:** Write a few paragraphs, first summing up an action you observed yesterday. It doesn't have to be anything momentous. It can be about getting your kids off to school or taking care of the bills. But first write it in summary form: The man went through his mail, weeding out junk, writing checks, etc. Next, try to interject a bit of dialogue or something active to bring it more to life: The man went through his mail. When he came to the blue envelope he stopped. "It can't be," he said to himself. Now try writing the whole thing as a fully developed scene. The man turned on the light and sat at his desk with an audible *hmph*. He took the pile of letters and placed them in front of him. He started with the first one—a plea for money from a homeless advocacy group. He threw it into the copper wastebasket at his feet. This exercise should give you a feel for three ways to write a narrative—summary, half-scene, and full scene.

## Thinking

There is too much thinking in narrative writing, so you just better stop it. Thinking is like telling. You need some . . . but if you use thinking to explain your characters—their motivations, their psychologies—then you fail your readers. You are saying, in effect, I don't think you'll get this on your own, so here is what Sally is thinking, and that's why she didn't go with her mother that day. We should be able to get why Sally didn't go with her mother from other things in the writing—the action, the sense of imagery and rhythm, dialogue, a feel for the character. If you have to tell us, then something is weak elsewhere in the story.

I was a teaching fellow at Bread Loaf one summer and attended a lecture given by Charles Baxter, who said something like: "The objects carry the burden of feeling." At least that's what I jotted in my notebook, and if he didn't say it he should have. It relates to what T.S. Eliot called the "objective correlative"—a way of expressing emotion through objects and situations instead of out-and-out stating them. If your writing is full of yucky heart-talk, see if you can express what you are trying to say through action or through objects instead. James Merrill wrote, "I always find when I don't like a poem I'm writing, I don't look any more into the human components. I look to the setting—a room, the objects in it." Emotional content is much stronger when it is grounded in something external, when it is not presented to the reader predigested: He is sad. You can't tell a reader, Feel, feel. The reader only becomes more cynical and set against you. As Chekhov wrote in one of his famous letters: "When you want to make the reader feel pity, try to be somewhat colder." He also wrote: "Shun all descriptions of the characters' spiritual state. You must try to have that state emerge clearly from their actions." In other words, writing is an art, not a lecture.

Lore Segal told me there is an order of vividness, of drama, in writing. At the top is action. Then comes conversation. Then comes feeling. The trick is to convey the meaning of your story as much as possible through the action. Action should serve as the metaphor for the meaning of your work. "If you read the Bible," she said, "you will see only action and conversation exist. The Bible is very vivid literature, and it is expressed—with a few interesting exceptions—in terms of what is *done* and what is *said*. You don't read, 'I think,' 'I feel.' Most of my students are more comfortable telling what they feel. It is much harder to write an effective dialogue. Aristotle says—I'm paraphrasing, of course, but he says, 'All our young writers can write these purple passages, but when there's some action, stop with the purple!' Two thousand years and teachers are still saying the same thing: Stop with the purple!"

**Try This:** Give us a character, real or invented, in an extreme situation—having a fight, expressing romantic interest, suffering a loss. You can use dialogue and action to express the character's emotions, but you cannot tell us explicitly what those emotions are. When you've worked on this a while, writing and cooking it, give it to a reader and find out what emotions and thought processes come across and what that reader does *not* get.

• Come up with an action or gesture to express the following emotions: love, jealousy, satisfaction, abandonment, rage. Don't go for the easy actions—expressing anxiety by having a character pacing, for instance. What if she fingered a loose thread in her sleeve until she frayed the whole cuff?

> Whatever is left upon the page without being specifically named there—that, one might say, is created. It is the inexplicable presence of the thing not named, of the overtone divined by the ear but not heard by it, the verbal mood, the emotional aura of the fact of the thing or the deed, that gives high quality to the novel or the drama, as well as to poetry itself.
>
> —Willa Cather

### Time Travel

Isn't it great to be a writer, to be so omnipotent you can read minds, be invisible, create meaning out of disorder? You can even travel in time. I don't necessarily mean by writing science fiction or historical romances, although there is that aspect of time travel available to writers too. I mean that you can give us, via flashback, scenes that happened to your main character in his childhood or yesterday.

The way to segue into this is usually by association. Something happens that kicks off a flashback, often a memory or daydream. You don't have to say, "Joe remembered the night his father came at him with the ax," although you can. Sometimes just seeing the ax will be enough for Joe to time travel. He might pick up the ax and fondle the handle. His father had an ax like that. Just like that, in fact. The night he came after Joe with the ax he'd been drinking. Joe was in high school then. Etc.

**Try This:** Write a narrative using association to help you time travel. Take a mundane, repetitive action—washing the dishes, bathing a baby, watering the garden or weeding. Describe the action in detail, but as you do so follow any association into memory. A bird flies by, and you remember your father whistling to red cardinals in the backyard. Your character then returns to the action at hand. Maybe slices a worm in half by accident with his trowel. This calls up the memory of the boy who would make worm stew. He was a neighbor's kid. His yard abutted the back of yours. Once they had a barbeque your family was invited to. As you pat the soil down around the tulip bulb you just planted, you hear a red cardinal's song. You look up in the tree, trying to see the bird. At the barbeque that neighbor had been talking about red cardinals—how he liked to whistle to the ones he heard in the backyard, how they answered him. You smile, digging the next hole. Poor Dad. He so much wanted to be in touch with nature, even if just on the weekends. But it turned out he'd been whistling back and forth with his neighbor for years.

It's harder to travel into the future, but when a writer succeeds in doing this, the effect can be wonderful. "She had no way of knowing, when she tripped over his foot, that Sam would end up marrying her sister. She didn't know she wouldn't see him again for three years, and by that time the romance that might have been would have fizzled, she having married and had a child a year earlier. But that would be later, and now was now. And when Sam apologized for his big foot and begged to take her out for dinner some night to make up for it, she knew only that she found him attractive in a goofy sort of way. And, smiling, she scribbled her number on the back of his hand."

## Verbosity
Writers are a long-winded bunch. Why use one word when three will do—especially if one of those words is a fancy Latinish one? And so

we use circuitous ways to say something simple, and then we decorate with adjectives and adverbs. We're trying to sound like Authors, people who speak with English accents and nineteenth-century vocabularies. That is why a lot of entertaining storytellers create stilted, dull writing on the page. That is also why it's a good idea to go back, after you've let a piece of writing cook, and take out all the unnecessary words. An excessive use of modifiers indicates a lack of confidence in your reader . . . and in yourself. You don't trust the simpler sentences to convey your meaning, so you add to them until nothing is left for the reader to imagine. It's not necessary, for example, to say "black night." We know nights are generally black. If you say "silver night," however, we may go with you a while. Why is this one silver? Does the writer have a purpose or is he just being, Heaven forbid, poetic?

Nouns sometimes do need to be qualified to present a complete picture; verbs are almost always stronger if they are not. Someone who whispers softly is whispering, period. The trick is to find a verb that does the work of a verb and modifier. Strong action words, evocative action words, and action words packed with secondary associations are better choices usually than common verbs with adverbs attached. The latter tend to show a lazy writer at work. A child *scampering* is a child *running playfully*.

Remember: It's okay to take the easy way when you're writing a first draft. It's in the revision stage that you want to delete the unnecessary words and find the strong verbs.

**Try This:** Make a copy of a piece of your writing from your Cooking file and delete *all* the adverbs and adjectives. Read it back. In the places where the loss of the adverb weakens the meaning, see if you can find a verb that will convey not just the action but will carry the action's modification within itself—a man galumphing instead of walking heavily. Reinsert only the most necessary adjectives and adverbs. If the meaning can be conveyed without a qualifier, leave it out. Put the original piece of writing and the revision back into your Cooking file. Look at both one week later—the revised version first. Did your writing benefit from this sort of cleaning?

You may occasionally want to make your own verbs, although if you do this too often the Literary Police will need to see your Poetic

License. Try conjugating a noun. Zack, as a baby, for example, liked to "broom" with his little Minnie Mouse broom and dustpan. "I brooming the floor" was one of his early sentences. This particular verb is probably not something you want to use in your own writing. But a character, hoping to impress her date with her intellectual gifts, might "magazine" the coffee table with the latest issues of *The New York Review of Books* and *Harper's*.

**Try This:** Experiment with this technique a bit. Make a list of five sentences using verbs you invent by conjugating nouns. See if you can make powerful new verbs this way, verbs that evoke an action and are readily understood.

> It is comprehensible when I write: "The man sat on the grass," because it is clear and does not detain one's attention. On the other hand, it is difficult to figure out and hard on the brain if I write: "The tall, narrow-chested man of medium height and with a red beard sat down on the green grass that had already been trampled down by the pedestrians, sat down silently, looking around timidly and fearfully."
>
> —Anton Chekhov

## Voice

Writing is based on voice—the voice you hear in your head, the voices you make up when you try to tell your stories, the voices you are drawn to when you are walking down the street, eavesdropping. Writer David Long once called voice "the mind of the story," and I think that is true, whether the story is fiction or nonfiction. In the same way, I believe we are all storytellers. Sometimes the stories we tell are imagined, sometimes they are taken from life. Lore Segal told me how one time at a party someone asked how she had come to the United States. Everyone was listening as she related her refugee-child experiences. "And I thought," she told me, "'I have a story!'"

All of us have a story, but not all of us manage to get our story down on paper. Only those of us who do are writers. You can't be a writer if you tell great stories but never write. But that sense of story, of inner voice, is as essential as paper and ink. When I say writing cannot be taught, it is that writing sensibility I am talking about—the inner dialogue, the attraction to one kind of material and not another.

That is what you bring to the page—your innate rhythms and vocabulary choices and ideas. Your narrative voice as well as the voices you are perhaps more consciously making up—character voices—are all part of the way you hear, the way you are heard.

For Zack right now that voice is about humor. "Writing should be funny," he told me, "not just blah-blah-blah-blah, blah-blah-blah-blah. That gets really boring." For you, tragedy may be the thing: The stories you love best are those that make you cry. But Zack just saw *West Side Story* for the first time a few months ago. I had told him it was based on a play by Shakespeare. He loved the music, he loved the story . . . until the end. Then he turned to me, his face wet and mottled with emotion. "I *never* want to see that movie again in my life," he said. "And I don't think I'd like *Romeo and Juliet* either."

## Waking Up
Never end your story with, "And then I woke up."

> Borges used to say that when writers die they become books . . . . I think they become voices. In many conversations with Borges . . . I realized sharply that to him I existed only as a voice. . . . [I]t is in voices, far beyond photographs, that the dead continue to live.
>
> —Alistair Reid

# SEVENTEEN

# POINT OF VIEW

**E**udora Welty writes that ". . . point of view *is* an instrument, not an end in itself, that is useful as a glass, and not as a mirror to reflect a dear and pensive face. Conscientiously used, point of view will discover, explore, see through. . . . Misused, it turns opaque almost at once and gets in the way of the book."

What that means is: Don't play with point of view to show off your brilliance. Use it to tell your story clearly. Figure out which point of view is the best one to do that with, not which one presents the most flattering image of you.

There are two main points of view in writing—first person and third person. There is also a second-person voice that, while acceptable in a nonfiction book that directly addresses the reader (such as this one), is used too often by fiction writers who want to show their originality. "People who want to be original," Lore Segal said, "don't understand that being original means looking inside yourself and seeing what's there. Instead, they look around to see what's original so they can be like that." That is what the use of the second-person voice, the *you* voice, is largely about in fiction—a writer trying to show that he or she can be as original as anyone else. That doesn't mean the *you* voice can never be used, just you need to make sure your reason for using it isn't trendy.

Most of the time the *you* is really *I* in disguise, but sometimes the *you* is meant to be a character who is being addressed, perhaps reading the story. Sometimes the *you* is the reader—you. When this last form of address works it can be intimate and spooky, but readers usually fight it. The writer says, "You went into the room and took out the portrait of your mother," and the reader says, "No way." This is all to say: Use the second-person voice only if it serves your story.

> **TIP:** Limiting your point of view to one central perspective makes your writing more accessible to the reader. The more points of view you use, the more you risk losing your reader.

## FIRST PERSON

First person means writing in the *I* voice. The trick here is to stay in the first-person head. *I* can't know what other people are thinking or doing if *I* am not there to see them or someone hasn't told me. My story is limited to what the first-person narrator is privy to. Sometimes the writer *can* reveal through that first-person voice something that the narrator is not conscious of but that the attentive reader will get.

First-person narrators are often the main characters of the stories they are in. The events happen to them. They are telling us what these events are. They may understand these events differently than we do. This happens a lot of time when the first-person narrator is a child. Jaded as we all are by experience, we understand the man in the overcoat stopping to talk to little Abigail better than she does. That can create suspense, as we worry about our innocent first-person narrator who is telling us things she doesn't get but that make our hair stand like porcupine quills.

Another use of the first-person narrator is to tell us a story about someone else. This narrator is an observer. He or she is moved by the experience of a friend, acquaintance, or family member, and tells us what happened to that person. Perhaps the most famous use of this sort of narrator is Nick in *The Great Gatsby* telling us about Jay Gatsby. Nick himself hardly enters into the action he relates, but it is his sensibility that infuses the story with poignance.

When using such a narrator it is essential not to violate point of view. That is the tricky part about a first-person observer. In real life, stories that happen to someone else are usually inconclusive. We can only relate what we think or what we heard about the events. And sometimes not even that. But narrative writing that leaves the reader feeling like something happened but darn if I know what is not going to be writing a reader will enjoy. The writer needs to satisfy the reader

Point of View

when offering a sideways glance into someone else's life, or else the whole thing seems pointless.

**Try This:** Write about something that happened to you the other day—an argument on the checkout line of the local supermarket or an exchange between you and your teenage daughter. In the first version write it from the point of view of a first-person narrator who experiences the event. In the second version make the event happen to other people: The first-person narrator is telling us what he or she witnessed. The emphasis in the first version is on a participant; the emphasis in the second version is on an observer. Which way of handling first person most suits your own writing? If you are writing a memoir, you may also choose to concentrate on your own actions—the narrator as actor—or the events happening around you—the narrator as witness.

## THIRD PERSON

Third person comes primarily in two forms—limited and unlimited. A limited third-person narrator is essentially a first-person narrator using the *he/she* voice. The perspective is limited to that one main character's consciousness, with the occasional outside look at him or her, although if you do the outside view too often people in your writing workshop will jump on you, saying you've betrayed point of view. I wouldn't worry overmuch about this. Just stick to your main character's point of view, and don't pop into other characters' heads for a look-see. But if you occasionally float up to the ether for a pan now and then, that's okay even if, going strictly by the book, that *is* betraying point of view. There's betrayal and there's *betrayal*. I mean, you can't tell us about events your main character doesn't know about. But I don't see anything wrong with describing your main character briefly as seen through the eyes of an unnamed observer. In a writing workshop, however, someone with a high, whiny voice will say, "Your character can't see himself so objectively. He wouldn't think of himself in such a self-conscious way." Just smile and nod your head, and remember Emerson, who wrote: "Consistency is the hobgoblin of little minds." But if *everyone* who reads your story is disconcerted by the way your point of view is jumping around, maybe there *is* something wrong in your handling of it.

119

Let's look at appearance again. A first-person narrator describing his own appearance will sound narcissistic or silly—sometimes that's the point. But writing that uses a third-person limited voice can get away with such description. It doesn't have to be read as how the character sees himself, although it can be. The reader can be told how that character walks, his gait, his body language, his attitude, what he is wearing, what he is whistling. Such self-consciousness on the part of a first-person narrator is like being with someone who's always looking into the mirror as he talks to you. But readers will accept such information about a third-person character more easily, even if you've been limiting yourself to that character's point of view till then. Most writers using third-person limited go in and out. They come in close to their main character's head, then retreat. That's why you choose third person. A true betrayal of point of view would be for the writer to dip into someone else's thoughts after establishing a point of view limited to one character. That's the sort of thing that makes readers fling their books into the distant sand. We can't see action or hear dialogue that our third-person narrator is not privy to.

Some writers get around that limitation by alternating point of view in different chapters of a book. The reader gets Joe's point of view in chapter one, and Mildred's point of view in chapter two. These two points of view may go back and forth like this, or the daring author may introduce other points of view in other chapters. *In Cold Blood*, which Truman Capote described as a "nonfiction novel," was written in alternating viewpoints, for example, a technique more commonly featured in novels today than when Capote first wrote his book.

The proviso is that you cannot violate point of view in any chapter, giving us Mildred's perspective during Joe's chapter, for instance. This limitation can create havoc with time, forcing the writer to give us a scene twice (or more), each time showing the same action from a different perspective. Also, if the action in a chapter is happening concurrent with the action in a different chapter, the writer needs to let the reader know that. The forward movement of time is assumed in the march of chapters, unless otherwise indicated.

Third-person unlimited narration is, of course, another way to offer the reader more than one perspective. This approach is difficult to do well and can have an antiquated feel to it. Natural enough, since it was more commonly used in the nineteenth century. You need to establish early on that you have an omniscient narrator who can pop into anyone's head at will. The writer of third-person unlimited narration often starts with an overview, as if the narrative voice were that of someone on a cloud, seeing from high above the actions of the little puppet people below. Then the roving eye zooms in to one character's perspective, bops out to give us the outer view, then pops into someone else's head for a few sensory descriptions.

Movement between heads in third-person unlimited can be done through the use of gesture and gesture-observed. If you have two characters speaking, for instance, you can have one of them push the hair away from her face. The other character noticing that gesture will give us entry into his head. Another way to create movement between consciousnesses is to mediate through the use of an outer perspective. It is easier to move from one head into space and then into another head than to try to go head to head.

**Try This:** Go back to the story you told in first person of an event that happened the other day. Now tell it in third person, picking any (or all, if you're ambitious) of the people involved as your limited point-of-view character. You might even experiment with moving in and out of the various heads—pretend you are the director of a play and can enter each consciousness at will. What flavors do the different voices have? What limitations?

One final thought on point of view: It is a bad idea to use the inner life of a pet—an old dog or a goldfish, for example. It is best to present such animal points of view in a fable-like or allegorical manner, Orwell's *Animal Farm* being a good example. That's not to say a more "realistic" approach can't be used. Chekhov gives us the points of view of the harbor pilot fish and the shark about to eat his main character's body in "Gusev." But you want to make sure, if you give us a nonhuman perspective, that your writing is more like Chekhov's and less like a Hallmark greeting card.

> A novelist can shift his point of view if it comes off, and it came off with Dickens and Tolstoy.
>
> —E.M. Forster

**EIGHTEEN**

# HOOK, LINE, AND SINKER

**F**irst of all, I don't fish.

Except for ideas in my murky unconscious where little swims but much crawls, I know nothing of throwing a line, dangling a hook, or jabbing Moby Dick with a spear. The *hook* I refer to is the thing you use in your writing to catch your reader. The *line* is the occasional burst of wisdom or surprise that brightens the page and makes the reader feel he's getting something. The *sinker*? Well, I don't know what the sinker is except a way to make a title for this chapter. Maybe the sinker is what brings the whole thing down. The disappointment after a buildup. The thing you don't want to do. All I have to say about sinkers is avoid them. They spoil a reader's day. I'm sorry if I've spoiled yours.

Back to hooks then.

Hooks are generally used in the beginning of stories, memoirs, feature articles, even screenplays, and at the end of chapters. There can be an element of mystery to them. They may state the impossible, and the reader reads on to find out how that can be so. They may hint at a later development, and the reader can't put the book down before finding out how that came about. The least interesting hooks, I think, pertain to plot, what E.M. Forster calls "story." He says that story answers the question, And then? while plot asks, Why? To me it seems the exact opposite, so I need to clarify my terms a bit. When the reader wants to know what's going to happen next, as one adventure leads to another and another, this is a function of what I call plot and is the basis of action novels. Airplane books that keep the reader going through a nine-hour transatlantic flight provide hooks at the end of each chapter that are of the cliffhanging variety. There's a bomb on board. The hero gets rid of it but has a heart attack. The heart attack is not fatal but there's another bomb on board; the first one was a decoy. The blast makes the door come off the plane. The heroine is falling out, held on only by a hair ribbon that's gotten caught on a jagged piece of metal. The jagged piece of metal tears the hair ribbon but the hero grabs her by the ponytail. Then the pilot has a heart attack. And on and on.

There's nothing wrong with such hooks. They don't add up to anything at the end, but if they help you make it across the Atlantic Ocean without having to jump out of the plane, they're worth it. But I prefer hooks with wiggling worms on the end: Something mysterious beckons. A seeming impossibility. A secret circled again and again, each time a little more of it revealed.

David Lodge in *Small World* refers to the Dance of the Seven Veils that writing does, enticing the reader with a tease of secrets revealed and delay in revealing them. The conclusion of a striptease, after all, is always the same. It's the dance, the play of revealing and concealing, that makes it exciting.

A writer involves me in his or her work by striking the right balance between being cryptic and being open. The important thing is the payoff. It's easy to be mysterious and not give anything away. I hate writers who seem to throw their hands up and say, "I wrote it. Now you figure it out." But I feel immensely satisfied when I read something like Toni Morrison's *Song of Solomon* and keep coming up against strangeness that leads me on, knowing as I do that eventually I will receive revelation. Novels like that are great to read more than once—the first time to be led along, the second time to watch the writer perform her tricks.

I'll again use a fishing analogy I have no right to since I don't fish, but you know those tugs fishermen do, when they let out a line and pull

The dancer teases the audience, as the text teases its readers, with the promise of an ultimate revelation that is infinitely postponed. Veil after veil, garment after garment, is removed, but it is the *delay* in the stripping that makes it exciting, not the stripping itself; because no sooner has one secret been revealed than we lose interest in it and crave another.

—David Lodge in *Small World*

it in a few times? They do this over and over till something is finally hooked. That's what catches me. I can never resist a dancing hook.

The hook can be a reference to what the reader doesn't know yet but will if he or she reads on. But the hook can also be the line; that is, sometimes we read for the poetry or the wit, because the lines are so great. It's not a matter of answering the questions, "And then?" or "Why?" We read for beauty. Or sometimes for laughs. Because the writer has a way of turning a phrase that makes us feel like *we're* on our heads.

A writer has to be careful with lines though. If they get too tangled the reader gets away, but if they lie too straight they never entice that reader to take the bait in the first place. You want to present the reader with a line that is true—the glint off the river that makes the reader say, "I've seen the river like that. That's just right." Or it might be a simple line that gains extraordinary power from its placement. A non sequitur. A refutation of everything that came before it. A confirmation of the same. A perfect succinct summary—three words that convey a paragraph of meaning. Sometimes the line is an aphorism. Sometimes a witticism. Whatever it is, the line stops the reader for a moment. He or she repeats it aloud, says it to a friend, circles it, writes it in a notebook. Or just tastes it a while before reading on.

One of the great pleasures of reading is the tasting of lines. Readers are fish who most definitely want to be caught. A hook dangles and we rush right over to investigate. A line is thrown out and we nibble at it. Your job as writer is to provide the hooks at the beginnings and ends of chapters, and to carefully place your lines. In short, to do whatever you can to keep the reader in a feeding frenzy.

I still don't know anything about sinkers, except it's best if your reader swallows yours along with the hooks and the lines.

**Try This:** Hook me. Make a list of at least five openers—a paradox, a bit of dialogue, a surprise that, in a sentence or two, will draw the reader in. See if you can come up with another list of chapter endings that will make it impossible for the reader not to read on.

**TIP:** Hooks at the beginning of chapters serve to engage the reader. Hooks at the end, in addition, can provide continuity in a larger work—hooking one chapter to the next as well as hooking the reader.

# NINETEEN

# EXERCISES

Writing exercises, like physical ones, keep you limber and burn away the flab. I always have a first-night assignment for my writing workshop, a one-page story or fragment with a theme that in some ways reflects the interests of the workshop. We go around the room reading these aloud, which is why I ask that they be so short. You don't have to limit yourself in terms of length. Below are some exercises I've used, and some I haven't yet. I use the term "character" to mean a person you are writing about. It can be invented, based on a real person, or a stand-in for you.

1. Meet a character from your novel, story, or book. Have him or her tell you a secret.

2. Take a character in a novel you have read and meet him or her someplace. If the character is from a contemporary novel, you may want to use a different name to make him or her yours. If the character is a classic, you may draw on the common pool of familiarity—somewhat like Woody Allen spoofing on Emma Bovary (and himself) in "The Kugelmass Episode."

3. Take a novel you have read and write a story that predates events in it. Again, if it is a contemporary novel you may wish to change character names and location to make it your own. If it is a classic novel you can keep the specific details, but give us the backstory. Jean Rhys's *Wide Sargasso Sea*, for example, takes the madwoman in the

attic from Charlotte Bronte's *Jane Eyre* and gives us her childhood in the Caribbean.

4. Write a third-person scene in which a character is lying. Make it clear through gesture and other action that he or she is not speaking the truth.

5. Write from the point of view of a character whose gender is opposite of your own. Have him or her confess something.

6. A key, a map, and a soda can—write a story that uses these three elements, making them in some way integral to the plot. You can use any number of disparate elements. If this sort of story exercise works for you, put the names of a bunch of things in a bag, choose three or four at random, then write the story.

7. Take a short poem and analyze it in terms of parts of speech (e.g., article, noun, verb), keeping the integrity of the line breaks intact. Now make grab bags of parts of speech and fill in the blanks. What comes out may spur a real poem. Feel free to play with it afterward.

8. Two characters meet and tell secrets or lies. Write the story first from outside, not going into either character's head. Then write from one character's point of view. Then write from the other's. You can start before the meeting, and you can continue past the meeting when you are writing from either limited point of view. Finally, try writing from both points of view, dipping in and out of the two characters' heads at will. Try to make the dipping seamless.

9. Take a snatch of overheard dialogue and go with it. Who are the speakers? What happens to them? Make a story out of eavesdropping.

10. You see someone on the street or on the bus who intrigues you. Give him or her a voice. Have him tell his story in an internal monologue. Listen in to her thoughts.

11. There is a knock on the door. Your character opens it. He or

she is surprised. Stunned, happy, angry, frightened? Go with it.

12. You are walking down the street. A child comes up to you and says, "Come quick." You go and find—what?

13. Write a scene in which the main character grapples with the death of someone. It doesn't have to be a deathbed scene. It's probably better if it's not. The further removed from the actual death it is, the more effective it may be.

14. Go to a public place and write what happens in the next five minutes. Remember to catch the senses—the smells, tastes, sounds, as well as sights and overheard dialogue.

15. Do an interior monologue from your mother's point of view.

16. Walk down the street, then recapture that walk. Again, pay attention to all the senses.

17. Pretend you are a time traveler from the distant future. Write what you see, being sure to include mistakes in perception and convoluted descriptions of things humans take for granted.

18. Read a folk story or fairy tale, and then write an updated version of it.

19. Write an urban myth. Crocodiles in the New York City sewer system (from all those tiny pet crocodiles getting flushed down the toilet) is an example of one. Let your paranoia run rampant. Make a story out of the myth.

20. Look in a story anthology. Pick a title (you may want to do this at random, closing your eyes and just pointing) and write your own story.

21. Open a book at random and let your finger fall wherever. Read the sentence and try to build a story around it. Alternatively, read the entire paragraph and see what it sparks off.

22. Write a recipe for love. If you like it, give it to a character. Have that character give it to someone else.

23. Write a story with a friend, taking turns supplying words, sentences, or paragraphs. This is fun to do with a kid.

24. Write a story in the present tense in which a character goes about his or her daily routine, then something happens to break the pattern.

25. Think of something you lost long ago. Suddenly you find it. What happens?

26. Something is lost, not long ago but now. What is lost? What does the character do?

27. Take a character from history and give him or her a voice. You might use an incidental character to tell the familiar story of the more famous person, with his or her own take on it. Thomas Mallon does this in *Henry and Clara* by giving us the eponymous characters who were with Abraham Lincoln at the theater the night he was shot.

28. You are given a magic object. What is it? What power does it give you? What happens when you use it? You can do this with different objects or granted wishes, using first or third person. It can be written as a fairy tale. It can also be modern macabre, a surreal take on surprising events.

29. How did your great-grandfather die? You probably only have the barest bones, so to speak, of the story, so you will have the freedom to invent. Write about other people from your ancestral village—those who didn't have children, who died young or unmarried, whose stories didn't get passed down.

30. You go into your room and discover a cupboard you never noticed before, although you realize it has been there all along. Open the door. What do you find? What happens?

31. Take a book of historical photographs and pick one. If there are people in it, make one your character. Bring him or her to life. If there are no people, people the place.

32. Look at an old photo album and pick a photograph at random. Who is the person in the picture? Make up a story that he or she tells to the photographer just before the picture is taken. Set it in the time period shown. Help us know the photographer by what the subject says.

33. Get an astrology book and read about the twelve signs. Now pick two and create characters with those astrological characteristics. Don't give us their signs. This is just for you to know. Take two incompatible signs and have them misunderstand each other. Have them fight. They may be members of the same family. They may be strangers who come in contact with each other in a bar. They both want something, but each wants in opposition to the other.

34. Eat a banana. Describe the event in detail. Try an orange. An apple. A kiwi.

35. Pick a favorite painting and describe it to a blind person.

36. Describe a favorite piece of music to a deaf person.

37. Describe a sensation to someone who is dead. Bring that person back to life by doing so. Reawaken him or her by reminding him/her of what's been lost.

38. A ghost comes to you. Describe him/her/it. What does the ghost say or do? Why does the ghost come to you? Make the story scary. Make it funny. Make it strange.

39. Have a third-person character tell a ghost story to a first-person listener. Does the listener believe the story? Describe his or her reactions, concentrating more on outer actions than internal thoughts.

40. Someone wrote something on your back but you can't read it.

You know it's there, and you need to convince someone to tell you what it says. The "convincing" is the story, but we also want to know what it says.

41. You wake up and find you have been transformed—into what? How do people react to you? What do you do? Kafka already made Gregor Samsa into an insect, so try something else.

42. Read a short poem you like aloud several times. Now pace slowly and see if any fragments of original poetry come to you. Woo the mood.

43. Did you ever disappoint someone you loved? Write the story of what happened, using the third person. If possible, write this in the voice of the person you disappointed.

44. Someone finds an old manuscript in an attic or basement or buried in the backyard. Who finds it? Who wrote it? What does it say? Why was it buried or hidden?

45. Someone buried something in your backyard, not knowing you were watching. What do you do after he or she leaves?

46. You are sitting in a coffee shop. A mysterious man or woman walks by and hands you a piece of paper. He or she leaves before you get a chance to read the note. What do you do?

47. Why did your parents get married? Give us two characters, two points of view. You can go back to the time of their courtship, or you can have them speaking now. They don't just *tell* you though. They hint, they accuse, they drop things. It's like a puzzle. They give you pieces but you still have to put it together.

48. Do a mosaic story, using fragments that somehow, when put in juxtaposition to each other, create a whole. You are not limited to first or third person in such a story. You can change tenses too. But there needs to be something to drive the story—mystery, suspense, poetry, theme. If the first-person character is also the third-person character

in other fragments you need to signal that to us somehow. This can be a more difficult story to read than to write, so you need to help the reader. That's where your ingenuity comes in.

49. The woman next door is planning to murder you. What do you do about it?

50. He wants a baby; she doesn't. They love each other but can't agree on this. They go out to dinner with another couple who tells them that the wife has cancer. The husband has been having an affair for a year and was planning to leave her, but because of the cancer he hasn't said or done anything. You, the writer, know this about the husband, but none of the other characters do. It may not come out in the story. It's just something to keep in mind as he speaks and does things. All four characters have something important inside, which may or may not come out. You know all secrets but may choose to keep the tension palpable by not revealing them. Still, it should be clear by the end of the story what is going on, even if it is never baldly stated. Try doing this story from outside all four characters. Later, monkey around with different points of view.

51. The above exercise can be done in any number of ways with any number of characters. Just give each character a secret, then have them do something mundane. Have them talk *around* what is troubling them. Have them say or do things that hint at the greater issues.

52. You find a child in your backyard. He or she cannot speak. What do you do? What happens? Where does the child come from? What happened to him or her? Do you find out?

53. You were abandoned or lost as a small child and raised by animals. You are found by humans and taken away from the animals that raised you. You are feral and never acquire the sort of language you need to tell your tale, but inside you are human and can express human qualities. Give us the internal monologue of such a character, remembering his or her limitations without trying to capture the language inability. (That would make you crazy.) The reader will need

to suspend disbelief here to believe in this voice. This is a variation on the if-your-cat-could-talk story, only less hokey, with more potential for emotional resonance.

54. Write a story about a villain, showing compassion for him or her without taking away from the atrocity of villainous action.

55. Write the Hansel and Gretel story from the witch's point of view.

56. Express an emotion through one of the following actions—eating a steak, buying groceries, feeding an infant, putting gas in a car. The emotion should have nothing to do with the action—love while feeding an infant is too easy—but should not be absurd—fear while putting gas in a car is too silly. The emotion should be in regard to something that happened before or after the action, not in response to the action itself.

57. Create an action that helps us understand the character doing it. The action can be a hobby or something the character does as part of a routine. Have it function as a metaphor for the character. Lady Macbeth washing her hands is a classic example.

58. You are invisible. What do you do? Where do you go? What happens?

59. You acquire the ability to change in size. How do you use this power?

60. How do you fly in your flying dreams? Describe it in detail. Make it as real for us as walking.

61. Describe walking. How do you balance, move your limbs? Describe any everyday action or activity to someone who has never done it—drinking tea, plucking eyebrows, urinating.

62. Take an early memory and have a character think about it while doing something. The memory is continually interrupted by the demands of the present activity. The reminiscing character should reveal through gesture or through perceived details of space something about the memory that isn't stated.

Sanity in a writer is merely this: However stupid he may be in his private life, he never cheats in writing. He never forgets that his audience is, at least ideally, as noble, generous, and tolerant as he is himself (or more so).
—John Gardner

# TWENTY

# WRITING TRANCES AND RITUALS

**W**e return our focus now to finding inspiration, time, and energy to write. To do so we need to look at the pleasure of writing when it's going well and explore ways to achieve that state of dream.

Soon after my husband and I started living together, he learned to make noise before coming into my writing space. He learned to do this because if he didn't I would get startled and scream. That would startle him and he would scream. It was *Night of the Living Dead* meets Edvard Munch till we worked things out.

When I write, especially when the writing takes off, I fall into a trancelike state in which I dream with my eyes open. This is why I write. It is the opium I crave, this entry into another state of consciousness. I used to think it meant I was a great writer, that it was proof of my "genius." I also used to think it meant I was a nut who zapped into hallucination as soon as her husband shut the door—*Diary of a Mad Housewife* with computer. I now realize it merely means I am writing.

Many writers I have spoken to experience this daydreaming-on-paper state, at least sometimes, and we all agree: This is the high of writing. Madison Smartt Bell goes "back and forth between dreaming the images and finding the words to describe them," but he considers all of it "part of the concentration on the writing."

I don't know about you, but I daydream very intensely. I didn't realize how intensely till I got married and my husband began watching me. "Who are you talking to?" he'd ask. Or, "Why'd you shake your head?" Or, "What are you making that face for?" Or, "How come you're smiling?" I'd want to punch him in the nose. This was worse than coming into my writing space without clearing his throat. He was entering my dream, and I hadn't invited him. Now the dream was lost and I was feeling self-conscious. Not only self-conscious but exposed. It was like finding out you talk in your sleep, then you're up nights wondering what you said and what you *might* say. No sooner did I break my husband of this habit than our son got old enough to do it.

Writing is a form of self-hypnosis. John Gardner says that good writing should read like a vivid, continuous dream. It should read that way because that is what it is. We dream on paper, and there is a flow, an organic shape to the dream. That doesn't mean you don't edit afterward. There is always the afterward in which you revise and pull your hair out. But let's concentrate on the fun for a while. Let's talk about the dream.

There are ways to induce the writing trance, and these can be silly and embarrassing to admit to, but I like you so I'm going to share this stuff with you. First of all, though, let me say that maybe you don't need a ritual to get yourself into the appropriate mood. Evan Russell just sits down and his fingers are flying. He has so much to say, he told me, that it's all he can do to get himself to the keyboard before he's writing. For the rest of us mortals it ain't so easy. But I can remember the days of yore when I used to start writing the moment my husband left for work; if he dared come back because he forgot his keys or something, I'd sling arrows of outrageous annoyance at him till he quickly left again.

Part of the ease of "trancing" then was due to the fact I was working on a novel. A first novel. The grand vessel for every rumination, fantasy, and desire I'd had for the past twenty-five years, which was how old I was when I started.

That old stream of consciousness doesn't babble as it used to, but when I am working on a novel and know my characters, I generally have an idea where I want them to go. Then I can sit down, crack a few knuckles, stare out the window, and get started. This is because I've induced the trance earlier, thinking about what I wanted to write. I've already dreamed it.

This is a good thing to do if you want to write but find you have trouble getting yourself to do it: Build up a head of steam first, thinking about your writing. Try to come up with a starting sentence or image. Maybe you'll throw it out later, but have something to get you going before you face that dreaded blank page. Some of the rituals I know may help you do that.

Walking works for me, although I live in an annoyingly friendly neighborhood and have to wear headphones and exercise clothes, and not make eye contact, to avoid my annoyingly friendly neighbors. But maybe you live on the edge of a deep dark woods. Maybe you can walk for days without seeing anyone but a muskrat. That sounds ideal for establishing a walking ritual. It will put a bloom in your cheeks and ideas in your brain—as long as you can walk in those deep dark woods thinking about your writing and not about ax murderers.

I plot while I plod, stopping occasionally to scribble a note. In other words, I work out an outline—first in my head, then on paper. It's a very broad outline, and it gets changed a lot. In the end I have a sheet of paper with arrows and asterisks and writing that goes up and down the margins, circles with lines shooting this way and that.

I was once working in the Periodicals Reading Room of the Forty-Second Street Public Library, a great temple of a place with vaulted ceilings, wood paneling and paintings, and long mahogany tables at which scholars write furiously and shopping-bag ladies snore in short, surreptitious snorts (if they're caught sleeping the guard kicks them out). The man next to me was working away. I assumed he was a scholar till I checked out his garb, which was sufficiently ragged for me to decide he was homeless. The way he was scribbling led to my further assumption he was crazy. Curious, I kept sneaking peeks at his scrawl. He was moving his lips, muttering to himself, writing up and down the margins, making arrows and upside-down sentences. The complete insanity of what he was composing was evident in the manner in which his squiggles decorated the page, even though I couldn't make out a word. That was when I looked down at my own sheets of chicken scratch. Like Chuang Tse, who woke up from a dream of being a butterfly and didn't know if he were a man who dreamt he was a butterfly or a butterfly who was dreaming he was a man, I didn't know if the man next to me was a writer or if I was crazy too.

Until you actually publish something, this doubt hides in the shadows of your mind, ready to jump you whenever you let down your guard. But dreaming a long work through can confirm your reality. It helps you see the sense in the concept. As you dream it from beginning to end, you shape it. The process of doing so helps the unconscious set the pace. Then when the writing takes off it may feel instinctive, this sense you have that this chapter needs to be long and that one has to have dramatic events, and after that there should be a serene flashback offset by sudden action. You feel it, the way a sculptor feels the need for a concave part here to balance the protrusion there. This is how it works for me. The writing has an organic shape, even if I end up moving pieces around. "Writing is really in the mind," Peter Rubie agreed, "like figuring out moves ahead in chess. Physically sitting down to produce words is the least of it."

## CREATING RITUALS

But I promised to tell you about rituals. First of all, let me dispel any hope you have for hocus-pocus, that there is a magic chant I can teach you that will enable you to write like Dostoevsky. Really, all I can tell you is that rituals sometimes help a writer overcome the initial dread and induce the trance. In the end you invent your own rituals, which may be as simple as brewing coffee, taking a walk, or turning on the computer and saying, "Okey-Dokey."

Don't frown at this. All rituals gain in importance the more you work with them. You don't have to sing "Row Your Boat" backward in Latin or smear the blood of a lamb on your laptop under a full moon. Go for simplicity. Go for what has meaning for you. When you find a ritual you like, stick to it for a while so that it becomes the "on button" to your creative process, the signal to your writing self that it is okay to take chances now. You have invoked the god of creation who will protect you from the god of criticism.

What might your ritual be? Breathing is a good one: It benefits the body and the soul. In yoga you breathe in through one nostril and out through the other, and whenever I try to do it I sneeze. It's like perfecting your crawl—some swimmers glide along so effortlessly you think you can do it too, and some swimmers snort water and have to be rescued by the lifeguard. You don't have to get fancy to breathe. Use breathing to center yourself, to quiet your self-doubts and anxiety. Inhale to the count of four, expanding your diaphragm as you do so. Then exhale slowly to the count of eight. Concentrate on the breathing and counting, not on how you're wasting time. After a few minutes, a sense of calm and well-being should come over you. Then you are ready to begin.

I know people who light candles and stare into the flames till they conjure the creative mood. Others don articles of clothing to signify they are about to undertake a sacred act. A hat can function as a creativity crown. A shirt as a robe of enlightenment. A ring given to you by a sympathetic aunt or a scarf that belonged to someone you love may remind you that these are the people you are writing for—not the ones who think you're a total drip. I used to put on my desk a talisman, a little toy animal that had been given to me by a writer friend. It served to remind me that someone believed in me. Steve Schwartz surrounds himself with pictures of writers he admires and people he loves, "those whose presence makes me try to be as good as I can be." A woman someone I know dated had a writing desk she wouldn't let anyone else use. She wouldn't even let others sit in her chair. The object or ritual itself doesn't matter as much as finding something that reverberates for you and using it.

In the end, once you are writing freely, able to detach yourself from the Watchers who perch on your shoulders waiting for any mistake, you may find you don't need a ritual anymore to get you going. Maureen Brady used to burn incense and speak to the voices that said, "Who do you think you are? What makes you think anyone wants to hear what you have to say?" She did this "to ritualize the notion that it was okay to write," but eventually she could just "light the match and skip all the wordiness." Now she doesn't even do that—she just writes when she has a free hour or two.

Lore Segal's ritual is the simplest of all: Seven o'clock in the morning she sits down to write, seven days a week. She has arranged her life around that. "My family knows not to get sick or need me in the morning," she joked. She accepts that sometimes nothing will come out during that time. But the ritual is the time itself. Seven o'clock is sacrosanct and has been for almost all of the years she has been writing. It started in her twenties when she was one of three couples who spent the summer in Connecticut. "Every day someone would say, Let's go to the swimming hole, let's go to the museum. And I would always say, I'm sorry, I can't go. I haven't written yet. Then I would tag along. There was a point at which my friend said to me, This is getting tiresome. You will get up in the morning at seven o'clock. You will sit at your typewriter for half an hour. You will either write or you won't write, and we will hear no more about it for the rest of the day. This was a revelation, and it is the basis for my answer to the question of how you can get yourself to write."

Your ritual doesn't have to be laden with *gravitas*. Lori Perkins makes popcorn. Ellen Dreyer has toy mice—a tiny bronze one and a fuzzy finger puppet. "I play with them," she said, "and they help me have, I don't know, courage I guess." Playing is as essential to writing as discipline. Free yourself to have fun, to fantasize the way you did as a kid, to fool around, like someone noodling at the piano till a tune comes along. Isn't that what drew you to writing in the first place— having a grand old time, making sentences that became stories? Writing is still a serious business—you need to put writing above cleaning the toilet or buying mangos—but the writing itself doesn't have to be serious. Have fun. Dare to be silly. Explore. If a funny thought comes into your head, write it. Something embarrassing? Great. Go for the scatalogical. Maybe it will come to nothing, but at the very least you will have a good time.

**Try This:** Write about a ritual you had as a kid. How did you do it? What was it for? Did you avoid stepping on cracks in the sidewalk because you didn't want to break your mother's back? How about a bedtime routine to ward off nightmares? A way to take tests so you'd pass? After writing about it, think about the ritual. Is there anything in it you can use for a writing ritual?

• Write about a magic object or place of power you had as a kid. How did you use the object or the place? What did it grant you? Can you develop a writing ritual out of that?

## RITUALS FOR SELF-CONFIDENCE
Two things operate in a writer's desire for rituals—the need for self-esteem and a method for finding the tunnel down. You may therefore develop different rituals for esteem problems and for self-hypnosis. I have a number of routines I do before writing. I don't *always* do them. Sometimes my self-confidence needs the boost; sometimes it doesn't. There are times when I can enter the dream in a zip. Other times I lose faith in my ideas.

Like Lore Segal, I find it essential to have a writing time. Some things are best done on automatic pilot. Sitting down to write is one of them. I don't think about it—shall I write or shall I make tuna fish sandwiches? There are no decisions to be made. I sit down, turn on the computer, and try to start writing before self-doubt has a chance to kick in.

But there are days when I sit at my desk at the appointed time. I crack my knuckles. I make coffee. I make tea. I look at the telephone as if I could *will* it to ring. At these times I need help creating the space in which to write.

The first thing I do is try to take some of the ego out of my desire to write. It's not about being great or famous, I tell myself. It's about being in touch with something (forgive me) *other*. I force myself to remember writing is a holy act. This may not help you, but it's how I think of writing—as a form of prayer. Barry Denny is another writer who finds this way of looking at it useful. Writing is a "substitute for religion," he told me. He uses Buddhist ideas about all beings seeking happiness as a way for him to enter the heads of his characters, and he says writing is "a vehicle to discover who I am and to help me be better."

So sometimes my writing day begins with a prayer. It's not something out of a book but more a talking in my head. I address the spirit I want to reach through the day—in my writing and in my being as fully alive as I can be. I pray for the ability to witness the mundane miracles, and not to surrender to laziness or despair.

It's hard to admit such a thing publicly. I'm sure it sends a shiver down some spines to know that they have been taking my words seriously till now and I've just confessed I think God and I go tête-à-tête over capuccino in the morning. But I am not proselytizing. I do not say you need to start *your* day with prayer. You can start the day shrieking curses at your aging mother if that feeds you. Prayer is how I enter the world of the dream. It is what puts me in touch with my voice. It gives me the sense of belief I need to face the page.

I sometimes close my eyes before beginning my writing day and try to imagine a blankness. I look behind my forehead. If I do this just right I sometimes see a nostril. One nostril. But what a nostril! It stands for a whole face. That one black hole sometimes lets me in. It is waiting, it is with me, it has chosen me. Whatever you do, the point is you want to come out of yourself and lose self-consciousness. You want to make your mind receptive to the voice that tells its story through you. You want to hypnotize yourself into belief—in your writing and in you.

You might try looking in the mirror, instilling self-belief by willing love for the person you see. Encouraging the child you once were. You wouldn't punch a kid in the nose who was trying to tell you something, so if you see yourself as your own child maybe you can stop beating up on the kid. "I believe in you," you might tell that child instead. "You're the only one who can write this. You have been *chosen* to write this."

Chosen by what, you may ask. Ah, now things are getting dicey. I do believe that something *has* chosen you, has given you the talent and the ideas and the experience to do what you are trying to. To me, that chosenness is about God, but if you don't believe in God you are still chosen. You chose yourself. You can address the *wish* inside you to write. The important thing in all this is love—for yourself, for the story you have to tell, for the world you want to reveal.

This is starting to sound like I'm telling you to put flowers in your hair and head to your nearest outdoor music festival. Well, stand back. It gets worse. Because the next thing I'm going to write about is mantras. I suggest you make a mantra for yourself, something that will enable you to believe in yourself and in what you are trying to do. "I am a good writer," said over and over, for example, can drown out the voices that tell you you are not. The thing is you have to say it until you believe it. You need to say it in the face of all the demons who come to tell you what a shitty writer you are, how you've never gotten anything published or, if you have, how you didn't get the good reviews you wanted, the recognition you crave, the admiration of your peers, that if you really were a good writer all those things and much more would have come to you.

These demon voices, they're not any more believable than the ones that tell us we are geniuses. We just give them much more credence, especially when it is morning in America and that blank page is grinning over our desks like a sardonic sunrise. You need a way to drive away the fear that you are deluded. Because if you let in the demons of doubt, they'll eat your heart still beating rather than let out what is in it. So, even if you feel ridiculous, standing in front of the mirror talking to yourself about how you believe in you, do it anyway. See the child you were. The child had stories to tell and no one listened.

You be the listener now. The loving grownup who didn't exist for the child when he or she was little. "You can tell me anything," you might say. "I believe what you are telling me."

You feel ridiculous, right? But feeling ridiculous is just another guise of the devil. He doesn't always wear the red suit with the tail and horns. That makes *him* feel ridiculous. Sometimes he likes to dress as a clown and mock you as you stand before yourself, trying to do something courageous. He will make fun of every word you put down, if you let him. So you have to banish him instead. You banish him with love. Love for yourself. Love for the kid you were. Love for the being who chose you. The muse. You want to know how you know you're chosen? It's simple. It's because you *want* to write. If you really want to write, if you really feel the urge inside you and it's not just that you wish to have written, to be famous for what you have accomplished, then that is a sign you have been chosen. You wouldn't have been chosen if you didn't have something to say.

Some people can't stand this sort of thing. "I want a better muse," Martha Schulman told me. "Something like Alice Walker's maybe. Where her characters talk to her or come to her in dreams. Or one of those demanding muses that doesn't let you rest. Mine lets me rest just fine."

It's like my son with the Tooth Fairy. I don't know why we persist in telling him the Tooth Fairy is coming for his tooth when he always says, "I know you're the one leaving the money under my pillow." If he did believe in the Tooth Fairy, we'd probably worry. Nonetheless we play this little game. He puts his tooth under his pillow and the next morning there's the buck. You be that way too. You don't have to believe in the muse to seek her help. Just keep looking under the pillow for the buck.

I think the problem is the way people envision the muse, like there's this naked lady who whispers poetry in your ear, and you get to smile at her, point and wink and say, "Got it," and just write it all down. There are no naked ladies floating around my head when I'm writing. People who think writing is about possession and not about hard work are in for some jolts of unpleasant reality. You *can't* wait for inspiration. Martha Schulman knows this. She paraphrased Flannery O'Connor for me, who said she just showed up at her desk at roughly the same time every day, so that if inspiration should visit, it would find her at home.

But, as Charlotte Bronte wrote in *Jane Eyre*, "The eagerness of a listener quickens the tongue of a narrator." This holds true for listeners we can see through as well as the fleshy kind. "My muse is the imagined reader at the end of the road or scene or even the good sentence," Evan Russell told me. "In a sense, I am my own muse."

For me, too, the *muse* is a listener. A receptivity. But the muse is also receptivity on *my* part, a will to wonder. A slowness. Fellow writer Emily Russell (no relation to Evan) told me that an hour spent watching a spider crawl up a wall . . . she would consider that, too, writing. So would I. The muse gives, but she doesn't give something for nothing. You have to be alive and aware and open to what otherwise passes unnoticed.

I have this feather I sometimes use to still the disparaging voices and enter the dreamy state. I found it when I was hiking twenty years ago. It is small, and when I found it on a rock by the side of the trail, it was brown and ordinary. I don't know why I picked it up, it was so plain. But when I did I discovered this shock of gold on the other side—a gift from the Tooth Fairy.

I have found that sometimes it helps to pick out one person—a real person you know, or an imagined person, and write to that one.
—John Steinbeck

**Try This:** Stand naked before a mirror and look at the person you see, not with judging eyes but with a sort of detached love and tenderness. That person is not you. It is not your place to look at the fat or the blemishes. A human being stands before you, frail and scared but worthy of love. That person has just been given a death sentence but doesn't know the date of the execution. Can you see her in a more sympathetic light now? Look into her eyes, deeply, and address the spirit there, the desire she has to write. Speak aloud to him. Encourage him, be his friend, accept him, believe in him. See past his body into the spirit that wants to be writing but is afraid. Tell her you won't laugh at her, you won't find her ugly or stupid. Tell him he can tell you anything, you will write it down. You will not judge him or mock him. You know he's going to die. These are some of his last words. These *are* some of his last words. Your job is to take down what that person before you has to say. Later you can shape and polish. But, just as you can't make a table without wood, you can't write anything without these words he has to tell you. Now sit down and write. Let him, let her, speak through you.

## RITUALS FOR ENTERING THE DREAM

After getting your self-esteem in order, believing in your chosenness, believing in a listener, you still have to *enter* the dream. You may need another sort of ritual for doing this, inducing the dream trance. I find that any form of mild, rhythmic exercise can help you enter that state. Nothing strenuous or complex. I wouldn't get out my ice skates and try a triple lutz, for instance. It should be something that can be done automatically so you can concentrate on your writing. Barry Denny uses T'ai Chi. I like to pace.

> Horseback riding; knitting; shuffling and dealing cards; walking; whittling; . . . All these occupations are rhythmical, monotonous, and wordless. . . . In other words, every author, in some way which he has come on by luck or long search, puts himself into a very light state of hypnosis.
>
> —Dorothea Brande

I used to have a perfect pacing apartment. It was a cube. The entry door led into the living room, which led into a hall that led into the bedroom and the office, and that led into the kitchen, which led back to the door. I could just go around and around till I'd thought my story out and was ready to begin.

My apartment now is *Y*-shaped, and so my pacing is more back and forth, with occasional excursions into the bedroom/office. I have to decide whether to take the leg that leads to the office or the one that leads to the living room. It's not as mindless as I would like. So we got a trampoline (Zack thinks it's for him), and sometimes I jump my thoughts out instead of pacing. I don't jump high or fast, or do the twists and kicks that are demonstrated in the accompanying booklet. I jump gently, doing careful little leaps that barely leave the rubber.

The important thing is the rhythm. I hypnotize myself as I jump, thinking about what I'm trying to write till a way to write it comes to me. I drum up a starting sentence. Sometimes I think about how I don't want to tear my meniscus again and how I should lift from my abdomen, then pretty soon I'm having Jane Fonda thoughts, so it's back to pacing from room to room, trying not to see dust or clutter. In this I am greatly aided by myopia: Without my glasses on I don't see *shmutz*.

Walking the dream is different from pacing. I walk as a way to gather thoughts and images for the next day. I plot, I tell myself the story I am writing, filling in some of the details and coming up with new scenes or images or bits of dialogue. If I know what scene I'm going to work on tomorrow, I walk that one around. But pacing is a bit more like talking to yourself while walking back and forth. Then, when something takes off, it's zip, to the computermobile.

**TIP:** If you combine exercise time with "writing" you will have more time for both. Use the mindlessness of automatic-pilot activities such as jumping or walking to think about what you're writing. Fantasize scenes while on the treadmill. Think through your outline while bicycling. The key is to find an exercise that doesn't demand mental attention and a lot of cheerleading. Jogging is better than running if you want to think about something other than breaking through the wall.

### RITUALS FOR THE SEDENTARY

Perhaps you're the sedentary type, though. If you mustered up the energy to go for a walk, that would be it for the day. How about knitting then? Marissa Piesman knitted while working on *The Yuppie Handbook*. Knitting seems to be the sort of activity one can do while plotting and dreaming . . . that is, if you are mildly adept at it. If your stitches get tight so that you feel you are going crosseyed trying to insert the needles into those hairy loops that suddenly open into great cobwebs of yarn, maybe knitting is *not* for you. But it can't be a coincidence that a yarn is a good, long story as well as the stuff you make into sweaters.

I sometimes doodle when I'm "writing." Not just a squiggle in the margin but a page of noses and eyes and lips, suns and moons that all interconnect in a grand Timothy Leary jigsaw puzzle. The problem is I can get so caught up in doing this that I forget to think about my novel.

Freewriting can also serve as your ritual for entering the dream. Try setting aside ten minutes in the beginning of your writing time to freewrite. That may be all you need to get you going. Along the same lines, you might write a letter or an entry in your diary. Or write down your dreams. Evan Russell read somewhere that struggling to remember your dreams was a good mental exercise, and so he got into the habit of keeping a dream journal. Ellen Dreyer also writes down her dreams as a way to put herself in a writing frame of mind. At the very least, it gets you over the first hurdle.

Dream writing is especially good if you can do it as soon as you get up; that is, you live alone. It's harder to capture your dreams if you've been up awhile, especially if you've been making French toast for your kid and hearing about his dreams while your husband is asking where his socks are and can you take his shirts to the cleaners.

Think about what sorts of things spur you on. What puts you in the writing mood? Are you a visual person? Maybe looking at old photographs or reproductions of paintings will inspire you. Some people are turned on by smells. For Jodie Klavans it's the smell of books. For me it's coffee—not the flavor so much, which tastes nowadays like stomach acid, but the smell of fresh-ground beans. One whiff and I'm back in the time when I was first married, writing like a madwoman the minute my husband went out the door.

Music does it for Sam Decker, who searches out songs that remind him of his characters or a feeling he wants to convey. He'll listen to those songs over and over. "Sometimes when I'm losing the feeling," he told me, "the music can bring it back again."

I stay clear of songs with words that fight the words in my head. I also find crescendos and descrescendos irritating when I'm trying to hear myself think. Peter Rubie, too, finds that, although certain types of music put him close, it is silence he really craves while writing. But he had a friend who wrote a novel about a serial killer while listening to whale sounds.

The important thing in all this is that you develop rituals that are meaningful to you. Hypnotize yourself into believing you can do it, then hypnotize yourself right into the dream.

**Try This:** What evokes a creative mood in you? Write about the sounds, smells, events that make you feel like writing. Use this piece of writing and the ones you wrote about childhood rituals, magic objects, and places of power to compile a list of inspiration/energy sources. You can add others to the list. Incorporating any of these elements, invent at least three writing rituals. Thinking of ways to woo the creative spirit should be a pleasurable activity for you.

Try the first ritual for at least five writing sessions. If it works, Zounds! you've found your ritual! Stick to it. If you're not sure, write about the experience—how did doing the ritual feel? What happened during the writing session that followed the ritual? Go on to the next ritual and give it a shot, again for at least five writing sessions. If at any point you find a ritual that works for you, you don't need to go further. But if you haven't, or if you just want to try all the rituals on your list, do that. Remember to give each ritual at least five chances. Rituals gain in power from being used *ritualistically*. And remember to write about the experience afterward, especially if you are unable to write anything else.

When you've gone through your list, write about the experience as a whole. Then go back and look at what you wrote about each particular ritual. Decide at that point on one of them and make it your ritual by default. Even if you're not quite satisfied, don't give up on it. You may find that it will start to work for you only once you have committed yourself to it.

> **TIP:** The ritual is any action of your own devising that enables you to feel calm and unafraid. The more you do a ritual, the quicker it works to put you in the state of creativity—a sort of Pavlov's dogs effect. A talisman does not have any power but what you give it. Choose anything, the presence of which pleases you because of its appearance, smell, taste, texture or weight, resonance, or associations it conjures.

# TWENTY-ONE

# NAPS, DREAMS, AND DAYDREAMS

Sometimes we struggle and strain, and nothing comes of it. At such times you can beat your head against a wall to a song with a nice steady rhythm—"Dock of the Bay" perhaps. Or you might try taking it easy for a change. Lie down, *dream* awhile. I'm not talking daydreaming, although that is a fine, *necessary* thing for writers to do. I'm talking about getting prone, closing your eyes, catching forty winks.

"I tend to get narcoleptic when I'm stuck," Emily Russell told me. "At such times I resort to the cat nap. A simple line will sometimes click during one and fall out of my brain."

My parents and uncle used to call the kind of napping old people do, falling asleep in the middle of a sentence, *kopping a dreml*, catching a dream. That's what you want to do. Use the nap purposively to catch the dream. It's like when you're trying to think of a word, and the more you try the weirder words start to sound, till you find yourself saying, "Dog? Dawg? Dag?" The word you are looking for will only come when you *stop* trying. There's probably a Zen koan for this struggle to not struggle, but I'm no Buddhist. In writing it means relax. Let your unconscious sift the sand awhile. Work at not working. Give yourself a half-hour snooze.

The idea, sentence, image that comes at such times doesn't come from nowhere, of course. This isn't magic. And sleep is not incubation, so it doesn't come from the gods either. It comes from inside you. You just couldn't get at it, blasting the surface with dynamite. But letting your fingers brush the earth, caressing the top layer and turning it over haphazardly, you may uncover what was waiting there all along. Think of yourself as being on an archeological dig. You stomp onto an excavation site with your pneumatic drill and someone's going to stomp you right off again: It's the patient sifter they want, someone capable of shaking out the soil, recognizing treasure in fragments.

Steve Schwartz also naps when he doesn't know where to go in his work. "It's amazing how often I wake up *knowing* exactly what to write next," he told me, although he did attach a warning to this: "Sometimes I wake up and still have no idea what to write. In those instances, it's important to power through."

I am not a napper. Oh, occasionally I have been known to fall asleep when I'm struggling to write, having managed to bore myself into oblivion. But I don't wake up feeling inspired afterward. I am more ashamed than exhilarated, and then I have trouble falling asleep later because of that early deposit in the sleep bank. So, while I love the *idea* of catching a dream, naps are not for me—too much guilt, too much caffeine.

But perhaps they are what *your* mind, and body, craves. Lore Segal told me that if your mind is in a muddle, your writing will be muddled too. Naps, and sleeping in general, are the quicker-picker-uppers of the mind. A dream has nothing better to do than stick a bunch of characters into an improbable situation and see what happens, then twist things around and do it again. Then comment on the action.

So if you are a productive napper, why are you reading this book? Put it down and go to sleep at once. But if you take a nap like someone sneaking into an abandoned building and wake up afterward starring in *The Lost Weekend* of your mind, naps are not for you.

> Thought is the greatest of pleasures—pleasure itself is only imagination—have you ever enjoyed anything more than your dreams?
>
> —Gustave Flaubert

Take heart, you non-nappers. Forty winks are not our only chances for dreams. Some writers program themselves to dream about their work at night. Peter Rubie does this: "Last thing, in the vain hope that my chaotic imagination will find some shape," he told me. Lori Perkins also uses this technique. "When I'm writing fiction," she said, "I can play the movie in my head. Sometimes I can see my novel as I go to sleep, which helps me to work out plot, character, dialogue."

Obsessions, generally considered bad things, are good for writers.

That is, it is good for writers to make an obsession of writing—to think about it all the time, the material itself, not the fame you hope the writing will bring you nor the weighing of value we usually obsess about. Obsessing about that will drive you crazy, but obsessing about the writing itself may bring you surprising aid from your unconscious . . . in the form of dreams. We do dream about our obsessions, after all. My husband, in college, was obsessed with playing bridge, and he would dream night after night of different hands playing themselves out. That's the sort of thing you want your sleeping mind to do—work out the different combinations of character and scene and plot, of childhood events reflecting adult complications. To try it all different ways. I told you, dreams have nothing better to do. This is what they're good at. It's like letting your dog lick the crumbs under the table so you don't have to sweep: Take help in whatever form it comes.

Try falling asleep thinking about your writing—the people you are writing about, the movement of your chapters. A lot of times nothing will come of this, but sometimes you may find inspiration. Bear in mind, though, that dreams don't directly answer questions. You want to know about your main character's love interest, your unconscious gives you a dream about marlin-fishing off the coast of Cuba. The unconscious makes things up, things that can seem meaningless. But a lot of times the dream relates to a different part of your work than what you are consciously thinking about. The Talmud says that a dream uninterpreted is like a letter unread. You want to be a person who reads his or her dreams, even if the handwriting is bad.

Don't be quick to dismiss a dream. The associations and puns of the dreaming self are not what the conscious mind is used to. The conscious mind thinks *potato salad*, and the unconscious is off and running with Sally surrounded by pots of a gelatinous, throbbing goo. So if the language of dreams is unclear to you, remember: It's meant to be unclear.

Last night, for example, I dreamt I wanted to go on a hike to see the lilies, but Zack wanted to see the oranges, and I had to go with him because he is too little to go alone. I don't know what oranges had to do with anything, but I woke up longing to see the lilies, especially the Blue Lily. It didn't take too much reflection to realize my mother, Lilly, was the one I wanted to see. The dream made real the central conflict of my novel-in-progress—the pull between being a mother and being a daughter. Perhaps this dream will work its way into my book, as a scene or as a dream my main character has. Perhaps it will not. But in any case it had me playing monkey in the middle between my mother and my son in the Land of Nod.

**Try This:** Start a dream journal. Keep it and a pen near your bed. Write down your dreams as soon as you can after waking. You can sneak off to the bathroom to do so if your spouse is a garrulous riser or likes to linger in bed, listening to the news. You don't need to analyze the dream right away—just jot down the details. Later, put the prism of your work to the dream and look at it again. Don't be put off by any seeming irrelevance. It's your job to detect the threads that connect the dream to your writing. If you are obsessed with your writing, or trying to be, the connections will be there.

## PROGRAMMING THE UNPROGRAMMABLE

Despite this talk of programming dreams, you must know that dreams are like writing. You can't really *control* them. You have to let them happen, with gentle prods in a certain direction. Dreams are not an alternative to writing, but sometimes they can be a tool to help you shape, understand, develop your work. What you are doing, trying to give yourself dreams, is holding out a bowl of fruit and letting your dreaming self choose what it wants to taste. Then, when you wake up, the dream holds the bowl out for you, offering you weird fruit without names that you get to sample.

"Dream and story come out of the same part of the mind," Lore Segal told me. "That has very little to do with what you intend. You can't intend what you are going to dream. In the same way, in a novel your story takes over." This is true, not just for fiction but for all kinds of writing. You have a map, but you take side trips and sometimes these turn out to be so much fun you change your itinerary.

In addition to "programmed" dreams, some writers are prone to the wisdom variety—unbidden advice from your sleeping mind. Such dreams may pertain to your writing, or to other matters of deep importance. When my mother died, for instance, I dreamt she called me on the telephone. I was telling her how we were pruning the tree of wisdom, tending the tree of life. She kept going, "Yeah," in this growly low voice. I didn't know why I told her that, but afterward it seemed that that was what death was about—it helped me see her death as growth, not only as loss. Maureen Brady once dreamt that characters in her just-published novel were serving unlimited amounts of lasagna. The dream came at a time of not knowing where to go for her next book, and it gave her a feeling of abundance and confidence. Ellen Dreyer, in the process of revising her novel, had a voice in a dream say, "Don't cut the heart out of it"—advice she's tried hard to take ever since.

Of course sometimes a banana is just a banana. "I so rarely remember my dreams," Martha Schulman told me, "that when I do I think of them as being in the province of my shrink more than my writing."

Whether your dreams are meaningful to your work or not, they are rarely meant to be taken verbatim from the unconscious and put in your writing. "The problem with dream imagery," Madison Smartt Bell told me, "is it usually makes sense only to the dreamer and has to be shaped and revised in order to be intelligible to a general audience." Good dreams, however, do find their way into our writing. In fiction they may become the dreams of our characters. "I did write a novel recently," Madison revealed, "that has a lot of actual dreams of mine dropped into the dream life of the protagonist."

Poets often use dream material directly. The connection between poetry and dream is so close, built as both are on wordplay, association, and startling imagery, that many poets mine the mountains of Morpheus for whatever gems they can find. Poetry, being less restricted by logic than other writing forms, may use the strange juxtapositions of dream imagery word for word, as it were—sometimes to great effect.

Madison told me he uses his unconscious another way to help him write. "One pretty good trick," he said, "is to use the twilight sleep period of waking in the morning to fix on an image of what is to be written about later, then think of a sentence or phrase that will begin the description or the dialogue or the scene or whatever. That way when I sit down to write I have already started, in effect, so getting over that hump is not a problem."

I've already told you how useful it is to have a starting sentence or image before you sit down to write. In addition to using twilight sleep, pacing, or jumping on a trampoline to find yours, you might try household chores. "Muses visit when I'm washing the dishes," Sam Decker told me, "not when I'm at the writing table." That way you get to write *and* do laundry—as long as you think about your writing while doing it and don't find yourself singing, "Ring around the collar."

Writing is daydreaming on paper, so you *can* be writing even when you're not. "I've been a devoted daydreamer since childhood," Madison told me, "and I work at it now that I'm a professional story-maker-upper. I make up stories while I'm doing other stuff, such as dishwashing, mowing the grass, driving, and so on. There are risks, such as wrecks or mowing over your own feet, etc., but the stories get worked out or at least well begun in daydream and can be committed to paper later."

Some years ago I read my old report cards. My third-grade teacher's comments seemed prophetic: "Marcia doesn't pay attention in class," she wrote. "She prefers to daydream out the window." What Mrs. Ehrlich didn't know, what I didn't know, was I was making up the stories that would teach me about being a writer. As Steve Schwartz told me, paraphrasing a remark by editor Burton Rascoe he'd read some years back: "What my wife doesn't understand is even when I'm staring out the window I'm writing."

**TIP:** If the writing won't flow, try to force it—freewrite, cajole, threaten, bribe. As a last resort, take a nap. When you wake up, think about your dreams and write them down. Use them to help you over the obstacle that's keeping you from writing. If you didn't dream, spend some time while you are still lying there to think about your project. See if you can find a sentence or image to get you started again.

# TWENTY-TWO

# SUPERSTITIONS AND BELIEFS

We writers can be a superstitious bunch. We have our hats. We have our hot drinks, steam curling from the cup the way cigarette smoke used to back when we were into unhealth. And so we go to the post office and stand in line for an hour to buy stamps that don't say "Love" or have an American flag on them. We believe editors, enamored of our stamps, will be compelled to buy our manuscripts. The Georgia O'Keefe poppy shows such taste, the Blondie comic such wit.

My favorite stamp right now is Bela Lugosi as Dracula. I tend to waste much time deciding whether to put Dracula on the SASE and the Mummy on the outer envelope or the other way around. After all, the outer envelope is the one that makes the first impression. But the inner envelope is clipped to the story for its return. I would never use two Draculas. I hedge my bets with one Dracula and one Mummy or Phantom. Sometimes I put the stamp on upside down, I don't know why. It's never done me a *lick* of good (that's a postal joke). I also always try to send something off on my birthday because once I got a novel published that way.

Evan Russell is another neurotic when it comes to the mailing process. "I debate which stamps to use and which post office to mail from," he told me. Since he also believes good things happen in a row he obeys "absurd rules to keep that roll rolling. And when, as inevitably happens, it stops I spend much time trying to figure out what I did wrong."

Ellen Dreyer's superstition takes the form of a lucky writing shirt, which is unfortunately getting rather worn and frayed. Soon she'll have to find another blend of inspiration and cotton.

Marissa Piesman, who wrote six mystery novels on the train on her way to work as a lawyer (but her closets are a perfect mess!), found after a while she could *only* work on the train. That was her belief—that her creativity was tied to the tracks, not that she wrote on the train out of necessity because the commute was the only time she had to write. When her daughter started nursery school, Marissa could no longer depend on getting a seat on the train after dropping her off, the nursery school being several stops closer to downtown. Her writing shut down because of this. Perhaps this is the difference between superstition and ritual. If it helps you, it is a ritual. If the disruption of the routine or the loss or fraying of the talisman hinders you from writing, it's a superstition. I realize this distinction is a bit fine. It is also entirely my own. The good news for Marissa is that of late she's been getting back into writing, although not on the train. I'm sure it's not coincidental that another of her beliefs is "the sloppier my handwriting, the less inhibited I am, the better the work flows." If you've ever experienced the jerks and jolts of the NYC transit system, you'll know the source of this belief.

> In relation to Gauguin, Van Gogh, and Rimbaud, I have a distinct inferiority complex because they managed to destroy themselves. . . . I am more and more convinced that, in order to achieve authenticity, something has to snap.
>
> —Jean-Paul Sartre

My own way to encourage good writing fortune is to pick up any little bug I find and put it out the window rather than squishing it and flushing it down the toilet (which is what I'd really like to do). Who knows but that bug might be Kafka come to invest my writerly soul with genius. I have karma concerns as well. I'm sure I was a cruel critic in a past life—there is no other way to account for my phenomenally lousy timing when sending things out. After consulting the *I Ching* and *Writer's Market*, throwing sticks and coins and blindly stabbing at pages, why else do I end up sending a story to a magazine that has just closed an issue on whatever theme my story is about? Maybe my kindness to bugs will convince the writing gods not to step on me.

For Sam Decker, knowing the title of a work in progress as soon as possible is how he makes his work real. For Martha Schulman it is refusing to print out a story till she has a "finished" version of it, although she can't decide if this is a paper-saving technique, a helpful practice that keeps her from "endlessly polishing the first pages" of a piece, or something "actively unhelpful."

Some writers find having the correct environment necessary for writing. One of my students told me a joke about a woman who wanted to write but couldn't because she couldn't find a garret. For Jodie Klavans "the smell of a library is very comforting" and helps her enter the writing mood. That sweetish dusty smell of radiators and mildew gets my heart pounding too, although I find the library too noisy these days and long for a time when librarians hissed, "Shhh," if you scraped your chair. Gone are the libraries of my youth, when you might be startled to find another person coming down the poorly lit aisle, the two of you sidling past each other like snakes, eager to be alone again.

Scratch any writer and you'll come up with enough flakes of habit, superstition, and belief to keep the New York Psychoanalytic Society and Dr. Zizmor the Dermatologist busy for years. Does any of this make us more productive or inspired than we would be without? Probably not. But writing itself sometimes feels like magic—the creation of something from nothing. So if we have our quirks and compulsions, the world will bear with us. Otherwise, we might just throw our arms up and say, "Okay, Mr. Smarty-Pants, let's hear you tell the story for a change."

**Try This:** Think about some of your superstitions and strange beliefs, not just about writing and publishing but about life in general. Are there good omens and bad omens in your life? Does finding a waterbug in your bathroom make you want to spend the rest of the day in bed? Does a full, vibrant rainbow seem a personal sign to have hope? Write a story, poem, or personal essay about this. You might try writing this as a humor piece.

## KEEP IT TO YOURSELF

James Joyce prescribed silence, exile, and cunning for himself, and I advise the same for you, with an emphasis on the first. This is a belief I take very seriously, although it's caused me grief at home. But I believe that silence on a creative project keeps the initial inspiration alive, the balloon of creation filling to the point of bursting.

People who talk about what they are going to write usually don't write—they talk. The need to write is diminished every time you tell someone your idea. Now you are getting the reaction, the praise without having to invest any energy in working on it. As Sam Decker says, "You talk it to life, then don't need to write it." Sam also keeps his silence on a creative project because he feels a loyalty to his characters. Talking about them before they're ready feels like an act of betrayal. "It's like they're being shown naked," he said, "before they are fully formed."

In addition to deflating the writing balloon, talking about a creative project opens you to reactions you may not be ready for. Cynthia Ozick once wrote that writers had "a little holy light within, like a pilot light, which fear is always blowing out." The role of one's first readers is to "help get the little holy light lit again." Unfortunately, not all our first readers know this. They think we want advice, criticism, harsh truth. The hell with harsh truth. We want lies. We want wild enthusiasm. We're not going to believe praise we get from our friends and family anyway, so give us a big dollop of the stuff. That is why family and friends mustn't raise so much as an eyebrow or even sneeze when reading our labored-over manuscripts. And that is also why you shouldn't show your work to anybody or talk about it till it, and you, are ready.

This said, I admit there are writers who find brainstorming helpful, who like to get input on their ideas before investing much time in the actual writing. Marissa Piesman, for example, used to read a chapter of her novel to her agent each time she finished writing it, although she told me she has since "outgrown" this. It is also common for screenwriters to pitch ideas verbally, before the screenplays themselves are written. In fact, most screenwriters don't write any of the screenplay till the ideas are bandied about, changed, approved. They write treatments, which are extended outlines, but they don't write the actual screenplays without financial commitments.

Memoirs written for publication, rather than simply as family history, may also have selling points that are discussed prior to their being started. The fame of the memoirist, the importance of the events lived through, the nature of the secrets to be divulged—such are the items often discussed before a writer begins such a labor.

Many works of the imagination are also sold on the basis of an idea and an outline, before being written. Mysteries, science fiction, historical romance, these are plot-driven genres in which it is not always the quality of the writing itself, high though this may be, but the ideas behind it that sells. For works of these sorts, there is no reason to keep one's own council. It is better to avail yourself of the advice of enthusiastic editors, agents, and other experts.

But there's another kind of writing—a kind that is increasingly difficult to get published, a kind the writer would choose to write even if it never got published (although fighting the despair this causes is a hurdle such a writer must jump every day). This is writing that "is not about, it *is*," as Ibsen put it.

Such writing can be spoiled by talk. It is not just that the need to write is lessened every time the writer tells people what he or she is going to write, but also that people who may not understand the ideas will offer input that changes the writer's concepts—not always for the better. If you are such a writer, you may find yourself no longer writing the book you had planned; the worst outcome is that you are not writing at all.

**Try This:** Spend a chunk of time without speaking, a whole day if you can manage it. You might tell your family you are doing an experiment. Or you might say you have laryngitis. Or you could plan not to answer the telephone or the door for a set amount of time when you are alone. Don't listen to music or watch television during this time or even read. You can write, though. In fact, you should, as much as possible. Write about the experience of silence—hearing it and dwelling in it. Do you feel any change in your energy or inspiration level? Is this a calming exercise, or do you feel like you're going to pop?

My husband and son find my reluctance to talk about my writing difficult to accept. They feel I should share my day with them the way they share theirs with me. They take it personally somehow—as if my unwillingness to share my work before it's ready means I don't trust them. It has nothing to do with that. It is only that I need to keep the fires stoked, the pressure building, by maintaining silence. As soon as I vent my ideas, the urgency is diminished. It becomes that much harder to write.

The other day, for example, an idea for a story came to me when

**TIP:** Some people are energized by the enthusiasm of others. If this is true for you, take advantage of your garrulous nature to combine sociability and productivity. You may even consider working with a collaborator as a means to spur you on and provide objectivity. But if you are a loner who finds other peoples' comments intrusive, learn to keep your mouth shut. People *will* say stupid things, stuff you don't want or need to hear. Try to come up, in advance, with a sentence that seems to sum up your current project without giving anything away. Change the topic to the other person's passion as soon as possible. This may even award you the reputation of being a wonderful conversationalist.

we were in the car. I got out my trusty little notebook and pen (which are always with me: see chapter four) and began jotting the idea down. It was complicated and took a few pages, during which my husband turned off the radio and generally showed himself to be the well-trained, considerate spouse of a bad-tempered, neurotic writer. My son, on the other hand, kvetched because he wanted to listen to rock music. "Can't you see Mommy's writing?" my husband said, at which Zack got quiet and remained so till I was through. Then it began.

"What are you writing?"

"A story idea."

"What's it about?"

"I don't want to talk about it yet."

"Why?"

"Because . . . because, it's not a story. It's just an idea."

"But what's it going to be about?"

My impulse was to put my hands over my ears and go "Lalalala" till he stopped, but I forced myself to remember this noxious prying creature was my own little love, that he was interested in my creative sources because he was interested in writing—and in me. I also knew that if I shared the story with him now it wouldn't make sense, and that would spoil it for later. I have done this in the past, thinking my reluctance to talk was a silly superstition. Superstition or no, the story was indeed ruined. "It's just an idea," I finally said. "I won't know what it is till I write it. When I do you can read it"—which may or may not be true. "It's about Grandpa Jack," I told him finally. "We were dancing."

This satisfied him for the time being, although I still don't feel we reached a good conclusion or that I handled this particularly well. As with all childhood questions, I wish I could push the pause button on life till I have a chance to think. Not that it would do any good. For now that I've had time to reflect, I still don't know how I should have handled it. Or what I should do in the future.

I must have a right to my own thoughts, don't you think, even though I am a mother. *I* must be the one to determine when to share those thoughts. So if I hemmed and hawed and sounded more like a Victorian woman talking to her daughter about the facts of life on her wedding night (I hemmed and hawed a lot less telling these to Zack when he *finally* asked) than a writer who'd just jotted down an idea, so be it. In time Zack will have his own secrets and I'll be on the other side, trying to wheedle them out of him. I suppose that's what I'm afraid of.

Which brings me to our very next subject.

> To name something is to destroy three-quarters of the pleasure of poetry.
> —Stéphane Mallarmé

# TWENTY-THREE

# MOTHERHOOD, AND OTHER TIES THAT BIND (YOU UP)

O nce there was a woman who was a writer. Every day she sat down at her typewriter and pounded out letters that formed words that became sentences that seemed to express her ideas. She knew she would do this every morning after her husband left for work and, although it was often difficult to begin, she was able to force herself through the first stilted paragraphs in the hope that something would take off. And take off it did, to the point where she was almost rude about shooing her husband out the door so she could start. In this manner she managed to write two novels, a number of short stories, articles, and interviews, plus do the freelance editing that provided income and a sense that she had a real job.

This was not a time of self-confidence brimming over the coffee cup of doubt. It was a time of self-doubt brimming over self-doubt. Almost nothing I had written had been published—or seemed likely to be. I periodically contemplated returning to full-time office work before it became apparent to everyone that I was insane. *The Shining* had not yet come out, but my life felt as if I were secretly penning "All work and no play makes Marcia a dull girl" over and over while my husband was at the office. I worried that I had no talent; I worried that I had bad writing karma from a past life; I worried that soon I would be too old to find a real job, my husband would leave me, and I would have to live in a Dumpster.

But I didn't worry I couldn't write. The work might or might not have been good, but I loved doing it. Often, after that first jump into the icy pool, while I was flailing around trying to find what I was trying to say and a way to say it, my thoughts would start to race. My fingers and mind were connected to the page, I fell into the writing trance easily, laughing to myself, crying, having a grand old time, watching movies on my mind screen. And since this state was real, I believed my writing was real too. That was all that mattered, or should matter—that plus finding a way to support myself while indulging in my addiction.

I turned out to be luckier than many. Some of my stories and articles appeared in magazines and books. I managed to find a publisher for one novel and started writing another. A pattern began to develop whereby I knew that if I worked at it I would get past the initial plunge, and my thoughts would take me someplace.

Then I had a baby.

It is my belief that the worst thing that can happen to a woman writer is also the best. I vaguely recall that before my son was born I would hover over my husband in the morning, trying to rush him along, so eager was I to run into the embrace of my typewriter. I remember it like a long-ago dream . . . dimly, fondly.

I was prepared for change once my son was born. I knew, after all, that he would have to be fed and diapered, dandled. But I imagined taking him for long walks, during which time I would be plotting and contemplating. I thought that when he napped I'd write. Perhaps I'd work on poetry. It is proof that I am no poet that I thought poetry easier to compose in the short time bytes allowed by a child's nap than the great chunks demanded by fiction. I didn't know that when he napped I would stare off into space, waiting for his next cry, like some torture victim listening for prison guard footsteps.

This is not to say I didn't love my son. I was besotted, and that was part of the problem. I smiled inanely every time I looked at him. Luckily this wasn't too often, only every other minute—for when I wasn't waiting for his cry I would steal into his room and watch him breathe. That first year I went from a solitary existence to one in which I was never alone. It was as though I had joined a religious cult. I got used to saying "we" when I meant "I." Soon all I could talk about was diaper rash and spit-up. Even when I was alone.

After a few months I realized I would never get any work accomplished if I didn't hire a babysitter. So I did—a wonderful, loving, intelligent, experienced babysitter who taught me so much about babies that I felt like she was *my* mother, even though she was ten years younger than me. She came two mornings a week and stayed three hours each time. I quickly discovered that the first hour would get whittled away, talking about how terrific the baby was, how her daughters and sisters and nieces and nephews were, making coffee, drinking coffee while she held Zack and my mind raced with how to escape without being rude. My husband said, "Just let her in, then go into your office and work." But I couldn't. First I had to establish a friendship with her before I could hand my child over. Then I had a friendship with her, which meant I had to console and advise and generally be a willing ear to the vicissitudes of her life—which, as a babysitter with two kids of her own and no husband, were pretty darn vicissitudinous. And so I tell you Rule Number One for writers new to the parenting game.

Do Not Make Friends with the Babysitter.

When I finally left Zack with her and went into my room to work, I discovered that I was a prisoner there. If I ventured to the kitchen to make myself a cup of coffee, there she'd be, my son in hand, full of pleasantries and advice, as happy as anything to take care of my child while telling me how smart he was, how he was doing stuff at three months that other kids didn't do till they were in junior high.

It's not like it was any better when I went into my office. I could still hear them. And if I couldn't I opened the door to make sure everything was okay. Or I listened in on the baby monitor and heard her sing, "Hello, My Name Is Zachary, How Do You Do?" along with his music tape. In short I did everything but write, and could just as easily have been taking care of Zack myself for all the work I accomplished. I kept thinking I just had to get into the swing of it, that eventually I would learn to let the sitter in and leave her to sit, tending my son while I tended my words.

In the end what saved me was preschool. When it was time for Zack to go—and I marched the poor kid off at two and a half, a baby businessman riding the A-train during rush hour with my husband—I found he could be out of the house but *never* out of my mind. Now he is eight, and I still spend an inordinate amount of time thinking about him—what he is going to eat, when I have to leave to pick him up; if he is safe; if he is warm. I arrange his playdates and his lessons and his haircuts; I make doctor and dentist appointments and take him to those places. And I figure I will be doing this for the rest of my life, or at least until I no longer remember what I wanted time to myself for.

## WRITERS WITH CHILDREN

Sam Decker says that he stopped writing for two years just to stare at his son. "Then I stopped writing because he talked all the time. Then I needed money, and the TV is on and family life, rich as it is, is all-consuming. I didn't start writing again seriously till my youngest began school, and I still go on class trips instead of to my office." Sam also said that, while he has to have a schedule to get stuff done, "anything family disrupts it greatly. I let them come first, on the assumption that the kids will someday grow up."

And so the world conspires against writers with children. You can never completely put your family out of your mind, or if you can do it one day there's no reason to suppose you'll be able to do it the next. There are sudden rashes and school holidays, there are concerns over your kid's learning problems or inability to make friends, there is always dinner to contend with and babysitters who come with their own load of rashes and concerns (if they come at all).

When my husband and son go out the door in the morning, I know I have till two in the afternoon to work. Then I have to go downtown to get Zack from school. I also have dishes to do and laundry to wash, beds to make. I have to plan and shop for dinner, even though I don't start preparing it till Zack is home. I have my own body to attend to—the food it demands, the ablutions and exercises it requires to keep it functioning. I have work-work to do—that is, freelance editing, teaching, correspondence. An ever-smaller portion of the day goes to my "real" work. If any activity demands more than its allotted time, my writing is the Peter I rob to pay Paul.

You might think that what with the hours I have left for writing so precious I would make the most of them . . . but you would be wrong. Writing is not a machine I can easily turn on and off. I can't look at my watch and say, "Oh good, I have thirty-six minutes till I have to go to get to school. I should be able to write the first page of a story by then." What happens is I say, "Thirty-six minutes. By the time I get started I'll have to stop. No sense in trying. Think I'll eat." That 2:00 deadline hangs over my head like the pendulum in my pit, swinging closer with every tock.

Being a mother and a writer is like being a ballerina and a concert violinist. That's not to say it can't be done. It's more that whatever you are doing, you think you should be doing something else. When my son was little, his babysitter would take him to play in the backyard. I would find myself watching them through the window instead of working. Here I was paying someone an hourly wage so I could spend time alone, trying to hear my voice, and the only voice I could hear was the one that was saying, "You are a bad mother." I would turn away from the window and try to focus on the computer screen, but the smallest cry sent me running to see what had happened, while every toddler shriek of glee felt like a ventricle torn from my heart. *I should be the source of such delight.*

The babysitter, as I said before, only came two mornings a week, so I had plenty of hours in between to play with my son and listen to him shriek with glee. But many was the time I'd find myself in the sandbox, filling another bucket, helping turn it over, thinking I was losing my mind. I plotted his naps like Sylvia Plath, only I never resorted to drugs (oh, maybe Tylenol once in a while if his temperature hovered around a hundred but didn't quite make it to the required one-oh-one). When he was sleeping I cursed the airplane whose roar would wake him, the shout of another child at play. I closed the windows, even in the summer, trying to dampen any sound, and walked on tiptoe into his room to make sure he was covered, that his pacifier was within reach, that the room was as cozy and sleep-producing as an opium den. I did so much of this hovering and shushing and tiptoeing around that I didn't work. That first dive into writing can be so cold. It's easier to put it off, focusing on the slightest noise that may bring the nap to an end. When I did manage to start, he inevitably cried the moment I coaxed the tiny thread of silk out of my soul. Baby ESP: Mommy isn't thinking about me—waaah!

The other side to the motherhood dilemma, of course, is fear. I am not the only mother who lives in terror of an obliging Angel of Death eavesdropping on her thoughts. Something else to worry about instead of writing! During his infancy I spent much time watching Zack's chest move while he slept. If he napped too long I started opening windows, enticing noise—come on, let's hear those helicopters churning up the airwaves. It would serve me right, I worried, to lose what is most precious because I kvetched about the lack of solitude I needed for my writing.

The facts of the matter are (1) things do get better and (2) but not that much. For it has been my experience that as soon as you have a routine something screws it up.

You can't tell a kid you won't be at the class play to hear him hoot like an owl in a chorus of hooting owls. Not that your kid will remember you were there, but if you weren't. . . . Point of view is not solely a question of craft. As Ruth Reichl said, "My family will tell you, with great sincerity, that I spend virtually all my time sitting in front of my computer. I, on the other hand, would tell you with equal sincerity that I spend all my time picking up after them."

Because of the almost illicit pleasure we have in writing, we feel shame indulging in it. Especially if we consider we are indulging at someone else's expense. If we are mothers of young children, if we have old mothers who are lonely, whatever our situation we feel guilty giving ourselves pleasure, writing. Then we feel guilty not writing. "Every minute I spend writing," Marissa Piesman told me, "I steal from my child." Write a masterpiece under that *guilt*otine.

"I'm in awe of those women who write in the dark, put five kids on the school bus, and go to work during the day in the steel mill—then publish a best-seller," Jodie Klavans told me. "Or the ones who've published thirty books because they carry their laptops to the grocery story and type while they help the kids do their homework. Who are these women, and would they be willing to donate their blood for a few quick transfusions?"

The truth is you need to be a little selfish in order to write. But the time you steal for your writing is not taken from anyone else. It is set aside. Make your writing time sacrosanct. You must not allow it to be whittled away by tasks only *you* can do (because you have the time to do them, right? Because you, after all, "work" at home. Susan Saiter told me motherhood worked for her because she got to stay home and write—but that's a double-edged sword if you have to take care of a kid, do all the household drudgery, be there for the repairmen, *and* try to write.)

Sacrosanct shmacrosanct, if the school calls and your kid is throwing up all over the desk and running a fever close to the temperature of the sun, you are going to close down your computer for the day and hightail it over there. You have to be able to discern major whittles from minor ones, and a major whittle is the serious illness or injury of a loved one.

When Maureen Brady's mother had a stroke, for example, she was glad she had arranged to go to a writers' retreat that week because it meant she had the time off to be with her mother. There was no question of what she was going to do, as much as she'd longed for that uninterrupted time in which to work. The Grim Reaper is the final arbiter of deadlines, after all. Eking out a few more pages could not compete with being with her mom at the end.

A minor whittle, on the other hand, is the telephone company coming to install a new line. Oh yeah, I know, sometimes they will tell you they can only indicate that they will be there on Thursday from eight till six. But if you nag and whine and pretend you have a real job in a real office in another part of town and a schedule that makes prison camp look like daycamp, they will narrow it down to morning or afternoon. And, horrible as this sounds, if they can't and you are working and it is flowing when the doorbell rings, *Don't open the door.* You are *not* at home: You are at work. You are at work just as much as someone who punches a clock. Afterward you can call the telephone company and explain you left work early and have just gotten home.

Here's the thing: If you put off your work till this other junk is out of the way, guess what—there's always more junk with your name on it, because you're home with the kids. No sooner is the telephone installed than your dishwasher springs a leak. When that is taken care of, it's time to paint, isn't it?

> The habits of a lifetime when everything else had to come before writing are not easily broken, even when circumstances now often make it possible for writing to be first; habits of years—response to others, distractability, responsibility of daily matters—stay with you, mark you, become you.
>
> —Tillie Olsen

I have to admit that when painters come knocking at my door I let them in. It's 8:00 in the morning. I'm still scraping the sand out of my eyes. I haven't brushed my teeth. My husband and son have left. But I know painters. They come early and they leave early, and there is no way around it. So don't paint, that's my advice. But if you have to because it's been ten years and even *you* are starting to feel like you're living in a Stanley Kubrick film, with paint peeling down like long fingers reaching for you, then try to schedule it during a time of revision. Try to have pages and pages of material to read over and correct, stuff you can take outside or to the library so you don't find yourself singing along with the painters' favorite oldies station while they scrape, plaster, and generally make a mess of your life. Don't try to write anything fresh while the painters are in the house. You *can* try freewriting. In fact, it's a good idea to freewrite about the painters, maybe have a fantasy about the cute one who loves all the colors you've chosen. Don't, however, leave your freewriting lying around on the off chance they read English, or you may find yourself wearing high-collared shirts and your ugliest glasses for the rest of the paint job.

**Try This:** Let other people take over. When I asked Lore Segal how she managed to raise her kids *and* write she said, "I had a mother." She went on to explain that her mother lived in the same building. "Every morning she would go upstairs and take care of the kids, and I would go down to her apartment and write." I've found that many women writers moan about how they have all the childrearing responsibilities, but when you question them you learn that they don't trust other people (i.e., husbands) to do anything. So let your husband or friend or mother or babysitter take over so you can write. Fathers can handle getting the kid a haircut. And if there is an excursion they're going on, you don't have to be part of it. That's hard for us. We want to go to the zoo too. Here's a chance to be with our kid *and* with other grownups. The sun is shining. It's a great day for an outing. Okay, but they don't need you. And it is better for them if you're not there: That way they can bond. You don't have to feel guilty about separating yourself from them. Tell yourself you're doing it for their sakes, so they will get to know each other deeply in a way neither of them would if you were there. And if Grandma gives your kid Coco Puffs for lunch, it's not the end of the world.

- Form a babysitting co-op. You take care of other people's kids in exchange for hours in which they take care of yours. Generally there's someone available for the hours you need. And when you're taking care of your own kid, it's actually easier to have playmates along.

- Form a mothers' writing group. My friend Jan Burstein told me about the one she belonged to when her kids were small. You could read aloud anything you'd written. If you hadn't written, you could read aloud something you wanted to discuss. Meanwhile, the kids would play. Yeah, they *would* always interrupt, which was frustrating. "I couldn't concentrate when the baby needed tending," Jan told me, "but we were all mothers. Nobody got bent out of shape if a kid interrupted. That was part of the flow of the group." Being in such a group made her feel productive. "Part of it was sleep deprivation, I guess, but I was always in a state of dreaming. Now I find it harder to get to writing. There isn't that intensity. I wanted to write so much then and I couldn't. I had to struggle for the time. Now when I have the time I find all these other things I have to do—like swimming."

• If you have an infant or a small child, try keeping a baby journal. Don't use that tacky thing your Cousin Ethel gave you at your shower. Get a notebook. In the back you might put the pertinent facts—weight, height, first tooth, rashes. But in the front write about your kid. You can address it to him, or her, as a present for some time in the distant future. I have such a journal for Zack. Some of it is addressed to him. Some of it is me talking about him. Because I plan to give it to him, I don't put down every passing paranoid thought. Also I tend to write things too long after the fact, so it's not as lively as I'd like. Still, it's something you *can* do during a kid's nap. And hey, you male writers, you can do this too, you know. We're not birds and it's not only the female who sits on the eggs and broods.

• Write books *for* your kid. You know the kind of book you wish you could find but can't? Write it. If you're artistic, do the illustrations. Maybe it's a storybook, maybe it's a book of poems or a counting book. When Zack was having nightmares I wrote a story for him called "Chicken Soup for Witches." It's all about a boy who's afraid to go to sleep at night till he becomes friends with a witch who has a cold and how he helps to heal her.

• Write books *with* your kid. Kids love to dictate stories. You can keep a notebook of his or her stories, or you can "write" the books with a tape recorder. Some stories will inspire you in your own writing. It's important when you're writing with a kid not to take over. Let him or her come up with the ideas. Later, you can write your own version, taking off from what your kid produced. Just keep the two versions separate.

• Some writers find they can work more easily when they are out of the house. They need a solitary island in which to write, someplace where they can't succumb to the lure of the vacuum cleaner. Jodie Klavans goes to a private "library that is a sea of calm and at which I cannot be reached. I phone my husband before entering to make sure I'm not needed, and then I take myself out of the real world." Her only problem with this is that "the real world keeps me from getting to the library more often than not. And I have to deal with balancing myself."

Many cities have writing rooms hidden in their nooks and crannies. New York, for example, has such rooms in the Mercantile Library and the Writers Room on Astor Place. Ask around. If such rooms are not available in your town, perhaps you can rent space from a neighbor whose schedule is the opposite of yours. Lore Segal, before she started using her mother's apartment to write in, would rent day hours in the apartment of a nurse. "It was miserable. It smelled of cats. But I could work there," she told me.

• Drum up a starting sentence while walking back and forth with a colicky baby. Try not to make it one that goes: Please, someone, shoot me in the head. Seriously, with a colicky baby you're not going to get much writing done. But if you have one that likes to be held and walked around, you might be able to think of a sentence or an idea while pacing. Be sure to put that sentence or idea on a slip of paper next to your computer. Then, when your baby falls asleep, try to start immediately. Pretend it's a race and the timekeeper has just shouted, "On your mark. Get set. Go!" Quick, let's see who finishes first—you or the baby.

• Do five-minute writing bits. Don't think of a whole book or even a whole chapter. Think of a scene. Think of a paragraph. You can weave these together later on, when you have longer chunks of time. (For more about five-minute writing bits, see chapter twenty-five.)

• There is always freewriting. The important thing is to keep writing. If all you can manage to do while your kid drinks his bottle and watches *Sesame Street* is some free association about Cookie Monster moving into your office and getting crumbs in your computer, go for it. It is good to do this. It will keep you sane. And besides, Me like Cookie, *humina humina humina*.

**TIP:** If you make a household chore schedule, someone else can do some of the chores you usually do, and that will buy you writing time. Your spouse planning for, shopping for, and making dinner two nights a week gives you that much more time to write. You can repay the favor by doing something special for him or her. But try appeasing the guilt gods *after* writing. If you take your kid to his favorite playground when you pick him up, you don't have to feel guilty about having dropped him off at the babysitter's so you could write. If you've added a class to your teaching load, which means grading papers at night so your family can afford a nice vacation, you are entitled to your morning spent writing.

# TWENTY-FOUR

# SADIE'S NOSE

**E**van Russell told me he doesn't want kids because he wants to write and doesn't care to invest the next eighteen years taking care of someone else. Instead, he and his wife used to look at their writing as their children.

"There were the beautiful newborns (most recent work)," he told me, "about which we were gaga. They were blameless and pristine, they could do no wrong and we bored the world blathering on about how adorable they were. Just one peek at the manuscript lying in its crib made our hearts swell and our eyes brim with happy tears: the wonder of creation! Then there were the older ones, the terrible twos who simply would not do what you told them to. They had learned to say no and were merciless. And we had our gawky, sullen teens, the older works that were an embarrassment, the ones you wished you could ship out of the country, the ones who were always being sent home from school (publishers)."

As far as kids interfering with your writing, he's right . . . and he's wrong. In the end you do what you do, and if you have one kid or ten, that's your life, that's your material; and if you don't have any, *that's* your material.

It *was* easier to write before I had Zack, but I have no regrets. Aside from all the love I feel for him, he has made me a better writer. I see my childhood through him. It helps me remember it in a less self-centered way. I am at once the child I was and the mother I am. Before, it was all about me—poor Nell, beset by villains. Now I realize the adults of that time were as confused and conflicted as I am now.

With Baby Zack changing daily before my eyes, I got to watch how a human being comes to be, how he acquires language and social skills. And now that he's older I see him developing a sense of his maleness, which is about sports and teams. I could dress him as a clown, complete with red nose, and he wouldn't notice, as long as he could wear his Mets baseball cap.

He is constantly granting me chunks of eight-year-old wisdom, as he thinks about black holes and interstellar space travel, time travel theories. He uses up all my aluminum foil to build rockets, and makes my heart quake with his theories about gunpowder and gasoline and electrical charges. I keep giving him reality checks—like when he was little and obsessed with Superman, and I kept saying, "You know you can't really fly, right, Zack?" and he'd look at me like I was crazy. (When he had just started preschool the music teacher asked, "Zack, what's your mommy's name again?" He looked at her with great earnestness and replied, "Lois Lane.") So now I keep saying he can't really set off his rockets with gunpowder and gasoline, right, Zack? And he hardly looks at me at all. But still he tells me his theories about what existed before time, why there is death, how he can get his aluminum-foil rocket to orbit the earth (237 little rockets filled with gunpowder and a giant balloon that inflates out the bottom of the big rocket when it reaches a certain elevation, or so I gather). He lets me in to see what is human. His fantasies are not mine; his obsessions are not mine. And that is what is wonderful about them. He is so totally other, and so totally willing to share himself with me. There isn't anyone else in the world who has been revealed to me so completely, from seed to bloom.

But the material I get from him cuts both ways. Because once I use something he has said or done, the character who says or does that becomes identified with him. I know that the character is exactly that—a fictional character—but I also know that Zack may *think* it is him. Since bad things happen to good characters, if I need to sacrifice a small child in my fiction I worry Zack will think it's him I'm trying to get rid of.

Madison Smartt Bell told me that when he began writing about the Haitian Revolution his daughter was an infant. He had to put in some material about "murderous assaults on infants," which were part of the historical record. Thematically it was important, but "I tended to do it at long range," he said. "It might have been more dramatically effective to have major characters lose infants in this way, or to have a child develop as a major character before being slain in a genocidal massacre . . . but I just couldn't do it, and I was very much aware that having a child of my own made it impossible for me to do it."

Madison's concern was not that his daughter would read what he wrote. It was a visceral reluctance on his part. For me the reluctance is both visceral and psychological. Zack isn't old enough to read my fiction now, but the kid has been pushing to do so since kindergarten, when my second novel came out. What I write is not appropriate for him. I need the freedom to write what I write, and if I think there's a little boy reading over my shoulder it freezes me.

Lore Segal found Zack's desire to read my writing unusual. "Most children," she said, "refuse to read what their parents write because they refuse to know." By way of example she told me how she had once been in a room full of Columbia University historians "and they discovered that their children had read the books written by the others but not by their parents." Nonetheless, she went on to say, "I am much troubled by writing child characters that my children would think were themselves. What you write about other people is a problem, too, and not just about children, but I have made my peace with that. I'm just going to do it and feel sorry."

Marissa Piesman's solution is to write about single people, not families. Ruth Reichl, on the other hand, finds having a child has freed her in her writing. It has made her more productive, even though her son sees "every book as the enemy," in that it takes her away from him. Because her memoir has painful childhood experiences in it, I was surprised to learn her nine-year-old son was reading it. "Initially I was unnerved," she told me, "but he asked if he could. Other kids in his class are reading it, so I said okay, and now I'm thoroughly enjoying the experience. He's never asked many questions about my family. This is a way for him to find out who I am—as a human being, not just his mother. He's finding out about my parents, whom he never really knew."

Autobiography comes largely from the impulse to share the story of one's life, which is perhaps why Ruth enjoys what I dread—our kids reading our books. *This is who I am*, the memoirist seems to say, *this is how I got to be that way*. People are who you say they are. There is none of this game of Spot the Source or Pin the Name on the

Character. People don't read between the lines and ask themselves, Is this me? Is that her? Is this how she really feels about me? There's none of the blending of the real and the imagined that makes readers who know us paranoid.

Because, yes, fiction writers *do* use material from life. And so people who know us read our work differently than those who do not, often making mistaken assumptions. Jodie Klavans told me she used to cry after a date with someone who had read her work. She felt so exposed *and* misunderstood. She still doesn't like her friends to read what she writes. "More often than not they believe you are your characters. If a character is a racist, I'm a racist; a money-hungry, sex-craving, calculating fool—yep, must be me."

If they don't see you, the author, at every turn they see other people they "recognize." They spot a trait and say, Stop! I know that man. So how can writers help but worry that some of what we write may hurt our husbands, children, parents. People take a nose for the whole person.

"I'm more guarded and afraid now," Jodie told me. "I know strangers read your work and can find you. My parents received a very threatening phone call after my first book was published. They actually moved in part because of that call."

Less ominously, my father-in-law asked me, after reading my novel *Secret Correspondence*, why I made the main character's father a baker when my own father was a butcher. I've been to weddings where cousins explain to me "mistakes" regarding family history that got into that novel. Sometimes they tell me stories, all prefaced with, "Listen to this. Here's something for you to write about, and it *really* happened." As if the reality of it made it better fiction. Reality doesn't make better fiction. Most of the time it gets in the way.

Fiction is a difficult concept for nonfiction writers to grasp. If you change something they correct you. No amount of saying that a character is a character and not a person will convince them otherwise, sometimes even when they themselves are writers. I had a reviewer refer to *Secret Correspondence*, which is written in diary form, as excerpts from *my* diary. And a well-known writer who had read the book told me he didn't keep a diary, implying he thought he was reading mine.

This is what you are up against if you are a novelist or a story writer.

The better your writing the more people will insist you took your material from them. You just keep insisting your writing is fiction, your characters are fiction, and even if your narrator has the same name and circumstances as yourself, he or she is not you. But things do get trickier when the reader is your own child, who remembers he said that about Grandma's wart. This is not a problem perhaps if you write lighthearted family stories where everyone loves everyone and only good things happen. You have other problems to deal with if that is what you write. But the solution to writing about your kid is the same as writing about other people—make composites and lie. There's just more at stake when the source of your inspiration is your own little darling, gazing back trustingly, telling you the secrets of his universe. You have to work hard to protect him from your cold writer's stare—disguising the origin of a character and an event that much more carefully.

Inspired by the foibles of family and friends, many writers find themselves frozen at the thought of exposing loved ones (and even not-so-loved ones) to the scrutiny of strangers. We use the material, then fear the sources will rise up against us. We're right to fear this. We're also right to use the material. You can't let guilt dictate what you write about, what you don't. You do need to take into account *how* you write it though. The best way to do this is not by diminishing the truth, but by learning to lie in the service of it. Mixing the quirks, changing the sexes, varying the situations—these are all ways we can write what we want and still protect our sources.

> If a writer has to rob his mother, he will not hesitate; the "Ode on a Grecian Urn" is worth any number of old ladies.
>
> —William Faulkner

The problem of identification is not restricted to kids, of course. We just worry about our kids more. But Uncle Harry has a few things to say about the way we make fun of his accent. And Little Molly wants us to know she wears a size-two shoe, not a four. Fiction writers don't create whole cloth: We take from life. All writers, with the possible exception of the Brothers Grimm, do this. If you write nonfiction you need to be as true to life as possible, keeping in mind that there is no truth—it is your perspective on the events and characters you are writing about. Still, you owe it to yourself, your readers, and your material to get your facts straight. And if you are writing unpleasant truths about them, it's best if your subjects are dead.

In fiction the secret to success is in the mixing of the real and the made up. It's better not to take Sadie Lipshitz and put her whole hog into your novel. That's like handing someone a cup of flour and an egg while singing, "Happy Birthday!" Bake the cake first. So take a handful of Sadie's comments and a few of Uncle-Joe mannerisms, throw in Phillip-Next-Door's ears, toss in a dash of dialogue and a sprinkle of zits. This is what you need to do to prevent hurt feelings and libel suits. Mix your material up so that no one is completely recognizable as anyone in particular, and events don't happen in quite the same way. If a man said it, have a woman say it. If he has red hair, give her brown hair. Then stick to your guns. This is not you. This has nothing to do with you. Yeah, I know your name is Sadie and her name is Sally, and she is married to Irv and you're married to Merv, but she's an accountant and you're a math teacher, so how could you and she be the same? Whatever you do, readers will still come along and say, "I know that's Sadie Lipshitz." Just laugh them off. Listen, they think they're so smart! You need to make them doubt themselves. Sometimes they're offended. "I don't uh-uh talk uh-uh like that." No one said you did. I said my *character* did.

"We are cannibals," Cynthia Ozick said at an Authors Guild symposium in October 1998. "I think it's a terrible thing to be a friend of, an acquaintance of, a relative of, a writer." And so I advise you to disguise the nature of the hors d'oeuvres you serve, then sit back and enjoy it with the rest of them. Remember, we may be cannibals, but others savor our offerings too.

Nadine Gordimer writes: ". . . this creature formed from the material and immaterial—what has breathed upon the writer intimately, brushed by him in the street, and the ideas that shape behavior in his personal consciousness of his time and place, directing the flesh in action—this fictional creature is brought into the synthesis of being by the writer's imagination alone, is not cloned from some nameable Adam's rib or Eve's womb. Imagined: yes. Taken from life: yes."

**Try This:** Write about someone you have strong feelings about, but disguise that person. If he's a man, make the character female. Or make him younger, older. At the very least change his hair color. Better yet, see if you can blend two or more real-life subjects into one made-up one. Remember, the idea here is to create a character, not be true to the real people he's based on. Test your deception by giving the portrait to someone who knows the person/people involved. Does your reader see through the mask or not?

> **TIP:** Some people will be flattered to find themselves in a book, no matter what you write; others will see any representation of them as a picture full of falsehood and venom. Be true to your material, then lie like crazy. I once went to a Halloween party where we were told to wear costumes to reveal the inner person. This had me so stymied I came as a mirror. But it's not a bad idea to pretend it's Halloween when you're writing: Dress your character up so her origin is unrecognizable but the inner person is revealed. You don't even have to buy green hair dye to do it.

TWENTY-FIVE

# "WORK!" CRIES MAYNARD G. KREBS

I've written about the difficulties of being a mother and a writer, but there are other constraints against a writer writing. A job, for instance.

I like to think that people who are rich suffer terribly from writer's block. How hard it must be to get up whenever you want and have the cook fix you something to eat, then have nothing to do a whole day but write. Yes, it must be horrible—not to have to get to work or meet a deadline or put breakfast on the table, do housework, shop for dinner. Not to have to do anything but write. A whole day. Whatever you want to write about. Never worrying about publishing markets and trends. Because you own the publishing house.

Somehow I don't think this form of torture is yours. I consider myself lucky because I work at home, but work I do—not just my own writing but assignments, editing, teaching. There are ways to make a living as a freelancer, but it's a meager one. John Gardner once suggested that if you are serious about writing you should find a patron, someone to support you while you write—a spouse, lover, or parent. I don't know if this is the best idea, but I do know that when I worked in an office I came home tired, unable to write at night. I wrote on weekends, but never as much as I wanted to—that is, I never accomplished what I set out to. I was lucky if I got to finish a story draft. I cried a lot. Sometimes, if things were quiet at work, I wrote there, but I didn't have my own office, so I had to be sneaky about it. I also had to type with my fingers in my ears—no easy task this. All in all, life was depressing.

Then I lost my job.

This was great, except for the fear of starving. The magazine publishing company I worked for closed. We all got a pittance as severance pay, but that pittance bought me a few weeks. And I had unemployment benefits. In effect, the government became my patron. That is not to say I wasn't looking for another job. I was. Only I was looking for freelance jobs. I was sending out resumes and writing samples, taking editing and proofreading tests, all in the hope of finding work I could do at home. And in the meantime I got to write every day.

It was a wonderful, scary time. I was figuring out how to be a real writer—which in my mind meant someone who wrote every day. I was learning self-discipline. I was learning that I could write in the morning, then I could set about trying to find work to support that writing in the afternoon. The hardest thing was making the telephone calls: introducing myself to people and asking for work. But I got better at it the more I did it.

The other wonderful thing that happened around then is I got married. And my husband was supportive of my writing career and has remained so through the twenty years that have passed. In effect I have found what John Gardner suggested finding—a patron. I contribute to our joint income, but if we had to live on what I make in a year we would be subsisting on moldy cheese and day-old bread. Whenever I get down on myself about this, equating money earned to value, my husband boosts my ego. "Someday your writing will take off, then I'll retire and live off the money you make." He also buys Lotto tickets.

The freelance life is not for everybody, especially if it is the only income in-coming. First of all, it tends to be a feast-or-famine deal. Many is the time I have had to juggle three and four editing and/or writing assignments only to finish up and not hear from anyone again for months. There is also a big lag between when you turn in an assignment and when you get a check for the work . . . if you get a check at all.

But one thing you get if you are a freelancer is time off to write. Lots and lots of time off. Nobody calls you, nobody makes demands of you. Nobody is paying you, and the bills keep on coming. Freelancers don't get vacation days or sick days—they get famine days, when there is no work to be had. If you can keep your panic in check, you can do a fair bit of writing during that time. If you can't, you will spend it calling everyone you know, panting with anxiety. And, like anyone else who works for a living, you still have to put aside your own work to accommodate Mr. Money Bags, no matter how close you are to finishing your opus. Martha Schulman, for example, does what she calls "goofy freelancing" in the afternoons or evenings so she has her mornings free to write. "If, however, someone paying me money wants me to do something in the morning, I'll do it."

Under the misguided notion that their love of language means they love anything to do with language many writers choose to work in fields related to writing. There are newsletter journalists who only want to write novels; business-magazine editors whose first love is poetry; literary agents who secretly want to be playwrights. For some people, writing for love and profit works fine. Tom Mallon, for example, told me, "I earn my living almost entirely by writing; have no children; live with a man who organizes our life together for my maximum comfort and productivity; have lots of friends but very little in the way of what might be called hobbies. I don't have the slightest idea of how to cook." Although he often has to put his fiction aside to work on something else, "The obligation is almost always another writing project with a more pressing deadline." When I asked him how he managed to find the time to write, he said, "By doing almost nothing else."

But for other people, working in a field closely aligned to writing can diminish or even spoil their original love. It's like working in a chocolate factory. The smell can get nauseating after eight hours immersed in it (or so I hear).

The last thing I feel like doing after writing an essay or editing a manuscript is to take out my novel for a read-through or, worse yet, to dash off a new chapter. I don't want to read, period. Not even *Jughead*. I don't want to speak. Or listen to songs with words. I don't even want to watch television—too much language involved. I just want to stare, glassy-eyed, at the ceiling fan—see if I can detect the individual blades from the spin.

Ruth Reichl, who was a restaurant critic for *The New York Times* as well as a memoirist, told me that juggling her two writing careers made her feel "sometimes I wish I'd just shut up." She'd find any excuse not to write. "Taking the cat to the vet is a good one." But because she *had* to get around this she did. She found "having a deadline really helps."

As a literary agent, Lori Perkins gets to use her love of reading as well as her desire "to help other writers get published well" in her work. But, as a writer herself, she occasionally gets "a little jealous" of the writers she represents. Whenever that happens, she knows it's time to devote herself to her own writing projects awhile.

The weird truth is that most writers have to do something else to make a living. Novelists work in bookstores, poets sell vacuum cleaners, and many writers edit and/or teach. Everyone wishes he or she had the freedom to work on a beloved project only. Perhaps we look at it the wrong way—there is inspiration to be gained from work we wouldn't rather be doing.

I joked before about the Poor Little Rich Writer who doesn't have to do anything but write exactly what she wants, being independently wealthy and owning the publishing house. But truly, how many heirs of the great robber barons are writers? With all that time and money, how come the Rockefellers haven't produced any literary geniuses? We complain about all the things we have to do, the way we complained as kids about the vegetables we had to eat before we could have dessert. I suspect we'd all secretly miss our spinach if we had to eat brownies three times a day, nothing but. And without the work that takes us away from our passion, we might find we had no food for thought, no structure to our day, nothing to write about.

I do fantasize about working at something less related to writing than teaching and editing. Being a carpenter would no doubt be a great source of nourishment for my writing. The problem is I don't know the first thing about carpentry. Sometimes I think I'd like to sell designer coffees or do leatherworking. Anything that has little to do with words. I could observe the world as I made my lattes and double skim capuccinos or tanned the skin of a cow and made it into a really fine belt.

Marissa Piesman, a writer who works in an area only indirectly related to her writing, advises, "Don't quit your day job without an irrevocable trust fund." She follows her own advice, continuing to lawyer full time despite the success of her mystery series. "The regular paycheck comes first," she said. "I write around the sides of that."

Anton Chekhov was a doctor, William Carlos Williams was too. Franz Kafka worked in insurance, T.S. Eliot in banking. Henry Miller was a telegram messenger. The notion that a writer must only write is a misguided one. Clearly there are ways to make a living and still write.

**Try This:** Write about your work, using the specifics of your job to serve as a metaphor for the larger meaning of the story, poem, or essay. Devote energy to the nitty-gritty of your job. Don't lose us in complaints, generalizations, or rhapsodies. Be specific. Pretend you are writing the piece for time travelers who've never seen an electrical outlet, let alone a computer. Don't take for granted that we know what an action entails, what the equipment smells like. William Faulkner said that his "own little postage stamp of native soil was worth writing about." This is true, too, for that tiny town you call your office and the landscape of desks and chairs you spend half your life in.

> It is good to welcome any region you live in or come to or think of, for that is where life happens to be, right where you are.
>
> —William Stafford

## FINDING THE TIME AND ENERGY

A few spaces do exist in the life of even the busiest gainfully employed person. Perhaps you've contemplated them. There's getting up early, for instance, writing for a few hours before work. I have nothing but admiration for writers who do this. Ruth Reichl told me, "I get up early in the morning, before everyone else, and get to it." I understand Joseph Heller managed to write *Catch-22* this way. Of course, you have to be a morning person to do it. And you must drink coffee. No one can get themselves going before sunrise without a cup of coffee. My friend Ellen Dreyer tried. She would make a nice cup of herbal tea around 5 A.M., then turn on her computer. They found her one afternoon in a cataleptic state in front of her screen. All she had written was the word *coffee* for ten pages.

Then there are the night types. Lori Perkins, agent by day and writer by night, said, "I'd rather write than do just about anything else, so I go without sleep to do it. I love to stay up and write while everyone is asleep, although I have also gotten up at the crack of dawn to write."

To write at night you must be the sort whose energy level peaks well after midnight. Perhaps you like to come home after work, have dinner and, instead of falling asleep over the newspaper, go into a room and learn another language. Or reread *The Odyssey* in the original Greek. Well then, night writing is for you. You clearly have the internal clock of an owl. Why fight it? Why toss and turn while the world snores, battling your mind's desire to create? Even if you are the tiniest bit groggy around 11:00, you have only to start to get energized by your creativity. Catch a wave of inspiration and you can go all night. The next day at work you'll be sleepy but fulfilled. Of course, if you do this regularly you'll begin snoring in the middle of meetings. Eventually you will be fired. But then you will have plenty of time to write.

Morning and night writers need to find ways to make their minds alert for their writing in the wee hours before or after work. Coffee is high on my list. In fact, it is higher than it has ever been, after cutting back for some months. I had been drinking twenty-four cups a day, and when I realized that I got scared. Of course they weren't real cups. They were what are called cups on the coffee maker, but really it takes two of them to fill a mug, so it was more like twelve.

There are other legal drugs to jumpstart your mind. I read somewhere that the army gives choline, a dietary supplement found in health food stores, to soldiers going into battle. I take choline when I have to talk to an intellectual. There's also ginkgo to stimulate your mind. It can be made into a tea that doesn't smell like vomit, the odor the fruit gives off when rotting in the park. Green tea supposedly fights lung cancer and dental plaque. It also happens to be chock full of caffeine. Sometimes I drink that instead of coffee—like whenever my pancreas starts to squeak. Occasionally I use these little homeopathic pills that promise Mental Alertness. The last time I bought them the guy in the pharmacy gave me change for a ten instead of a twenty: I guess he thought I was fair game.

If sleep deprivation is not for you, what about food? Perhaps you can write during your lunch hour. I know from having worked in an office that the lunch *hour* can last anywhere from fifteen minutes to half a day. Don't waste yours eating. Gobble something at your desk—a yogurt, a nutrition bar, some nuts and berries—then take that "hour" outside. Go to the library, the park, the local Starbucks. Go where you can sit down and write.

You may also find the odd chunk of time to write on your commute to work. I thought it unusual that Marissa Piesman wrote six novels on the subway on her way to work. Then Lori Perkins told me about her friend who wrote his first novel commuting on the E-train. *Standing up.* "I followed suit," Lori added, "and now I always have time to write what I need to, although I may not have time for 'luxurious' writing."

I can imagine writing on an Amtrak, where they give you those little pulldown tables to use as a desk. But standing up on the subway? To do it I'd have to lean my notebook on the back of the person in front of me. Even if I get a seat, it's not easy to concentrate, squeezed as I usually am between a sullen teenager who thinks he's a cowboy, his legs spread wide enough to accommodate a bronco, and a half-naked Sumo wrestler sweating onto my page, making the ink run. But inspired by Lori's and Marissa's examples, I have taken to freewriting on the train—only if I get a seat, however. And only if the person next to me isn't muttering curses in Serbian. To protect my privacy I've cultivated a handwriting so bad even I can't read it.

If your job causes you to travel from appointment to appointment, you might try to schedule some writing detours on the way. A friend of mine who works in the field—social services, not agriculture—is in the habit of popping into libraries on his way to appointments, stealing the odd half-hour in which to write. If your job allows you to do this, you might try a little library-hopping too. Avoid guilt feelings by thinking of it as taking all your coffee breaks at once.

And of course there are weekends, sick days, and vacations. Peter Rubie, for instance, manages to do a rough draft on weekends as best he can, then he can more easily "sit down and start working off the page with a pencil" at other times. Barry Denny takes the occasional sick day to find the continuity in which to bring things together.

## THE FIVE-MINUTE WRITING ROUTINE

You say you need privacy in which to write? Well, there *is* a private little room somewhere in your office where not even Simon Legree would follow you to see what you are doing. That's right—you can write in the bathroom at work. Maybe not novels (unless you're constipated). Maybe you can't stay in there an hour. But you may be able to steal five minutes a couple of times a day—enough time to write a few notes or a rough paragraph, maybe sketch out a scene.

The important thing about writing is that, while it's best to do it every day, you do not have to write for long periods of time. Look at your life and figure out what is reasonable for you to do. Can you find fifteen minutes in your day in which to write? You don't even have to work for fifteen minutes at a stretch. You can do five minutes in the bathroom and ten minutes on your coffee break, maybe in an unused stairwell for quiet. The important thing is the commitment. If you write every day for a predetermined amount of time, you can feel good about it. That is an accomplishment. And you can get a lot done. Perhaps the most important thing is that you are taking some of the weight off the upcoming vacation.

What happens to writers who work in an office is that they invest all their creative energies into thinking about their vacation. They plan how they are going to sit at the computer, writing all day so they can finally finish that novel. This doesn't sound like a vacation to your imagination, it sounds like a threat. If I were inspiration I'd hightail it out of there. And that is what inspiration generally does.

If you haven't been writing all along you are probably going to come down with one major writer's block during the two-week stint you plan to spend at your computer. Instead of writing, your time will be spent beating your forehead on the screen. When you get back to the office people won't ask about your vacation. It will be clear from looking at you that you spent your time in prison or the National Reserves.

Five-minute writing chunks are good for keeping the impending writer's-block/vacation-in-hell at bay. You can write a lot in five minutes, though probably not the "luxurious writing" Lori Perkins despairs of having the time for. You can write notes; you can freewrite. You can even write a quick first draft of a scene, knowing that on your vacation you can take out that sketch and work it up into a full story or chapter. If you get a pack of five-minute sketches, your novel will almost write itself as you stitch them together. If it's an essay, you'll have your major themes in paragraphs you can then polish.

Because the mind freezes in fear of the blank page, you need to find ways to ward off that fear. Your packet of five-minute pieces is your torch to scare away the vampires of doubt. Read over the bits you wrote in your stolen moments. Try arranging them in some order. Any order. Kenneth Atchity, who first turned me on to the five-minute writing block in *A Writer's Time*, suggests using index cards to write on—they make it easier to shuffle the deck.

I'm talking about the worst scenario—five-minute writing breaks for people who can't really write anything in five minutes. Of course, if you're writing for five minutes and you don't want to stop and don't have to (e.g., no one is pounding on the john door), then *don't*. But make a commitment of a certain amount of time you will spend each day writing. If five minutes is all you have time for, so be it. Do your five minutes and feel good. There are a lot of five minutes wasted in a day.

**Try This:** When you find yourself daydreaming at work, grab a pen and start taking dictation. We all daydream, so don't tell me you don't. The more deadening your job, the more time you waste doing it. Instead of staring out the window watching the pigeons mate, jot down those woolly thoughts. Daydreams don't have to add up to the Great American Novel. The important thing is that you are writing. Your synapses are full of current, your inspiration cells are juicy.

**TIP:** Make an outline of scenes and/or topics. When you only have ten minutes to write, pick one and go to it. You can write a rough first draft of a scene in that amount of time. It's a sketch, not a finished painting. Later you can add shadows, light, and Technicolor.

## OTHER GOALS

A variation on the five-minute writing slot is to set a goal for yourself of pages written rather than time consumed. Lori Perkins, for example, tries to write a page a day. That page can be anything—a page in her journal counts. Freewriting counts. If she doesn't make this goal, she doesn't beat herself up about it. She just tries to make that goal the next day. Some people set weekly goals instead, or monthly ones. That way, if they can't get to the writing on Monday, they can write twice as much on Tuesday. They can do it however they want, as long as they finish the appointed number of pages within a certain time frame.

Making a writing commitment, whether it is a daily amount of time or a weekly number of pages, keeps writer's block from building. It keeps the finger-mind connection alive too, so when you want to write the serious stuff you remember how. It will even help you lose weight.

After all, how many cookies can you stuff in your mouth if your fingers are dancing?

> The only way to learn [to write] is to force yourself to produce a certain number of words on a regular basis.
>
> —William Zinsser

Some people will shake their heads at this, insisting there are not five minutes in a day to spend writing down their daydreams. They rush from here to there, and don't even use the bathroom. Frankly, I have just the slightest bit of doubt about such people's commitment to writing. I know I said it's possible to write and still make a living, but there are jobs and there are *jobs*. If you don't have any time to write, maybe you are in the wrong kind of job. Have you considered housecleaning? Louise Rafkin, author of *Other People's Dirt: A House-cleaner's Curious Adventures*, supported her writing for eight years by cleaning. The twenty to fifty dollars an hour she charged for doing that (fifty dollars!—she must have cleaned for J.P. Morgan) beat the seven bucks an hour she could get working in a bookstore. House-cleaning not only enabled her to write, it fed her imagination. The snooping instincts most writers have were given free rein. She could open medicine cabinets and drawers, "tidy" desks (reading what was on them), assembling clues about people by what they saved or threw out. She always found a story in the mess.

Evan Russell believes writers need to take work that is unglamor-ous but pays better because nobody wants to do it, a crummy job that lets you buy time off to write. "To buy time you have to sacrifice," he said. "You have to be poor, not have pretty things, not drink the best hooch, not travel. Stick with the old piece-of-shit stereo. You have to work part-time at a job that is the opposite of fulfilling because jobs that reward the spirit pay poorly and/or are intellectually taxing. You have to seek out the kind of horrendously awful jobs that are just demanding enough that management has to cough up a decent wage."

This may sound a bit self-righteous, and Evan did admit he initially started writing when he broke his back and was on disability for six months. (He was mighty cheery last time I spoke to him, when he told me he'd been in a car accident and was on disability again, con-templating a new novel—I don't recommend this.) So if you don't want to quit your low-paying, glamorous job to work sixteen-hour stints doing computer data entry two days a week, you don't have to. But if you *really* want to write you have to find a way to make a commitment to that. There's sleep deprivation, lunch deprivation, coffee-break deprivation, bathroom deprivation. You can write fifteen minutes a day in five-minute chunks. You can promise yourself to write a certain number of pages a day or a week or a month. You can write your daydreams instead of just having them. You can write on the train. If you commute by car you can try to "write" by talking into a tape recorder.

> People say, "Time is money," but I say, "Money is time," for every luxury costs so many precious hours of your life.
>
> —Israel Meir Kahan

But here's the thing: If you really want to write, you get to do that. And you *can* still hold down a job. It takes a lot of energy, but remember: Writing is your love. It's like making time for sex or food. It is what you enjoy—that is why you want to do it. You may need to question yourself, however—is it the writing you love, or the fantasy of having written? If it's the latter, I can't help you because writing takes time and effort, and if you're working at something else you're not going to want to give up anything in order to write. But if writing is what you love, then that is what you *want* to be doing. You will make sacrifices to do it, not because you're a martyr but because of a secret you and I share—writing is a deep pleasure.

**Try This:** Look at your life and figure out a reasonable writing schedule—half an hour before work? Fifteen minutes in three bathroom breaks? Twenty minutes during your lunch hour?—or page quota—two pages a day, five days a week? Thirty pages a month, no matter what? Once you have figured what you can reasonably do, make a chart and mark off each time you fulfill your commitment. Do this for at least a month, till it becomes as much a part of your life as brushing your teeth. After a month look at what you've accomplished—the growing pile of pages, the higher self-esteem, the greater sense of purpose. This should enable you to make a commitment for the next month. The schedule or quota may change from month to month. During busy periods at work you may only have five minutes a day to write. During months with vacation time you may be able to write for a few hours at a stretch. You can always do more than what you've committed yourself to. The schedule or quota is the bare mimimum you can manage. And if you fall off your schedule, just get back on the next day. It's like a diet or Alcoholics Anonymous: The sooner you get back on track, the better.

And if not now, when?

—Hillel

## TWENTY-SIX

# IT'S ALIVE!

Unfortunately, there does come a time in every writer's life when she must put aside the writing she'd rather be doing to work on something urgent. Whether that is taking care of a kid or a parent, working against a pressing deadline, making money or hors d'oeuvres for a party of two hundred, some obligation will raise its ugly head and look at you, and you will have to go to it.

Like parents whose child has just left for sleepaway camp, writers often worry what will happen to their inspiration during such a break. Will it return to them alive? Will there continue to be a relationship between them, or will it from that point onward look at them with the cold eyes of a stranger?

While there are no easy answers to these questions, perhaps there is solace in realizing most writers live with such enforced hiatuses. Oh, perhaps John Updike doesn't. Somehow I can't imagine a *New Yorker* editor calling him in a hissy-fit because he took time off from writing an extraordinary essay to write an extraordinary story. But most of us are not John Updike.

Those of us who are not John Updike must juggle the work we do for love and the work we do for money. All we need are big red noses and baggy pants to complete the ensemble. Despite intentions to write at dawn or dusk, writers with regular jobs may find themselves writing mostly on weekends. Handyman-freelancers may have to put writing projects aside for months in order to turn in an assignment on time. Kids get chicken pox and holidays. This is the nature of the beast we live with. All I can say is learn to love yours, because it's not going away. It may change from time to time, depending on your obligations, the project you'd rather be doing, and your menstrual cycle. But it is a permanent companion in the writing life.

You *can* see past the fangs though. I sort of like my beast because when it's not around I am immersed in a daily fantasy world, little of which sees the light of publication. After a while I start to feel the slightest bit unreal. Having an assignment to turn in or a teaching gig to go to gives me credibility, at least in my own eyes: *Hey, I really am a writer—look, there's my byline.*

That's not to say your writing project won't swoon into a deathlike sleep while you're off in the mines, digging for gold. You have to learn to be Prince Charming *and* the seven dwarves to respond to this. But your kiss *does* have the power to awaken Snow White. Your writing only looks dead till you plant a wet one on her. Your thoughts will bring her back to life.

I asked some writer friends what they do to keep inspiration alive during the times they can't be writing. Ellen Dreyer, whose work as a freelance editor and writer often makes breaks from her novel necessary, said, "At times I feel in mourning for the lost continuity." To get around this she tries to keep her novel in mind by "jotting ideas in my journal, sticking Post-it reminders and encouraging words on my bulletin board—keeping the project visible, not shut in a drawer."

Emily Russell also finds it important to keep a work in progress open on the desk. "Having it around, I tend to sidle up to the page at odd times and inadvertently get something done. Sweeping it out of sight, it becomes *peripheral* to life rather than a central element."

I am an anti-clutter sort of person, and my desk has limited surface area, so such an approach does not work for me. When I take on an assignment, my novel goes into a folder and gets stashed away. But I try to keep the ideas alive by thinking about them during the odd interstices of my day—running, washing my face, buying milk and cottage cheese. None of these activities demands much mental power. I am capable of sniffing a cantaloupe and daydreaming about my character sniffing a cantaloupe.

Sam Decker keeps his postponed work alive by thinking about it all the time and writing in his journal. "When I was first writing poetry the poet Alice Neely told me to always think about poetry—so I do the same writing stories, as I cook, shower, drive."

If you learn to switch to the daydreaming mode during the blank times in your day, your project won't seem so foreign when you get back to it. Madison Smartt Bell told me he fights laying projects aside for very long, but "When that is impossible, the daydreaming habit helps keep the work mentally alive and in touch."

In addition to daydreaming, perhaps you can find a five-minute break in your day in which to write about your ideas. You may not have the energy or concentration to sink deep into the dream, but you can tickle the itch. Not only will this keep your project alive, but when you do return to it the notes will help you reenter that particular dream.

I find it frustrating to have to put my writing aside, especially during the heat of creation, but I also look forward to the time away from it. I try to finish a draft before I take on an assignment—if not a complete first draft of a novel, then whatever section I am working on. This isn't always possible, but knowing I have work coming on such-and-such a date often functions as my deadline for finishing a draft. If I have to steal a day or so from an assignment in order to finish up or get my notes in order, I do. It's part of that anti-clutter thing. Just as I can't keep a project open on my desk while I am working on something else, I can't leave my writing in the middle of a chapter. I need to finish my thought for the time being. It doesn't have to be perfect; I know I will get back to it. But I can't leave it in a complete muddle.

This book you are reading now, for instance—I have had to put aside a novel to write it. At first I thought I would be able to work on both projects at the same time, but deadline constraints didn't allow for that. Plus the verbal part of my mind is used up by the afternoon. I don't *want* to write my novel after writing about writing. Instead, when I'm running or doing other mindless tasks, I switch to the daydreaming mode. As a result I am thinking out subplots I sketched earlier. I knew they were needed, but I couldn't be bothered thinking about them before. They felt like a distraction from the main story. But now I have ample time to ponder the strands of plot, twist them, tie them. I am also looking at my characters from different angles, making them rounder, more complicated.

I know from experience I will end up with reams of notes in my various notebooks by the time this manuscript is handed in. When I first start going through these notes they will seem the ravings of a lunatic. Still, I will mine them in search of the odd gem—a revelation or a phrase. When I see something I like I will circle it. After I complete the search mission I'll type the circled notes. Everything will be a mess for a while, and I'll fantasize about becoming a lumberjack, a Paul Bunyan of a woman, cutting down all the trees so no one can make paper. But I will force myself to keep contemplating my outline, dreaming the book through, making changes. Eventually things will start to clear, my notes will take on an order, and I will rearrange them (aren't computers wonderful?). At that point I will be ready to re-immerse myself in my novel, reading over what I've written.

Although it is not ideal to be reading first-draft material before the draft is complete, I will do it to reestablish the narrative voice, as well as to remind me what has taken place. By the time I finish reading, trusty notes and outline in hand, my murky thoughts will have clarified, and I will be ready to start writing new material.

This is how I kiss the Sleeping Beauty after working in the mines. It is frightening at times to see that dead figure before me, realizing I'm the only one who can bring it to life. But I've done it before, and I know in the end I will have a richer book for all the enforced departures.

Emily Russell told me she finds getting back to a piece of writing after putting it aside "excruciatingly fear-ridden," but instead of allowing that to freeze her she tries "to fall in love with the process, viewing it as another part of the necessary passage." If you view the intervals between writing as opportunities for reflection, not as going on vacation without leaving food in the pet bowl, you'll find the breaks nourishing. Remember, even when you're not writing you can be "writing." Daydreams and note-taking are just as much a part of writing as tap-dancing the keys.

## RETURN OF THE ICEMAN

Perhaps you've seen the movie *The Iceman*. In it these scientists find a Neanderthal frozen in Antarctica or someplace like that, only he's not dead. He's in suspended animation, deep frozen like Walt Disney's head, but they manage to bring him back to life. That's what it feels like when you pick up a writing project you've put aside. You brush off the layers of snow and ice, and come up with this cold, dead thing. It looks like your project but it's inert. You're sure you'll never be able to get it to breathe, to move around, to make jokes again. Well, you can. I don't remember how the scientists did it to the Iceman, but you can do it to

> Mary Wollstonecraft Godwin Shelley wrote *Frankenstein* after failing to write the ghost story Lord Byron requested. "I saw the pale student of unhallowed arts kneeling beside the thing he had put together. I saw the hideous phantasm of a man stretched out and then, on the working of some powerful engine, show signs of life.... His success would terrify the artist; he would rush away [hoping] this thing ... would subside into dead matter. He sleeps; but he is awakened; he opens his eyes; behold the horrid thing stands at his bedside, opening his curtains."

your writing by performing eye-to-page resuscitation, a.k.a. rereading.

Even writers who write every day read "the last bit of stuff I wrote," as Lori Perkins put it, to enable them to pick up the train of thought. For Barry Denny, who rarely gets to write every day (only on "those rare occasions when I take a week's vacation to write"), and whose work "is an ebb and flow of interruption," rereading is a way to bring his characters back to life and to remember at what point of the development of his ideas he stopped.

How far back you read has to do with the length of time since you last wrote. If I'm writing on a daily basis, I don't read back too far, just a paragraph or so to help me reenter the voice. I've found that when I read back further I get caught up in editing. Since the piece in question hasn't had a chance to simmer long enough for me to gain enough objectivity, this is not the best approach. But if I've had to leave a piece of writing for a long time I will probably have to read from the beginning to go forward.

## STOPPING IN THE MIDDLE OF A . . .

Some writers advise stopping in midsentence as a way to establish continuity and enable you to more easily reenter your writing. Instead of trying to complete the first draft of a chapter or story, no matter how sketchily, you are advised to stop writing in a place where you know what comes next, where the excitement and the urge to finish are high. Doing this is supposed to help you pick up where you left off. As I mentioned earlier, this was Hemingway's approach.

I can no more stop myself from finishing an exciting scene than I can stop reading one. It seems to me stopping this way, at the height of the creative urge, defeats the purpose of writing. I don't write because I believe the world needs to read what I have to say. The world has shown too little regard for what I write for me to believe that. I write because it gives me pleasure. It helps me remember things, to understand them. It creates order in this otherwise sloppy monologue I call my mind. So I always try to finish a draft in a sitting—a chapter or a story, or sometimes just a scene. Then I go back and fill things out, revise, move stuff around. I like to have the whole blob of clay before me to shape on the next go-round. I could never leave a nose lying on the table because I was really excited about the eyes and mouth and cheeks I was going to get to do next time.

But some writers have such tight schedules they have no choice but to leave the work before they're through. Lori Perkins, for example, always has to leave her desk before she's completely finished. Jodie Klavans says, "If I didn't have to close shop at 2:00 to pick the children up from school at 3:00—or worry about dinner, baths, homework, field trips, birthday parties—I'd finish a first draft of a chapter in one sitting. But I do, so I don't put time pressure on myself."

If you have to leave work unfinished because of your schedule, why not try stopping in midflow, at a high point where you know what comes next? Perhaps it will help you achieve continuity in your work and get back into it more easily the next time. If, however, you develop a nervous tic and start kicking puppies, I'd suggest you reconsider the approach.

## TO THE FINISH

The scariest thing about putting work aside is that you might *not* finish it. You really might not find a way back into it. It does happen. Marissa Piesman told me, "Everything I've had to put aside has not been finished. I lose momentum easily." She also joked that "The first unfinished manuscript horrified me. Then you get used to it."

Sam Decker's perspective is more philosophical. "It doesn't bother me anymore. I've outgrown ideas because I was too slow in bringing them along. That's sad, but the story and its purpose in my life are still there, and still important to me."

Not all works are meant to be finished. We change over time. Our needs and obsessions change. Sometimes writing half a novel is

> **TIP:** You may need to reread in order to pick up the thread of your writing, but there's only so much rereading you can do before it becomes counterproductive. If you write solely on weekends you need to limit the number of pages you reread or you will keep reading and polishing the same ten pages. Maybe you can start on the last page of what you've written. Remember, rereading is seductive. It's easier to read what we've already worked on, to play with punctuation and substitute a word or two, than to head off into the Great Unknown. But the latter is what you have to do. So reread only as much as you have to in order to reestablish the voice. Chances are you're going to have to revise your early pages by the time you get to the end anyway.

enough—we have already benefited from writing what we did and now we are ready to move on.

Jodie Klavans told me that when she puts her writing aside to tend to some other obligation, "My inspiration changes, and I have to deal with that. Certainly it was much easier when I was twenty and had no obligations—but then it was all about me and by the time I was thirty I couldn't go on like that any longer."

Peter Rubie remembers his earlier writing as being less troublesome. "I've used up most of the easy stuff, the easy characters," he said, "so sloth looms large and I have to dig down deeper." Easier or not, you can't go back to what drove you ten years ago. Writing begun when you were single probably won't be relevant to you when you're a grandparent. If you put something away for long enough, you may simply have to let go of it. That doesn't make it a failure. You've gotten out of it what you needed, even if that was only learning how to move from A to B. You've sucked the juice from the orange; now it's time to throw away the skin.

Madison Smartt Bell says he doesn't have trouble finishing projects because "Most of my unrealized ideas never make it out of the mental toying stage. If I pick up a stylus to begin something, I usually have a complete enough idea of the whole thing that I finish it."

Steve Schwartz also says he tends to finish projects because he's picky about starting. The things he hasn't finished he thinks of as "still in process." He doesn't have the luxury of doing this with projects for which he's paid, but "I feel a little looser about things I'm writing for me. I feel even if they've been in the drawer for years, when the time is right I'll pull them out and finish."

As we get older we get choosier about the projects we start. Once you've worked on your first book you know what that entails and are less inclined to start work that doesn't drive you. "I don't write novels that don't haunt me," Peter Rubie told me. "So when I start, I begin to quickly feel like some modern version of Charles Dickens' Ebenezer Scrooge. The damn book won't leave me alone. At its most benign it's like a nagging child despite whatever gets in the way." On the occasions when he does experience trouble continuing or finishing a project, he curses, weeps, and thinks a lot. "I always start to rethink my characters; who they are, what they want." He also moans to friends, "and in so doing sometimes talk out the problem until it's solved."

There are some people, however, who have psychological barriers that keep them from finishing work, and that is a different sort of problem. It's not that the material doesn't drive them, or that it isn't relevant, or that they weren't suitably hot before starting. It is more a sort of separation anxiety. They fear their work being out there, alone, without them to protect it. What will its reception be in the world's eyes? Will it make friends easily? And it's gotten to be so pleasant having it around, now that it no longer demands a 2:00 bottle and a rethinking of the outline. The work is almost done, the book is about to go off to college. As it nears completion they find themselves panicky. It's the empty-nest syndrome. When they don't have it to work on anymore, what will they do?

When Maureen Brady was having trouble finishing a book she'd been working on for a long time, her therapist suggested she write a letter to it. In the letter she described "all the book had meant to me on a personal level." This was "To get it ready (ask it if it was not ready) for the graduation to becoming public." The approach enabled her to finish the writing, to *force* herself to do it.

The operable word here is "force." If you find yourself unable to finish *anything*, it may not be due to separation anxiety or having outgrown the project. You may be experiencing a test of faith. You lose confidence in your ideas before you can complete them because you are unable or unwilling to let anyone else reject them before you do. What you need to do if this happens to you regularly is *strong-arm* yourself to finish a first draft. Do not allow yourself to give up. As dull as the writing seems, as murky as your ideas have become, slog on through till the end, then give yourself a couple of days to recuperate. (You may promise yourself a treat while you're slogging and spend those few days doing things you love—movies, trashy novels, dinner with friends.) After those days are up, read what you've written. Usually you'll find that once you have something on paper, bad as it may be (and it's almost never as bad as you imagine it beforehand), you can work with it. But if you allow your self-doubt to rule, you will never finish anything. Then at the end of your life there you'll be, surrounded by your incomplete manuscripts, and you'll get to look up from your deathbed and say, "At least I didn't make a fool of myself."

"For years," Jodie Klavans told me, "I couldn't finish anything. This came after what I consider a great success with a Hollywood deal. Everything I began seemed good at first, and then I couldn't go on because it didn't feel good enough. Eventually I forced myself. Now I'm rewriting and I feel good about the process." So good, in fact, that when I ran into her the other day she told me she had finished her novel and sent it off to her agent, who hadn't heard from her in five years and had stopped sending her Christmas cards. "She was enthusiastic," Jodie said. "I still need to do some restructuring, but she was optimistic and encouraging. I had to force myself every day to sit down and write, but I did, and it paid off."

**Try This:** Brace yourself. It's time to take out one of those half-finished manuscripts and finish it. You are not allowed to put it away without an ending, no matter how bad. Read over what you have and let the momentum carry you through. If it doesn't, make a list of all the possible things that can happen to end the piece. Choose one and write it. After you have finished that ending, you may choose another and write *it*. What you may not do is put it away without an ending. You are going to force one out, or you are going to throw away the fragment.

> **TIP:** Threatening yourself with discarding an unfinished project will often frighten away your resistance to finishing it. *Hey, she means business*, the unconscious thinks. *We better get cracking before she throws out the baby and the bathwater*. You don't have to like the ending you come up with. You can change it later. You can write a different one. But for now you are going to work on coming up with an ending, period—any ending.

# TWENTY-SEVEN

# WHAT TO DO WHEN YOU JUST CAN'T DO IT

Sometimes you just can't write. You sit and stare, agonizing and accomplishing nothing. You bang your head on your desk, gently at first, then with greater intensity. You hear the mantra begin: I hate myself, I hate myself, I hate myself.

You don't have to hate yourself. You don't have to give up. There are things you can do at such a time. Go to a movie. Go to a museum. Read a book. Call a friend. Paint, sing, bake. Clean a closet, organize your files, update your computer.

Most important of all: Be kind to yourself.

Sometimes you are empty. You need to nourish yourself before you have something to say. That's where movies, books, and museums come in. Listening to music is another source of mind food. It's okay to do these things. It doesn't mean you are sloughing off, doing what everybody secretly thinks you do all day anyway—nothing. You are feeding yourself. You are giving your mind a chance to play. Let your imagination roam away from your desk. Lie on the couch and day-dream. Doodle and let your thoughts wander. Sometimes you can't write because you don't know what you want to say. If you stop telling your mind to think, think, damn you, it may come up with an idea on its own.

You have to trust your unconscious sometimes. You have to leave it alone to do the work in its own playful way. It's cooking, but you can't smell the fragrance yet. You can't force it, anymore than you can force a cake to rise before its time. If you try you will end up with gloppy batter that not only tastes bad but will probably give you salmonella because of the raw eggs.

"I never think of myself as 'blocked,' " Steve Schwartz told me, "even though I've had long periods without writing. It's more that I have nothing at that moment to say."

Sam Decker agreed. "I don't believe in block. You either write, or you don't. Sometimes you aren't creative; sometimes you don't have ideas. Then you do."

When you're having a hard time getting your work done, take stock of what you're doing. Maybe you need a break. I don't want to sound like an astrologer or someone walking around in a purple gown, but this may be a good time to dream—and to pay attention to your dreams.

The unconscious speaks in a different, non-rational language than the conscious, ambitious ego. Its manner of speech is more akin to jokes than work. Puns, nonsequiturs, fantasies, archetypes, symbols—this is how the mind fools around. Let it. Stop being such a strict parent. Stop with the No More Monkeys Jumping on the Bed.

When he's having trouble writing, Barry Denny goes to the movies. "But I have a tendency to do this too often," he admitted, "and that's running away from the hard work of writing." Now, listen to me. I am *not* telling you that you can go to the movies every day and still call yourself a writer. To be a writer you have to write. I wish you could be a writer just by buying a computer and some stamps, but you can't. Writers have to *write*. You can't write, however, without living. You can't write only from the head. You have to go places, even if it's only a walk around the block. You have to do things, whether that's open-heart surgery or digging for worms. Take things in while you dig for worms. Smell the dirt; feel the tickle of worm on hand.

So, if you have tried for an hour or however long you've determined to give to your writing each day, and nothing is coming out, well, maybe there's nothing in there. You're running on Empty. It's time to get some fuel. One thing is certain—if you sit there any longer you will begin to hit yourself over the head with a ream of paper, you may even open your wrists with your rapidograph pen. Neither of these is a good idea of what to do when you just can't do it.

If art feeds your spirit, go to that exhibit you've been dying to see. If it's anthropology, go to the Museum of Natural History. Even a simple thing like taking a bath or shower can get your creative juices flowing again. Legend has it that Archimedes' "eureka" regarding the displacement of water got shrieked in the tub. On a less exalted plane, Ruth Reichl often resorts to taking showers when she's not sure how to proceed with a restaurant review. "I get great leads standing under the water," she told me.

Does social activity energize you, do you need a few laughs—why not invite a friend to lunch? Do you get turned on when you're alone in some eerie place? Head over to that cathedral near your son's school. They don't know you're not praying. Go in there and soak up the atmosphere—just don't wash your face with the holy water.

Or try exercise. Walking is good because it can be done on automatic pilot, leaving you and your mind alone. You know how I feel about plotting while I walk or jump or run. I don't know why this works. Maybe it's the increased blood flow to the brain. Maybe it's the endorphins. Maybe it just gets you out of the self-hating mode so you can stop reciting the I-hate-myself mantra. Whatever it is, something about pushing your body helps your mind relax and start thinking again. And after all, that is what your mind *likes* to do.

You can get past a block not just by doing physical exercise but by doing writing exercises. Evan Russell, while working as a typist in a law firm, used to see a series of books in the conference room called the *List of Digest Topics*. "On the spines were the first and last digest topics in each volume—*Abandonment* to *Burglary*, for instance. Intrigued, I photocopied all the titles (there were hundreds) and then made myself sit down and write a little vignette for each one. I never made it through the *B*s, but still I wrote a lot. And the topics were so juicy: Abandonment, Abduction, Abortion. It was simply an exercise, like calisthenics, but one or two worthwhile short stories were born from it."

Martha Schulman wishes there was a writing service that assigned exercises. Every couple of weeks a new exercise would come in the mail, and she could work on it, then share it with other writers. It would be a sort of *Mission Impossible* of the imagination—Your writing exercise, if you choose to do it, is. . . . And there it would be.

I don't know of any such service, although it sounds like a good idea (entrepreneurs, take note). But you can be your own taskmaster. Assign exercises to yourself. Go to a bookstore or the library and browse the many writing books that offer exercises. Some are to help you with a particular problem. Others are to help you find the fun. I threw some your way in chapter nineteen, but it's easy to make up your own, based on your own interests and needs. Lori Perkins used to invent exercises to get her "writing juices flowing." A couple of her topics were: "Describe the interior of the local butcher store" and "Document the stories on the local TV news." What interests you? Can you invent an exercise that engages that interest?

**Try This:** Collect or invent writing exercises. Put these, each on a separate slip of paper, in a story envelope. Then it's a simple matter to pull one out when you want to write but don't know what to write about. Remember: These are exercises. They are not for anyone to see but you . . . unless you choose to show them. Knowing this may help relieve some of your self-consciousness and self-doubt.

> Writer's block is only a failure of ego.
>
> —Norman Mailer

## THE WRITE TIME

Writing is life. When you are a writer, you are a writer all the time. If you can't actually sit down and write you can still observe. "Try to be one of those people," Henry James said, "on whom nothing is lost." Write in your head. Memorize a snatch of overheard dialogue. Note the details of your desk, where it's scratched or warped, where it shines. Look for material in the world around you. It would be nice if you were surrounded by flowers and baby lambs. Maybe you are surrounded by Formica, dog poop, and burnt coffee pots. As much as you hate your job, there must be something you can use for material. If you work in a fast-food restaurant, take us into its hidden recesses. A friend of mine worked at McDonald's when she was in high school. She said the manager had photographs on the wall of himself at McDonald U. Eventually he fired her, telling her she wasn't taking her job seriously enough. "I'm selling burgers at McDonald's and you want me to take that seriously?" she asked, flinging down her apron. There are absurdities in your job. Odd inspirations. Take note of them.

Novelists are luckier than short-story writers because a novelist has a book inside that she carries, like a pregnant elephant, for a couple of years. Every day the novelist knows what she is going to write. There's the next chapter, another scene, a new character. She doesn't always know how to move the plot along, but she has the basic storyline, characters, locale, and mood.

A story writer, on the other hand, has to frequently think of a new story, and sometimes new story ideas just won't come. The best thing for the writer of short pieces to do is to rotate stories. Write something new, then let it simmer while working on other stories in the Cooking file. That way you can always be working. The Astronomer Royal of England, Sir Martin Rees, uses such an approach to avoid "theory block," the scientific variation on the theme. "The way I overcome it is to work on several things at once. I follow several areas of a subject in parallel. I'm on three or four at the moment. . . . If one thing goes badly, then I shift to something else." If this works for the Astronomer Royal of England, it will work for you.

Now, let it be known there are some writers who have never experienced writer's block, lucky souls, and a few go so far as to dispute its existence. Tom Mallon, prolific and level-headed, called it "an invented malady that writers invoke as an excuse." But those of us who have undergone such periods of incapacitating self-doubt know otherwise. "It's been several months since I had an ongoing story I was deep into," Martha Schulman told me. "It seems I'll never think of a story again. Still, I try to write, I play with old things, I try to make something up. I whine. I nap. I turn on NPR. These last behaviors do not free anything, but they pass the time."

Evan Russell likened writer's block to "a huge case of overself-consciousness. It's like if you start thinking about walking or eating, how you look when you walk or eat. Before you know it you can't put one foot in front of the other and you're biting your tongue and stabbing yourself with the fork. Just walk, just eat. Same with writing: Keep writing, even if you aren't penning *War and Peace*. The important thing is the act of writing. Hitting the keys, wallowing in language."

The main cause of writer's block is perfectionism. We don't want to make the messes we will later have to clean up (revise). We want the perfect story, the perfect article, right away. Emily Russell's block came on after one of her stories was published. "The shock of having been exposed essentially paralyzed me for several years. I kept trying to go back and reenact whatever the 'thing' was I'd gotten right on that first story." This happened even though she believed and still believes that "that 'thing' is different in every story and you're sunk if you try to repeat it."

**Try This:** What helped Emily get past her block was she would handwrite passages of writing by other authors she admired "just to demystify the process. Seeing something handwritten somehow reminded me that it was only words. That a story gets written sentence by sentence." When you come across writing that affects you, try writing it out in your notebook. Be sure to ascribe it correctly though. Some years ago a writer was accused of plagiarism because he mistook words he had copied into his journal as his own. I keep a notebook devoted just to quotes, which I often mine for encouragement and solace—group therapy with the dead.

• Notebooks are useful to all writers, but those experiencing blocks often find in them the key to unlocking their prison. "The journal has proven invaluable over the years," Lori Perkins told me. "In it I document my block and how I get out of it, so the next time I find myself in that emotional space I can read about how I got out." Your journal can serve as a laboratory for writing exercises, but its most important function is as a *kvetch*atorium. No one wants to hear you complain about how you can't write. But your journal doesn't mind. *Give me your tired, your humble, your bored and dull thoughts yearning to be free.* One doesn't get an offer like that every day, not without paying a hundred bucks an hour. So take out that notebook and write pure dreck—self-hatred, mother-hatred, and don't forget Christmas while you're at it and yapping dogs.

• Some writer's blocks are caused by the vacuum we write in, the sense no one cares. It can help to know there are magazines looking for work on particular topics. Thematic literary magazines run issues on predetermined subjects or themes. The literary magazine *Witness*, for example, had an issue some years ago on American Humor, another one months later on the Holocaust. Other magazines will give you a title and ask that you come up with the story. "Scrawled in a library book" was one such title in *Thema*. Knowing there are magazines out there with stated interests on particular themes can relieve that feeling writers sometimes get of screaming under glass. It's not that your stories are any more likely to be published in thematic magazines than non-thematic ones. It's still a hard sell, but at least the market is limited to those writers who are mining a particular vein. And the theme may inspire you to write something you might not have thought of without prodding.

Along the same lines, the magazine *Poets & Writers* has a classified section in which many different magazines and anthologies post calls for writings in specific areas. Editors may be looking for manuscripts on Childhood or Assisted Suicide. This may touch off a story idea in you.

• Sometimes writers are just sick of being alone in their rooms. We feel like we're being punished. There's no reason why you can't write in public. Go to a Starbucks. Many writers do (which explains why I can never find a seat among all the people already scribbling). Or take your laptop to the park. You don't have to be alone to be alone with your thoughts. Try writing in the subway. Marissa Piesman found that the only way to relieve her writer's block was "to get back on the subway," although after six novels even the subway stopped working for her. I never actually *go* to the train station to write. It's usually that I have a train I need to take, but there's no reason *you* can't go there just to write. Then you can hop on the train after you're done, celebrating by going to a favorite place.

• Arbitrary deadlines can help you get over a block. I don't mean the ones that say, "I have to finish this by next Tuesday or I'll kill myself." I mean, how about writing whatever comes into your head till the train comes, till the microwave goes off, till the waitress throws a bacon, lettuce, and tomato sandwich on your notebook?

• Maybe you need to change writing modes. Put your memoir away and write a letter. It can be to a real person, living or dead. It can also be to an invented character—someone in a novel (your own or someone else's) or to a demon of doubt. Writing a letter to a character, or writing a letter to yourself from a character, can help you get to know that character. The same is true for a dimly recollected figure from your past—a parent or a weird neighbor. If you write to a real person you have the freedom to say *anything* because you have no intention of sending the letter. Maybe that person is the reason you are having trouble writing. He or she said something disparaging about your last story. So write a nasty, angry letter. Tell him what you think of *his* writing. Tell him what you think of his nose, how it's pugged just like a piggy's. You don't have to be mature. Write anything you want. About how he's a drunken has-been who never was. Vent.

Gail Godwin's wonderful essay, which I've already told you about, "The Watcher at the Gate," is one I often read at the first meeting of the writing workshop I teach. In it she describes the Watcher who keeps us from writing, and she suggests writing a letter to your Watcher to find out what he or she is afraid of. When she asked her Watcher this question he replied, "Failure." You might try writing to your own Watcher, and getting a reply.

> Watchers are notorious pencil sharpeners, ribbon changers, plant waterers, home repairers and abhorrers of messy rooms or messy pages. They are compulsive looker-uppers. . . . And they'd rather die (and kill your inspiration with them) than risk making a fool of themselves.
>
> —Gail Godwin

- If you're a novelist, try writing a poem as a way to free yourself. Maureen Brady took a poetry class to cure herself of a block. "Working with words at the barest level," she told me, helped her "remember that writing is about language." If you're a poet, try writing a book review. Write a review of your own book. Give yourself a great review. Tell yourself what you've accomplished—or will accomplish. Talk about themes and symbols, the poetry of the language, the emotional resonance of the scenes. Take your work seriously in this review. Then hold on to it. During those moments of self-doubt, it can work as a life preserver to keep you afloat.

• Another thing Maureen did to help herself over her block was she took a winter off from writing and just read books that had been recommended by a mentor. She went to museums, plays, and readings. Being "the recipient of other people's art" helped her get back to her own.

To sum up, when you have those times when you just can't do it, stop doing it. Figure out what nourishes you and do that instead. Figure out what frightens you and fight back.

**TIP:** Daydreaming is writing. Lie down and fantasize about your characters or subject. Let your mind roam. When you hook a good one, reel it in by writing about it.

# TWENTY-EIGHT

# PUBLISHING, A NASTY BUSINESS

**W**hen I ask my students what prevents them from taking themselves seriously as writers, the number-one response is: Not having been published. This is what causes good writers to lose faith in themselves. People seem to feel that if only they could get something published they would be filled with self-confidence and affirmation, and that *that* would be enough to send them gleefully to the computer every morning, bursting with ideas.

'Tain't necessarily so.

I used to be an unpublished writer. In fact, I was an unpublished writer for a damn long time. And every day something would sidle up to me when I was trying to get started and whisper, "How can you do this? Let's face it, you can't be any good or you would have published by now."

I would try to refute this by pointing to all the truly terrible writers who were published. "You see, publishing doesn't mean anything. That's the marketplace. Look at who gets published."

And that voice would reply, "What do you know? You *think* they're terrible writers because you are. After all, they're published *and you're not.*"

An argument I could never win.

Now, I won't say that when I finally got my first novel published I didn't feel terrific. It's only that the feeling lasted for about two months. By which point it had become obvious that no one was going to read the damn thing. The reviews I got, good though most were, were it. There was no hoopla, no fanfare, no tickertape parade. In order to continue being a published writer, I had to write another book. As

Peter Rubie says, "Getting published is like having sex the first time—you want to do it again, and soon, but do it right this time."

It *was* better being a published novelist than not being one. I received congratulatory letters from friends. And now my family didn't look at me like I was secretly sleeping with unemployed actors during the day because I never answered the phone. And when that voice started in with, "You aren't any good," I could say, "Yeah, but I've published a novel." The voice would be quiet for a minute before replying, "But nobody read it."

This was hard to refute, even though I knew it wasn't exactly true. Some people did read it. I even got a couple of fan letters—one from a guy who signed his note "Marquis" and wanted to "meat" me, but okay, I'm sure he was a very nice guy and his intentions were honorable even if his spelling sucked.

I don't want to be like the beauty queen complaining how hard it is to have perfect skin and hair and all. So yeah, it *is* better to be a published writer than not. I just don't want you to think it's the answer to all your prayers, or, if you have been published, to feel you're alone in your disappointment. In the end you still have to learn to turn those criticizing/aggrandizing voices off and write. In the end it's still you and your thoughts.

We put weight on getting published because we don't know how to read ourselves, and so seek validation from someone else. "There would be a big wavelike vacillation," Madison Smartt Bell told me about when he was first starting out. "I would feel something was brilliant when I finished; the next time I looked it would seem nauseatingly bad." Unpublished writers think getting something published will take them off this oscillating ride, but it doesn't. It just lifts you to a higher rung, and then you dangle back and forth between good reviews and bad, comparing yourself to every other writer you've heard of, living or dead.

The way to get off the ride is to see you can never have true objectivity regarding your own work, *and it doesn't really matter.* W.H. Merwin asked John Berryman how he could know if his poems were any good and wrote a poem about reply: "You can't you can never be sure/you die without knowing."

"I've worked with many great writers—some of the best of our times," Jodie Klavans told me. "And they all suffer from depression, self-doubt, and have little objectivity. I tell myself over and over, 'You are not alone.' And do you know what? In the end, if your work sucks—so what? Your life was complete doing it."

I've noticed, however, that some people complain about not getting published, but if you ask them what they have sent around they give you a dumb look, as if you'd asked them about the ever-expanding universe or string theory. They seem to think that when you finish a piece of writing the telephone rings. "Hi, I'm an editor," says a throaty voice. "Got any manuscripts?"

To get published you need to send things out. This is a royal pain in the butt, but there is no way around it. I used to send a story out and wait. I rarely sent anything out at the time, so my thinking was that when I finally did the first magazine I sent it to would gobble it up. Life became very exciting around the old mailbox for a while. Every day there would be mail—not the mail I was looking for, but who cared? There was the anticipatory excitement of opening the box and looking in, hoping for that thin business envelope. And every day it wouldn't be there, giving me another day to look forward to the mail. Until one day there it was, but it wasn't thin and it didn't have an embossed return address. No, it was thick and the handwriting on it was familiar. It was the dread Self-Addressed Stamped Envelope, and in it was my rejected manuscript, now coffee-stained and wrinkled, returning home like a bedraggled cat I'd tried to drown.

My advice to you is this: Don't put a shitload of numina on a manuscript you finally send out. Don't spend an inordinate amount of time choosing the stamps and perfecting your signature. Don't write cute, whimsical, thoughtful letters to go with the manuscript. Show you are professional, not eccentric. And most importantly, get into the habit of sending things out—regularly, and often.

Lore Segal told me that when she was first starting she and her writer friends had a list of magazines to send to. "We sent manuscripts to every magazine on our list. To *The New Yorker*, of course. I remember I sent them a letter once that said, Is there anybody there? I know there's a pencil because he writes 'thank you' at the bottom on my printed rejection. And they wrote back that yes, there is somebody here. In fact, every story that comes to *The New Yorker* is read by two people, a male and a female—I wonder if that's still true. It can't be. . . . The first thing I published was in a little magazine, and my payment was two copies. But editors read the little magazines. No one else reads them. Your colleagues may not read them. But editors and agents do."

More and more magazines will accept multiple submissions, so if you have a good story, send it to more than one place at a time. I hate magazines that will not consider multiple submissions . . . as if we writers aren't treated badly enough. Most magazines, especially the little literary ones, pay you a pittance, if anything at all. They know you're an addict, that you would write even if they charged you to read your stuff. So guess what? Now they do—in the form of the reading fee or the story contest. They do this, of course, not because they're looking to exploit writers to make a profit but because the little magazines are barely staying afloat themselves. Nonetheless, it was with great annoyance I watched the practice of charging a reading fee (in the form of a literary competition) escalate from the occasional to the commonplace event.

I hate the publishing end of the writing business—I don't mean I hate my publishers or editors. I mean I hate the business I need to do in order to publish. It seems to me I should write all day, that is my job, and the other stuff—well, somebody else should do that. Ideally my agent (but he won't).

Agents do not market stories. Oh, some do, I suppose. Joyce Carol Oates isn't busy self-addressing return envelopes and licking stamps. But you and I, we have to do our own licking. And the sooner you get into a routine of doing this, the better your chances of getting published. This goes for essays as well as stories; novels too, if you don't have an agent. You need to send things out. As Maureen Brady put it: "Consider that if you are receiving a lot of mail addressed in your own hand, you are doing your job well. You're getting your work out there, in the marketplace, you're getting your work exposed."

I don't know how much time you can devote to the *business* of

> You cannot let your writer's ego be affected by the publishing process, which, by nature, entails repeated rejection. . . . You need to develop a special part of your mind and your routine to deal with publishing and professionalism.
>
> —Kenneth Atchity

writing. It's secondary to the writing itself, but it needs to be done. Can you spend an hour a day? Half an hour? Ten minutes? Can you spend an hour a week? Whatever it is, make a schedule and stick to it . . . as much as you can stick to any schedule if you have kids, a demanding job, or you're getting your period.

My students always ask how to figure out where to send stuff. I try to look wise, like I really know, but the Crazy Eight Ball seems as good a place as any to turn to for advice. Even to do this you need a list of magazines to ask about.

The best source for finding the names and addresses of places looking for particular kinds of work is *Writer's Market*. In addition to the general *Writer's Market* there are specialized versions for poets, fiction writers, children's book writers.

After going through the *Writer's Market* you will have a list of places to send your work that reaches roughly from New Jersey to Mozambique. To shorten it you might check out the various "best" anthologies, especially if you are a fiction writer. There's the *Best American Short Stories, Best American Essays, The Pushcart Prize*, and others. Reading these collections will help you see what various magazines publish. They will also acquaint you with prize-winning writings in your genre. At the end of the anthologies, the magazines that were consulted for work are listed. The ones with the stories that interested you most are the ones you should send your work to first.

Some magazines, like *The New Yorker*, are a long shot, but hey, we're writers, we don't audition in person. Paper rejections don't hurt any more than paper cuts. So if you have a story you think slick enough for a slick publication, send it. But know you're more likely to get your work published in a rinkytink leaflet. Even if the payment is only two contributor copies, agents, editors, and publishers *do* read these little magazines, looking for fresh blood. You're bleeding, aren't you?

**Try This:** Maureen Brady tells her students to address a whole bunch of envelopes with a submission plan, "so they don't stop after one or two rejections." Make a list of at least ten magazines you are going to try before reconsidering your manuscript. Have the envelopes stamped and ready to go. You are less likely to cop out on a stamped envelope.

## REJECTION DEJECTION

The more you send things out, the greater are your chances of getting published. The greater are your chances of getting rejected too, but you need to inure yourself to that—to the point where when something comes back, you dash off a letter and send it out again without doing a whole lot of soul searching.

Soul searching is one of the worst responses to a rejection letter. Unless the editor has made constructive criticism, which is a different level of rejection letter and should make you feel pretty good, you don't need to rethink your story, and your life, with every *no* that comes along.

"There are many different forms of rejections," Steve Schwartz told me. "It's important to learn the differences. A form-letter rejection doesn't carry much meaning. If, however, all you ever get are form-letter rejections, the message is that many people don't think your stuff is worth wasting time on. That's a strong message, and you should ask yourself why. If the rejection comes with a personal letter or phone call, then listen carefully to what they liked and didn't like. Take sustenance from what they liked. Listen with an open mind to what they didn't. Finally, if the rejection has to do with commercial reasons, it's useful for me to listen. I don't just write, I earn my living writing. I think I have a better chance of doing that when I'm aware of conditions in the marketplace. Ultimately I trust my own instincts, opinions, and aesthetic. I trust if I care deeply about something, regardless of the current fashion, other human beings will also care. What's unmarketable today may be the next big thing. And anything done superbly will always be welcome in the marketplace."

Lori Perkins concurred about the joys of a good rejection, although not about the meaning of getting a lot of form rejections. "A good personal rejection can be an inspiration. A lot of form rejections just means you haven't found the right agent or editor."

"If my mailman only knew what lurked in my wicked heart," Evan Russell said. "Every day that he brings me nothing I am this much closer to strangling him. But good, polite, intelligent rejection letters are wonderful. We all know the feeling of calling up a friend and saying, 'I just got the most fantastic rejection letter!' "

Rejection slips are pieces of paper. Don't give them magical significance. Some people do just that. They wallpaper their bathrooms with them. I don't know why. Why would you want to have them staring you in the face, especially if you're constipated? Sam Decker used to paste rejection slips on the wall over his desk. Instead of causing him to howl at the moon, he told me they helped him feel like a real writer. "I got into seeing what color, size, and particularly what wording the slips contained. It took the sting out. When I looked over my wall I felt good that I was actually sending my work out. My collection was proof that I was taking myself seriously."

Now me, I file my rejections—who knows why? I have rejections from twenty years ago: What am I saving them for? Maybe it's a nose-thumbing thing. When I am recognized as a *Great Genius* I want to know who exactly wrote what nasty things to me, and I want to remember to absolutely refuse to let them have any of my stories, no matter how much they beg.

No one likes rejections, even when there is praise involved. Praise, ha! Most writers are deaf when it comes to compliments. "He's just being nice," I'm apt to say of an editor I've never met, dismissing as an old softie someone who, for all I know, tortures bunnies in his spare time. But a negative comment, now there's something I can suck on for years—*What did she mean, I left a modifier dangling?* I'm still mulling over that one. If I hadn't committed the dastardly crime would she have *taken* the story? So okay, I'll undangle it, but where is it? It's like a Sherlock Holmes mystery—"The Case of the Dangling Modifier." I've been all over the manuscript with a magnifying glass and a dogeared copy of *Elements of Style*, and I still can't find it.

Even a writer as successful as Ruth Reichl finds rejection a bitter pill. "I never have any sense if something I've written is good or bad," she told me, "and once I've been told it's a failure I can't overcome it. I'm awed by stories of writers with drawers filled with rejections. Humiliation may be good for the soul, but I have never found it to be anything but humiliating."

## TRAGEDY: THE EDITOR HAS A PAPER CUT

Let's just think about editors for a moment. I used to imagine they were wise men and women who thoughtfully considered my story, perhaps discussed it with one another before sadly, with regrets, slipping it into my self-addressed stamped envelope (chuckling over my choice of stamps, wondering at my lovely handwriting, my unusual signature), returning it to me.

I don't think so anymore.

An editor is a person. He or she may be smart. He or she may be stupid. He or she may have just had a fight over a parking spot before tearing open your envelope and reading the title. Then he or she may have put it into the SASE and sent it back to you with no more thought than they would give the potato chip they crunched on the sidewalk next to their parking spot.

I'm not saying this is always the case, only that it may have been. You have no way of knowing what happened just prior to the editor opening your envelope. Why assume it is your work that lacks merit? Why make this stranger so powerful that his or her judgment validates or invalidates your writing?

I've been on both sides of the selection process, so I can tell you the process is nothing if not subjective. As there are more students who want to take my class than there are slots for them, I weed through manuscripts deciding who gets in. Although I'd like to say I study each story and weigh it against the feather of truth, it's not so. I myself don't know why I choose one student's writing sample over another. It seems based more on where in the reading order the story finds itself. Early stories may be scrutinized more carefully than later ones that sneak in with a good opening. Sometimes it's the later ones that get turned down because I'm too tired to be fair. And gothic horror stories will often get rejected not because they aren't well writ-ten but because they give me a creepy feeling about the writer. What I'm saying is, in the end, judgments about your writing are subjective. That's why you can't read them as if they were postcards from Maat, who's just weighed your heart. Rejection notes aren't pages torn from the Egyptian Book of the Dead.

Emily Russell knows firsthand how subjective the submission pro-cess is, after having had a story rejected several times before it was ultimately accepted for publication. "Part of having a piece accepted is crossing paths with the right reader at the right time—nothing less miraculous than having a meteor land on your house. Looking at rejections in this light demonstrates they are a means to an end."

So why do we make editors the final arbiters of our talent when we don't know who they are and don't know their criteria or the mood they were in when they read our stuff? Why do we give them the power to decide our fates, whether we will believe in ourselves as serious writers or not? Why do we do this?

Because they do not love us.

They do not hate us either. They do not know us. They are the anonymous reader, and if we make such a person smile, and he or she offers to let us make other people smile, then we know an objective outsider thought our writing was good enough. Therefore, it must be.

This would be fine if editors were truly objective, if they were looking only for high-quality work, as they say they are. And they are. In book publishing they are looking for high-quality work *that will sell well*. But the high literary standards are often secondary to the bedroom scene, the murder, or the author's celebrity that they think will make the book sell.

"It was George Garrett who pointed out to me that rejection is part of every writer's life forever—you just have to learn how to deal with it," Madison Smartt Bell told me. "What I preach is that the marketplace for writers has become so inimical that a writer can no longer depend on it to furnish a sense of validation. Rejection by the marketplace has nothing to do with the quality of work submitted. (Well, it might, but you have no way of knowing if it does or not.) In that situation, your judgment of your work and your sense of its worth has to come completely from within. Which is maybe a better position to be in, in the long run."

That's not to say there aren't self-indulgent writers who would never deign to thrill the reader, who think their work should be approached as just that—work—who intend for their readers to scratch their heads, puzzling out the hidden meaning of symbols and convolutions. Geniuses, in other words. Well, just remember: Geniuses are generally misunderstood and unrecognized in their time. So if this is you, why are you reading this book? You should be smoking a pipe by the window, laughing raucously at the thunderstorm as you twirl your cape and finger the hangman's knot you habitually make with that length of rope you keep by your desk.

I believe writing has to be about something more than pleasing the reader, just as food has to be something more than dessert. Please the reader for sure, excite him, make her laugh or cry, but most importantly, make the reader think. See connections not noticed before. Find meaning where there seemed to be none. Experience a life outside of the limited one each person must live.

Ideally, this is what an editor should respond to. Some do. Some don't. In the end you have to believe in yourself, in your own work. Then you take it to market, and if this little piggy cries *weee weee weee* all the way home you don't cut off your toe. You realize the buyers out there are buyers, not gods. They pass things up for good reasons, but they also pass things up for silly reasons—because they're hungry or tired or swamped, because they're jealous (many editors are writers, remember; writers with jobs, therefore angry writers without the time to write). Because they're afraid, because they're ambitious, because if they publish your story they won't have room for the story of a friend or publishing colleague who might be in a position to publish *their* story. These are not the *only* reasons stories are rejected, but these are *some* of the reasons.

Editors are human beings. They make mistakes. In some cases, two hundred stories may cross someone's desk a day, only to be followed by two hundred more the next day. No one wants to pass up a great piece of writing, but editors get tired too. That is why you can't let rejection hurt you or make you soul-search too deeply. It can't have more meaning than what we give it. Ideally we should know the worth of our own work and merely shake our heads at the inability of some editors to recognize it.

Alas, the sad truth about publishing is that through no fault of your own you may find it difficult, even impossible, to get published. That doesn't mean you are a bad writer. That doesn't mean you should stop sending your stuff out. You need to keep working at it, getting responses from fellow writers, putting it away and looking at it again. You need to send your writing around on a regular basis, so that the rejections don't grow too powerful, so that they're like rainy days in Seattle. They happen. A lot. So what, it's still beautiful.

Listen, the miracles happen too. Coincidences don't always work against you, making you send a story about your father dying to a magazine that's just closed an issue on death. Sometimes it happens that an editor is looking for a funny story and yours crosses her desk. Or you send a piece about your pet mink to someone who's an animal-rights activist. The most important thing to remember, though, is that an editor is a person, not a god. His or her judgment is merely his or her judgment, not the objective Truth about your talent.

"For years I was more concerned with publishing and money than the passion of writing," Jodie Klavans told me. "Before I was married I worked at a large publishing company and I was very involved with the business. But now I realize the pleasure is in the doing—not the selling."

So how does a writer keep going in the face of rejections? "Faith in my own talent, as modest as that sounds," Evan Russell said. "Also I understand the really important thing is the writing itself, and not the publication. Depressing as it is to utter the words, I do believe that even if I never get into print, never make one dime at this, my life writing will have been well spent."

**Try This:** Write down a response to a rejection letter immediately. Ellen Dreyer finds this helps her get past it more quickly and back into sending things out.

- Remember how many good writers had trouble getting published. Keep a list of such rags-to-riches stories. It will enable you to continue to believe in your writing despite the naysaying of so-called "experts." Whenever you hear of a neglected writer's rise to fame, write it down. Consult the list when you start to believe your critics know your "true" unworth. Barry Denny, for example, always remembers that William Kennedy had *Ironweed* rejected thirteen times before it was finally published and went on to win the Pulitzer Prize for fiction.

**TIP:** If there is the slightest bit of praise or encouragement in a rejection letter, write it down. A word scribbled at the end of a rejection slip is worth remembering, even if that word was "Sorry." It meant someone cared enough to write a word to you. That's a connection. Don't dismiss it.

# TWENTY-NINE

# FOR THE RECORD

et me be practical here for a moment and add a word about record-keeping. You need to send things out, this is true. But you also need to know where you sent them, when, and what the reply was. There are computer programs to help writers keep track of their work. Why? Do you really need a *program* for this? There must be a good reason to spend forty bucks on such a thing, but I don't know what it is.

I keep a record in the back of my daily notebook (where I write lists of who to call, what to do, appointments—my cheapo version of a desk diary). I write the year on top, then I make four columns—two thin ones for date sent out and date returned (or accepted—let's not be pessimistic); a thick one for whom (I sent it to), what (it was), where (the magazine is located), and why (I chose that magazine—e.g., recommendation, query, *I Ching*); and another thick one for the response—e.g., form rejection, personal note (with enthusiastic quotes from the latter).

In addition to this paper record I keep files in my computer—two, to be exact. One is of submissions, the other is of magazines. The submission file has the name of each story I am sending around. Under each story title I list where I have sent it and when, the most recent places being closest to the top. I never delete the names of magazines that reject a story. I add pertinent information instead, the date of rejection, quotes from the rejection letter (if there were personal notes), and other comments. I play up the positive remarks. I need as much encouragement as I can give myself. Negative comments burn into my brain without any additional help from me.

The second file lists magazines I've submitted to, with the ones I like the most at the top. The jerks I keep under a subheading called "Jerks." I keep note of what stories I submitted to each magazine, when, and who the editor was. There is a lot of duplication between these two computer files, and between them and my handwritten record as well, but this system works for me. I don't always want to turn on the computer to enter a rejection. Generally after getting a rejection I don't particularly want to live anymore, so it's all I can do to write "No" in a column with a date. Later I get my energy level back up (by consuming half my weight in chocolate). Then I enter the information in my computer files.

On days when I'm sending stuff out, I can see where I've sent that story before. I can look at the magazine list and see where editors have been most receptive to my work. I have the name of the editor who made such kind remarks, poor fool, that I'm sending him something else.

## BOOKIES

Although I have been writing mostly in this chapter about sending out short pieces, much of what I've said applies to longer works as well. The main difference is you can't send out as many copies of your book at a time.

You have two possible approaches when marketing a novel, memoir, or other book. One is to look for an agent, the other is to try to find a publisher yourself. Both of these searches are best done with a short query letter, maybe a sample of the book in question—a chapter or two, the first ten or twenty pages. As with shorter submissions, it is important to enclose a stamped, addressed envelope for a reply and/or the manuscript's return. If you don't care about the manuscript's return—if, for example, the return postage costs more than the price of copying—you can enclose a stamped, addressed business envelope for the reply, giving the editor permission to recycle the manuscript pages.

## FALLEN AGENTS

My students always want to know if you need an agent in order to get a book published. My own agent isn't going to much like my reply, but no, I don't think you always need an agent. It does make getting it read easier. An agent has contacts in the publishing field and generally makes telephone calls to editors before sending them manuscripts. Editors tend to read manuscripts sent by agents first—and sometimes *only* manuscripts that reach them through agents. The assumption is that if you don't have an agent, you mustn't be good enough to get one. So unagented manuscripts are allocated to the slush pile. Readers at the low end of the publishing totem pole read through the slush pile. These may be college interns or secretary/receptionists working their way up. They are encouraged to reject manuscripts because the editors above them don't want to have to read slush. As a result, it is hard to get out of the slush pile. But not impossible.

One way to get out of the slush pile is to address a particular editor with a query letter. Then, if he or she expresses interest in seeing the whole book, you can send it to that person with a note reminding him or her of that interest. It might still go to a reader first, but generally this reader will be a step above the slush-pile reader, maybe an editorial assistant instead of the receptionist.

The other way to get out of the slush pile is to find a generous published writer who responds to your work and is willing to help you. This is a hard way to go, and it seems to have more to do with luck than anything you can *do*. Sometimes you will meet such a writer in a workshop or a class, or at a writers' conference or reading. Most writers are not terribly eager to read your manuscript. And if they read your manuscript, even if they love it, they won't necessarily help you beyond offering words of encouragement.

But Susan Saiter's first story was published in the Columbia University magazine when she was taking a class there. And her first novel was accepted by a publisher she met at a party. "It probably helped that we were both from Michigan and he 'got' what I was writing," she told me. Madison Smartt Bell's first published story was selected by George Garrett in connection with a workshop Garrett was teaching. "I felt my writing fiction was legitimized to some extent by that acceptance," Madison said. "A good thing, as I did not manage to publish anything else for about five years."

Evan Russell, "in a fit of pique" at not having gotten anything published, sent a hundred pages of his stories to Charles Bukowski, a writer he greatly admires. "Here was this disgusting, lecherous, smelly old drunk, who basically only wrote about how disgusting, lecherous, smelly and drunk he was, but who had, by sheer stick-to-itiveness and a fine poetic sensibility, made it. I mailed the stuff off, asking for his opinion. I'm not sure what I expected, but a week later I received one of the kindest and most thoughtful letters I've ever gotten. He was critical of my writing (in a way that made it clear he'd read it), but also sympathetic and supportive. And from Bukowski? Who'd've guessed? I can't tell you how much that letter meant and still means to me."

My first two novels were initially unagented. I had an agent for my very first novel, but she was unable to sell it and soon stopped returning my telephone calls. When I finished my second novel and sent it to her, she sent it back with a note saying she wouldn't know how to find a publisher for it. I wandered in hell for a few years, trying to get the energy to write a third novel. Which I was doing when I took a writing workshop with Madison Smartt Bell. When he learned I had a completed second novel, he asked to read it and subsequently sent it to his editor, who took it on. I was then in the happy position of looking for an agent for a novel that already had a publisher. As you might expect, in such circumstances it was fairly easy to find one.

This agent negotiated my contract (by saying yes to everything the publisher offered) and was my liaison with the house, but when my editor was laid off and my book was orphaned, there was nothing he could do to make the situation better. Which is how *Secret Correspondence* came to be published and forgotten. Editors do not like orphaned books. They have their own projects and view their predecessor's acquisitions as bags of garbage someone left in their backyard. They don't *have* to do anything to get such books noticed. And they don't. And he didn't. And it wasn't.

So I wandered in hell for a few more years, during which I finished writing a third novel. My agent sent it to a few places, got a few rejections, became easily discouraged and dropped me as a client. (Agents are so easily discouraged. Good thing they're not writers.) In the meantime Madison told me of a small press looking for a novel like my third one. I sent a query letter, then the manuscript, and soon I was the proud writer of a second novel accepted for publication without an agent. This time I decided not to work with an agent at all. The advance was measly enough without having to give a fifteen percent fee to somebody for reading the contract and saying, *Mmm hmmm.*

*Wishbone* managed to get no reviews. Oh, surely I exaggerate. There must have been one or two. One for sure; I'm not sure if there was a second one. The problem was that the publisher had a tendency to call the editor of *The New York Times Book Review* and berate her for not reviewing any of the books she published. She believed this was because she was from Texas, so she came to New York, marched up to the offices of the *Times* and berated the editor in person. This was a tad impolitic, although I don't know that anything would have made a difference. My publicist at the press was somebody who, the week before becoming my publicist, was a bookkeeper in a shoe store. Nice guy. Very young, very sweet. Eager. He seemed to be working hard for me, making calls, setting up readings. He promised he'd have one hundred reviewer copies sent out—all he needed were names of people I thought should get copies.

Five years later I'm still hearing from people on that list who are surprised to learn I published a second novel. I understand the publicist went back into shoe sales soon after my book appeared. Well, that's shoe business.

Now I have an agent who is also a writer. He seems to come to the business with more sensitivity and less greed (which is why he lives in the same neighborhood I do). He returns my telephone calls. He reads my stuff and responds to it. He talks about me to editors. He thinks of me when he hears of work. This is all to say that yes, Virginia, there is a Santa Claus, even if you're Jewish.

There are good agents and there are bad agents. Having an agent is like getting published—it helps you feel like a writer . . . for about a week. During that week you say things like, "My agent says" and "I have to check my machine, I'm expecting a call from my agent." It's like when you first get married and find yourself saying, "My husband says," a lot. It's a credential. I have an agent, therefore I am a writer.

But an agent who doesn't return your telephone calls is not better than no agent at all. And if he or she reads your stuff and is negative without giving clear reasons, well, do you really need another negative person in your life? Isn't your mother enough? One of my previous agents used to talk to me only about how hard it was to publish literary fiction these days, how bad the publishing scene had become, how only self-help books were selling. He'd sound so down I would spend my time trying to cheer him up. Don't get discouraged, I'd say. Have you thought of going into retail, maybe opening a Ranch 1 Chicken restaurant? I couldn't ask him if he'd sent my book out to any other places. It was too depressing for him to talk about.

So this is all to say again (and I hope I don't sound too much like my old agent), publishing is a nasty business, but someone's got to do it. So concentrate on your writing, first and foremost. As Sam Decker told me, quoting the wisdom of Henny Youngman about old age: "Consider the alternative." If the writing pleases you enough so that you don't care about publishing, wow, you must do a lot of yoga. I admire you. Don't trade that peace in for lowly ambition such as plagues me and every other writer I know.

But if you want to write and get published, you need to do just that—write, and work at getting your stuff out there. Sustain yourself with "small victories," like the ones Steve Schwartz listed for me. "Finishing a screenplay, getting my first agent, getting rejections accompanied by positive comments, winning a contest." Your small victories will be different but as valid. As far as rejections go, look, just be grateful we're not actors. We don't have to *hear* the snickering; they don't tell us thanks but no thanks to our faces.

Send the stuff out. Open your mail when you're alone. Send the stuff out again. And most importantly, keep writing. If you don't give up, something will happen. Maybe. And then, of course, there's always yoga.

> No wonder poets have to seem so much more businesslike than business men—Their wares are so much harder to get rid of.
>
> —Robert Frost

**Try This:** Make a record of where you send things to, when you send them, and what the response was. Your primary record should be listed by manuscript, but you may want a secondary list of magazines and publishers you have sent stuff to. Make sure you record the names of all editors you wrote to as well as those who wrote back to you (they are not always the same); their titles; and the responses, especially any favorable comments. Record also if someone recommended you send the piece to that particular person or place.

**TIP:** If you keep your record on computer, type the magazine or publisher information as if you were addressing an envelope. Then when you are addressing the envelope you can highlight and copy that directly onto the mailing label as well as the letter. Remember to verify old information when sending out something new—is the same editor there? Has his or her title changed? Has the address changed? And by all means make sure the place is still operating.

## THIRTY

# WHY DO IT

Writing is hard and publishing not guaranteed, so you may well ask why do it. But if you have to ask, then you probably should do something else. You owe it to yourself. Writing is not martinis and lunch in four-star restaurants with your editor who only wants to talk about how marvelous your writing is and when will we see your next book. I once had lunch with an editor in a fancy resaurant. She didn't eat anything because she was an Orthodox Jew and the place wasn't kosher. I spent the whole time unable to talk and chew, worrying I had food stuck in my teeth or that I was going to belch.

"There was a point a few years ago," Steve Schwartz told me, "when I was having no success and slowly going broke. My wife suggested I give up and go back to my former career. What she suggested made perfect sense. But I couldn't do it. The way you keep going in the face of disappointment and rejection is you have no choice. I was constitutionally incapable of quitting and doing something else. I think there's so much pain involved in making a living writing the only reason to continue is it's impossible to stop. If it's a choice between writing and selling real estate or something else, well . . . do the something else."

You write, not because you think you'll make a zillion bucks doing it. Not because it's glamorous. Getting published is a plus—but you can't even count on it. In the end you write for love.

"It's very pleasant to have someone in love with you," Lore Segal said, "but it's you being in love that's the event. In the same way it is wonderful to be published, but the event is your writing. That is what's happening to you."

Write because you have to, write because you *love* to. Fame, fortune, and finger foods have little to do with it. If you get published you will still have to diet. So write because it's a wonderful gift, and if you do not share it you're a miser and will die a miser's death, clutching your thoughts to yourself. Write because it's fun, because it makes you laugh and makes you cry. Don't write because you think you can make a living at it. A meager living it is, for most of us. Write because it's something you are passionate about.

"Enthusiasm is like gold, like religion," Evan Russell said. "I have become so sentimental and weepy over the last few years and I just fucking love it. This has everything to do with writing. Writing has made me so happy and also put me in touch with a larger feeling of human wonder and sorrow that is like a pool one can tap into for nourishment. And as I've matured this way my writing has improved. It's just like learning how to love and grieve honestly, I guess, and also to play. Without getting Alan Wattsish, writing is like playing, and as I've realized this living itself has become more like playing. I'm not being a Pollyanna. For Christ's sake, my life is a complete mess: Dead broke, strangled with impotent rage a lot of the time, hopeless alcoholic, the works . . . but somehow, more and more lately, I'm coming to understand that none of that's really the point. The writing is the point, and if it works all the rest, all the so-called 'unhappy' things, become a source of humor, almost of happiness and strength."

What Martha Graham wrote of dance is true for all creative work: "There is a vitality, a life force, an energy, a quickening that is translated through you into action," she wrote to Agnes DeMille. "Because there is only one of you in all time, this expression is unique and if you block it, it will never exist through any other medium. . . . The world will not have it. It is not your business to determine how good it is, nor how valuable, nor how it compares with other expressions. . . . You do not even have to believe in yourself or your work. Keep the channel open."

So if you'd really rather be writing than anything else, that's what you have to do. Don't let fear of rejection, lack of time, self-doubt, children, and parents stand in your way. Try to get published if you want, but don't make a god of the lowly editor. He just spilled hot coffee on his pants before opening your envelope. You expect objectivity and consideration from *him*?

I asked Lore Segal whether she would still write if she knew none of her stuff would be published. She paraphrased Isaac Asimov in reply. "Asimov was asked, If you knew you were going to die would you still keep writing? And he said, I'd type faster."

I think a lot about a writer friend of mine who died suddenly in his early forties. Single, childless, he had nothing in his life but his writing, and he complained even about that—how all his characters wanted to do was call each other up. I imagine him on the day he died, plugging away at a book he would never finish, trying to get his characters to *do* something besides make telephone calls. What would *he* have done if he knew in a few hours he would have a heart attack? Would he keep typing and faster?

I don't know why death surprises us. If there is one thing we know in life, it is that we are going to die. What do you want to be doing those last hours? If typing faster isn't the answer, what is? Me, I'd like a hot fudge sundae with wet walnuts and whipped cream, but I can't live my life like that. So I write. No one is making me. If I stop writing I can't blame anyone but myself.

Here's the thing: If you'd rather be writing, you can. It's as simple as that.

**TIP:** Writing is the Open Sesame that will roll the boulder from the cave mouth. There is no other. Write, and you will be writing. Don't write, and the boulder grows more embedded before you.

**Try This:** *Write!*

- If you can't write because are worried about your parents, write about that.

- If you can't write because you are preoccupied with your kid, write about that.

- If you can't write because you don't have the time, write about that.

- If you can't write because you doubt your talent, stamina, and intelligence, write about that.

- If you can't write because you don't have a garret . . . all right, maybe you can't write then. So give it up. It's not for you. But if reading this makes you angry, if it makes you all the more determined not to relinquish your dream, good—write about *that*. No one can stop you. You can only stop yourself.

# INDEX